Reading for Our Time

Sleeping Ariadne in the Vatican Museums, a Roman Hadrianic copy of a Hellenistic sculpture of the Pergamene school of the second century BCE. It figures in an important way in *Middlemarch* and is discussed in this book in a section on Dorothea as Ariadne.

Reading for Our Time

Adam Bede and Middlemarch Revisited

J. Hillis Miller

EDINBURGH
University Press

For Julian and Christina
old friends who have cheered me on

© J. Hillis Miller, 2012

Edinburgh University Press Ltd
22 George Square, Edinburgh

www.euppublishing.com

Typeset in 10.5/13 pt Sabon
by Servis Filmsetting Ltd, Stockport, Cheshire, and
printed and bound in Great Britain by
CPI Group (UK) Ltd, Croydon, CR0 4YY

A CIP record for this book is available from the British Library

ISBN 978 0 7486 4669 2 (hardback)
ISBN 978 0 7486 4728 6 (paperback)
ISBN 978 0 7486 4670 8 (webready PDF)
ISBN 978 0 7486 5440 6 (epub)
ISBN 978 0 7486 5439 0 (Amazon)

Contents

Foreword: Required Reading or "Some of Us, at Least"

Julian Wolfreys

Why should anyone care about George Eliot? And why should Eliot concern any of us today, especially? These are the interrogative motifs by which J. Hillis Miller introduces and concludes; they are the questions underlying what Miller calls the rhetorical reading of *Adam Bede* and *Middlemarch*. Acting not only as motifs—"Prelude" and "Coda" might give us insight into the nature of this brilliant, complex, and disarmingly probative reading of Eliot—but also as framing devices, substrates, or both, the questions of Eliot's significance, the significance of the rhetorical reading, and the concern with why good reading not only matters but must matter, inform and determine *Reading for Our Time*. Indeed, the urgent, ethical, and historical concern is markedly announced in a title, which itself bears the hallmark of all Miller's writing: at once apparently straightforward, yet also profoundly enigmatic and resistant to the bêtise of so-called common sense—which "time"? whose "time" exactly? who are "we" that the time is perceived as "ours"?—the title, and the study of one of the few novelists for grown-ups (to paraphrase loosely Virginia Woolf) to which this title serves as a gateway, make it clear that "our time" is also that of George Eliot.

To put this differently, the title, which resonates with a seemingly Dickensian echo, invites us to understand that we are not yet done with Eliot's time. We are not past, post-, or after the moment of Eliot's text and the careful reading of that text, for the very reason that the questions Eliot asked of her society are questions of overarching importance to us also. That Miller apprehends the necessity of returning to Eliot because she is no more done with in our time than we are done with hers is there to be read also in the title, if we read the title in different directions, as Miller would require that we do. For if the title, *Reading for Our Time*, brings pressure to bear on the very idea of thinking the notion of a period in any discrete manner as being problematic through its implicitly, not to say immanently, abyssal opening of the moment or the idea of such a determinable moment, it also operates on the question of the reader's responsibility in other ways. Responsibility in reading is crucial for Miller's understanding of Eliot and what Eliot does (as it is elsewhere in Miller's work), and this is a responsibility already in place in Eliot's writing, to which Miller responds, and for which he assumes responsibility. To come back to the title, this is advertised in those terms "reading" and "time" but also in the play of the title in its entirety. We need to read *for* our time; we must take responsibility for reading what is taking place in what we call the present. This is what George Eliot teaches us, says Miller; and this, therefore, is also what Miller has to teach us, if we listen. But, equally, George Eliot is, in the language of college reading lists, required reading. She is required reading *for our time*. There is no escaping this, and there can be no doubt about this requirement. (Why Eliot is required reading, for our time, and for times to come, as she was in her own time, remains for us to understand.) A stronger, stranger reading of the title might suggest that our time is being read by *Adam Bede* and *Middlemarch*, that these are texts which, if we give close attention, can be read as reading *for* our time, reading for times to come, for a time that can arrive at any time, through reading a time that was Eliot's, a time comprising both that which had been, that which was, and that which was to come.

Still, that said, what does Eliot have to do with "our time" or times? How will reading *Adam Bede* or *Middlemarch* help, apropos global catastrophe, climate change, increasing disparity between rich and poor nations, and all the various worldwide problems that appear often as inevitable as they seem insurmountable? What—to state this as baldly as possible, as nakedly, indeed, as Miller himself puts it before us—does reading a literary critic reading a Victorian novelist reading her times have to do with adversity, tribulation, and calamity on a worldwide scale? And why indulge in rewriting, revising, revisiting material on said Victorian novelist, some of which has already been revisited as Miller confesses, in order to produce a book which the author calls a palimpsest?

To ask such questions, as Miller implies we should, is not to avoid answering, but to accept responsibility, to use that word once more, for those questions, even if there appears to be no direct correlation between the troubles which prompt the questions and particular novels first published in the nineteenth century. That there might not appear to be answers initially is itself part of the difficulty, and taking responsibility for those questions does not necessarily mean that answers are reached, or can be attained. That there *are* questions, Miller would have us understand, is—or should be—where reading might search for a beginning, or, to employ a formula of Eliot's from her final novel, the make-believe of one. For any beginning is also a moment *in medias res*, and our time can only be understood if we begin by recognizing that we are in the midst of an untotalizable process, and so must take up that make-believe of a beginning, and in looking back maintain on the one hand an affirmative openness to the coming of the other, and on the other hand, in response to the possibility of such a coming, an endless, illimitable "yes"; hence Miller's consideration of the process by which *Reading for Our Time* has arrived. For the reading that *Reading for Our Time* is "for"; that is to say the reading it advocates as well as that which it signals it is searching after—"for" in the title making a gesture "toward" a time to come, which can always arrive at any moment, in a manner not dissimilar to that implied in Marcel Proust's use of "du" in the title of *À la recherche du temps perdu*—this "for" directs us toward a reading that remains to be read in our time, while affirming its own advocacy: this is the reading *for* our time, this is what reading is *for*. This is what good reading should be in our time, and in times to come. "For" signals therefore, with a singularity that is very much the signature of J. Hillis Miller, a seeking-after of a reading to come in another time, in other times, other tempi, in the other's time. Reading is the search as well as the research, the one always already finding itself involved in the other. In being *for* such a reading, such a reading is already moving in the direction of the times it seeks. The reading is actively *for* that time, in the sense that *for* signifies this forward gesture, a motion, the smallest of steps. Affirmation therefore *and* a motion toward, *for*, the undecidable future, in our time; and which "future" can only arrive through the patient effort to read closely, apparently anachronistically, backwards, belatedly, in a gesture that is as much one of remembrance and attestation as it is the signature of a hope, an opening on to that which remains to come. In apprehending the other's time within our own, we might, Miller teaches us, in learning how to read, come to read the signs, if not of *the times*, then at least of our times in the times of the other, in the times of George Eliot.

No one is pretending, though, that reading George Eliot will either change your life or save the planet, J. Hillis Miller least of all. To reduce what Miller says, or what I am seeking to say as a foreword—a foreword which is also a response—to Miller's exhaustive reading of Marian Evans and George Eliot, is as willfully stupid as it is reductive; not that this will stop some people from being both, often at the same time. But a first step, even if we pause to turn around, looking over our shoulders into the past, in order to seek a way forward, involves the labor of reading. Reading is not a one-shot deal; it's not something you do once and then put down the book, thinking that you've done. At least, not in the work of J. Hillis Miller, for whom reading is always a process, always in process, revisiting, returning, reiterating, and, with patience, attentiveness, care, and responsibility, a continual explication: an unfolding, which, in being open to the coming of the other, in saying yes, unfolds the possibility of readings that remain, to come. This is in evidence throughout *Reading for Our Time*, as it is in all Miller's work: reading as an ethical act, demonstrating in its incompletions and returns a commitment to the other through the work of what the critic calls with disarming straightforwardness "rhetorical readings."

So what does the maintenance of reading, of "rhetorical" or "good" reading, teach? What can Eliot teach us? What can Miller teach us about what Eliot can teach us, if we learn how to read aright, without falling into the mistaken simplicity of a blind belief that one can close the book on reading? Not least—and this is much—in reading carefully J. Hillis Miller reading carefully George Eliot we might come to learn how to read the ways in which those concatenations of events, subjects, experiences, and interpretations we call "society" or "history" are directed by what Miller calls "ideological presuppositions"; such presuppositions, such blind spots in the act of social, political, historical, and ideological reading, where reading comes to a halt in favor of economic calculations, are everywhere in Eliot's representations of society, social groups, and their complex interactions. Learning how to read those interactions, and the often powerful myopia of self-interest by which they are generated, can, as Miller argues, "make some of us at least Ariadnes awakening." Reading Eliot can make you see, if you choose to; but reading Miller can make you want to see. J. Hillis Miller can teach us how to see what we have not seen, how, like those creatures of George Eliot's, we make mistakes in how we read and act according to those misrecognitions and misunderstandings, often with detrimental, and occasionally disastrous, effect. Insight can arrive, even if belatedly, as hindsight. Miller can make you want to see. But you have to *want* to see. You have to say "yes" to seeing clear-sightedly, and this is never easy, nor can it be guaranteed that you will always see at one moment with the insight you have gained at another. But we all have to begin somewhere, and J. Hillis Miller reminds us—he shows us patiently, with good grace but also an ineluctable will toward clear-sightedness that is the hallmark or signature of his work—that we can see. You have to *want* to see, you have to choose to want this. You see?

Prelude

Can reading *Adam Bede* and *Middlemarch* today be at all justified, in this time of irreversible global climate change, worldwide financial meltdown, with a new financial bubble already building, and the bamboozling of the American electorate (and other electorates around the world) by the media, advertising, the politicians, and hidden right-wing contributors into voting in ways exactly contrary to their interests? What use is "reading for our time"? The Republicans in the last United States general election in November, 2010, took over the House of Representatives and increased their number of conservative Senators. They are determined not just to defeat Obama in the next presidential election, but to repeal the healthcare reform bill, to privatize or abolish Social Security, to phase out Medicare, to repeal or weaken further the already weak financial regulation bill, to keep tax cuts for the rich, to continue to stalemate any climate legislation, and to carry on indefinitely our war in Afghanistan and our continued presence in Iraq. They have some help in all this from Democrats. If we follow this path, we are throwing ourselves over the cliff. In order to go along with this program of self-destruction, "we the people" have to be persuaded to believe that lies are truths. What possible use can rhetorical readings of *Adam Bede* and *Middlemarch* in these bad times be? Such readings would seem to be a big waste of time. We have far more urgent things to do. In any case, in these days when so many people are glued all day to their iPhones or Blackberries, who has time any more for an attentive reading of a novel of more than nine hundred pages like *Middlemarch*? Our attention spans are being reduced to the length of a sound bite or of a 140 character "Tweet."

To this resistance I give two incompatible answers.

On one hand, it may be that reading George Eliot's novels, for those who like to do so, is a good in itself, an end in itself, as Immanuel Kant said all art is. People who play computer games, or watch films, or listen to popular music do not try to justify doing so. They just like doing it. I immensely enjoy reading *Adam Bede* and *Middlemarch*. I want to pass that pleasure on to others. Even in these bad times, we need a little respite from anxiety and handwringing.

On the other hand, it is just possible that some few readers here and there might learn something about how to unmask the lies that bombard us in the real world by reading *Middlemarch* or *Adam Bede* as models for how to do that. Certainly these novels abound in characters that are taken in by self-generated illusions. Demystifying those illusions for the reader's benefit is the chief goal the narrators' analysis of their follies pursues. Paul de Man, in a celebrated (for me at least) statement in "The Resistance to Theory," said: "What we call ideology is precisely the confusion of linguistic with natural reality, of reference with phenomenalism. It follows that, more than any other mode of inquiry, including economics, the linguistics of literariness is a powerful and indispensable tool in the unmasking of ideological aberrations, as well as a determining factor in accounting for their occurrence."[1] The narrators in *Adam Bede* and *Middlemarch*, as I shall show, use the linguistics of literariness as a tool for just such unmasking of the self-destructive mistakes of the main characters. As the narrators of these novels show, the characters fallaciously assume that their words refer to phenomena outside their minds. Lydgate, the country doctor in *Middlemarch*, in a discussion with Farebrother, the country clergyman, attacks medical men "who truckle to lies and folly."[2] This formula could be generalized to apply to all the men and women in the novel, except perhaps to Farebrother himself and to Caleb Garth and Mary Garth, along with a few other quiet clear-seeing people. A rhetorical reading of *Middlemarch*, I am arguing, can teach the reader a lot about resisting lies and folly such as have put the United States in such a pickle today.

Nevertheless, it would not do to be too hopeful about the benefits of reading *Adam Bede* or *Middlemarch*. De Man more than once plausibly asserts, with examples, that ideological aberrations magically re-form themselves even when they have been "unmasked." One forceful statement comes at the end of de Man's reading of Rousseau's "Profession de foi" in *Allegories of Reading*: ". . . if we decide that belief, in the most extensive use of the term (which must include all possible forms of idolatry and ideology) can once and forever be overcome by the enlightened mind, then this twilight of the idols will be all the more foolish in not recognizing itself as the first victim of its occurrence. One sees from this that the impossibility of reading should not be taken too lightly."[3] This does not encourage me to believe that I have read *Adam Bede* and *Middlemarch* right or that a right reading of these novels will cure people of ideological mystifications. Farebrother's response to what Lydgate affirms about lies and folly is to say that perhaps impossible obstacles stand in the way of curing people of their addiction to these dangerous aberrations. "You have not only got the old Adam in yourself against you, but you have got all those descendents of the original Adam who form the society around you" (17: 193). The old Adam, as we know, is humankind's ineradicable propensity to believe lies and to act self-destructively on the basis of that belief. *Middlemarch* does not have the putatively standard novelistic pattern of illusion followed eventually by clear-seeing wisdom: "Then I believed falsely; now I know how wrong I was." Dorothea, the main protagonist of *Middlemarch*, is not cured of her propensity to be deluded. She just, luckily for her, shifts her belief from a bad object of her devotion (Casaubon) to a good one (Ladislaw), as I shall show.

In spite of the dark wisdom that *Adam Bede*, *Middlemarch*, and de Man teach, we can permit ourselves the audacity of hope, the hope that reading *Adam Bede* or *Middlemarch* might do more than give a pleasure that is an end in itself. At least we may learn to understand better, as de Man promises, how ideological lies and folly come to occur and how they might be unmasked, at least in others, if not in ourselves. Putting this book together and revising it sentence by sentence has renewed my admiration for George Eliot's writings and my desire to do them justice by close attention to what they really say and to how they say it. I want to pass that just reading on to my readers. I claim that doing this may possibly help readers to come to terms with our present situation and even to act to ameliorate it. Though I do not deny the value of knowing as much as possible about the life and times of an author, *Adam Bede* and *Middlemarch* are still literary works. They are works of fiction, not sociological treatises, works of history, or disguised autobiographies. To be understood and made useful today, *Adam Bede* and *Middlemarch* must be read slowly, closely, and carefully, with much attention to linguistic detail, tropological and otherwise. I have tried to do that as best I can. My claim is that the strangenesses in the stylistic texture of Eliot's novels become more apparent when relatively short citations are abstracted from their place in the narrative flow and set side by side with similar passages in other parts of the novel. I claim also that the possible benign performative force of Eliot's novels on present-day readers can only be felicitously activated in this way. Moreover, I want what I say about *Adam Bede* and *Middlemarch* to be paradigmatic, however faulty it may be, for such readings. I want what I say to be in addition exemplary of the human, social, and political utility of reading for today.

It won't do, however, to be too solemn about the joy of reading and of readings. You will remember that the first excuse I gave for reading *Adam Bede* and *Middlemarch* today is that doing so gives a pleasure that is an end in itself. It is the pleasure, as Nicholas Royle says in a quite remarkable recent book,[4] of "veering," of veering, that is, into a make-believe world (amazing phrase, if you think of it: "make-believe"; it makes you believe, while at the same time you know it is only a pretend believe), and into the intricate layerings of imaginary narrators and of characters telepathically known by those narrators, not to speak of the sheer joy of tropological word play, a wild turning not by any means absent from Eliot's work, as I shall show, in which everyday words like "stars" and "light" swerve into strange linguistic constellations.

I had thought at first of calling this book *Ariadne Awakened*, but decided that title would lead to confusion with the title of an earlier book of mine, *Ariadne's Thread*. My frontispiece, however, is a photograph of the statue of *Sleeping Ariadne* in the Vatican Museums. This statue appears in a notable scene in *Middlemarch* discussed at the very end of this book, at my book's climax. My frontispiece puts *Reading for Our Time* under the aegis of Ariadne, with a suggestion that good reading today is a way of waking from sleep.

Deer Isle, Maine
June 27, 2011

Acknowledgments

In 1982 I published *Fiction and Repetition*, a book that had been many years in the making. It was readings of seven British novels from the perspective of a theoretical and formal issue: repetition. The original manuscript, when submitted to Harvard University Press, opened with chapters on two George Eliot novels: *Adam Bede* and *Middlemarch*. These chapters were judged to make the book too long. They were therefore excised. Over the years I have published a series of essays on *Middlemarch*. These were to a considerable degree abstracted from the lost chapter on *Middlemarch*. Pieces of the manuscript were revised and published as separate essays in various places, always as the result of solicitations from colleagues or editors. These essays are specified below. The *Adam Bede* chapter has so far gone unpublished. It is included in much-revised form here as a first section of this book. The original chapter on *Middlemarch* made a continuous argument. It was, I hoped, a full rhetorical reading of the novel. I have over all these years had the dream of putting the dispersed pieces back together, like Isis reassembling Osiris's *disjecta membra*. I have now elaborately revised the whole in the light of what I think at present about *Adam Bede* and *Middlemarch*, as well as what I think now about the theoretical issues my reading raises. I have also taken account of the abundant work on *Adam Bede*, on *Middlemarch*, and on Eliot's work generally that has appeared during these decades. That Isis failed to find Osiris's phallus in her work of reconstruction may be relevant to what I say about gender reversals in *Adam Bede* and *Middlemarch*, not only in Marian Evans's choice of a masculine pseudonym, but also in her critique of phallogocentrism in *Middlemarch*.

Examples of recent work on George Eliot in its somewhat wild diversity are Neil Hertz's wonderful book, *George Eliot's Pulse* (Stanford, CA: Stanford University Press, 2003), Karen Chase's comprehensive *George Eliot: "Middlemarch"* (Cambridge: Cambridge University

Press, 1991), Gillian Beer's *George Eliot* (Brighton: Harvester, 1986), Alexander Welsh's *George Eliot and Blackmail* (Cambridge, MA: Harvard University Press, 1985), Kay Young's chapter on *Middlemarch* in *Imagining Minds: The Neuro-Aesthetics of Austen, Eliot, and Hardy* (Columbus: Ohio State University Press, 2010), and Barbara Hardy's latest book on Eliot, *George Eliot: A Critic's Biography* (London and New York: Continuum, 2006). To these may be added two admirable recent essays by Nicholas Royle on telepathic insight in Eliot, "On Second Sight," in *Telepathy and Literature: Essays on the Reading Mind* (London: Blackwell, 1991), 84–110, and "The 'Telepathy Effect': Notes Toward a Reconsideration of Narrative Fiction," in *The Uncanny* (Manchester: Manchester University Press, 2003), 256–76. *Middlemarch in the Twenty-First Century*, edited by Karen Chase (see the list below), is a good place to find bibliographical references to the best work on *Middlemarch* up to 2006, as well as a collection of recent essays on the novel. Chase's book does not of course list even more recent work that has been important to me in my current work of revision, for example Avrom Fleishman's admirable *George Eliot's Intellectual Life* (Cambridge: Cambridge University Press, 2010), plus his *George Eliot's Reading: A Chronological List*, in *George Eliot-George Henry Lewes Studies*, Supplement to No. 54–5 (September 2008). For *Adam Bede* see Josephine McDonagh, *Child Murder and British Culture 1720–1900* (Cambridge: Cambridge University Press, 2003). Perhaps the best recent essay on *Adam Bede* is Rachel Bowlby's "'Hetty had never read a novel': 'Adam Bede' and Realism," in *George Eliot Review*, 41 (2010), 16–29. A revised version of this essay was published as the second part of Rachel Bowlby, "Introduction: Two Interventions on Realism," in *Textual Practice*, 25:3 (2011), 395–436. Bowlby's essay was first presented in 2009 at a one-day conference organized by Josephine McDonagh to mark the 150th anniversary of the publication of *Adam Bede*.

In the work of present-day extensive revision and reassembling, as I have said, I have joined as a prologue to my *Middlemarch* reading my excised chapter on *Adam Bede*, also substantially revised. Parts of this book have been published in earlier forms in the places listed below. I am grateful for permission to reuse this material in much revised form. Without more than a little derisory self-irony, I can describe these preliminary essays as *parerga* or *hors-d'oeuvres*. *Parerga*, meaning beside or outside the main work, is Casaubon's name, in *Middlemarch*, for "the pamphlets—or 'Parerga' as he called them—by which he tested his public and deposited small monumental records of his march" (29: 311–12) toward the never-to-be-completed "Key to all Mythologies." Casaubon remains perpetually in the middle of his march. Neil Hertz has speculated on how George Eliot saw herself in Casaubon, as does Hertz himself. Don't we all, all we scribblers in whatever genre? The difference, however, is that I have finally finished the *ergon*, or main work, such as it is, with much help from the following *parerga*:

J. Hillis Miller, "Narrative and History," in *ELH*, 41:3 (Fall 1974), 455–73. © Copyright 1974 by The Johns Hopkins University Press.

J. Hillis Miller, "Optic and Semiotic in *Middlemarch*," in *The Worlds of Victorian Fiction*, ed. Jerome H. Buckley, Harvard English Studies, 6 (Cambridge, MA and London: Harvard University Press, 1975), 125–45. Copyright © 1975 by the President and Fellows of Harvard College.

J. Hillis Miller, "The Two Rhetorics: George Eliot's Bestiary," in *Writing and Reading Differently: Deconstruction and the Teaching of Composition and Literature*, ed. G. Douglas Atkins and Michael L. Johnson (Lawrence: University Press of Kansas, 1985), 101–14. © by the University Press of Kansas. Also in J. Hillis Miller, *Victorian Subjects* (Hemel Hempstead: Harvester Wheatsheaf, 1991; Durham: Duke University Press, 1991), 289–302. © J. Hillis Miller 1991.

"Reading Writing: Eliot," from *The Ethics of Reading*, by J. Hillis Miller. Copyright © 1987 Columbia University Press. Reprinted with permission of the publisher.

J. Hillis Miller, "Teaching *Middlemarch*: Close Reading and Theory," in *Approaches to Teaching Eliot's Middlemarch*, ed. Kathleen Blake (New York: Modern Language Association, 1990), 51–63.

J. Hillis Miller, "The Roar on the Other Side of Silence: Otherness in *Middlemarch*," in *Rereading Texts/Rethinking Critical Presuppositions: Essays in Honor of H. M. Daleaki*, ed. Shlomith Rimmon-Kenan, Leona Toker, and Shuli Barzilai (Frankfurt, Berlin, Bern, Brussels, New York, Oxford: Peter Lang, 1997), 137–48. Reprinted in a longer version in J. Hillis Miller, *Others* (Princeton: Princeton University Press, 2001), 65–82. Copyright © 2001 by Princeton University Press.

J. Hillis Miller, "A Conclusion in Which Almost Nothing is Concluded: *Middlemarch*'s 'Finale,'" in *Middlemarch in the Twenty-First Century*, ed. Karen Chase (Oxford: Oxford University Press, 2006), 133–56. Copyright © 2006 by Oxford University Press, Inc.

My frontispiece is a photograph of the statue of *Sleeping Ariadne* in the Vatican Museums, a Roman Hadrianic copy of a Hellenistic sculpture of the Pergamene school of the second century BCE. The statue was widely known and copied, though it was at first thought to be Cleopatra.

See http://en.wikipedia.org/wiki/Sleeping_Ariadne and http://commons.wikimedia.org/wiki/File:Sleeping_Ariadne_2.jpg, both accessed June 27, 2011. The photograph is credited to Wknight94 and comes from the Wikimedia projects.

History is therefore . . . the emergence of a language of power out of a language of cognition.

(Paul de Man, "Kant and Schiller")

Chapter 1

Realism Affirmed and Dismantled in *Adam Bede*

Signs are small measurable things; interpretations are illimitable . . .
(*Middlemarch*, Ch. 1)

Ultimately, man finds in things nothing but what he himself has imported [hineingesteckt] into them: the Something is called Knowledge [Wissenschaft], the importing—art, religion, love, pride.
(Nietzsche, *The Will to Power*, 606)[1]

Under the influence of linguistic and anthropological structuralism, a better knowledge of Russian formalism and of Prague structuralism, accompanied by a renewal of rhetorical criticism, new study tools and terminology for interpreting fiction have proliferated in the last decades. Sometimes it seems as if we may be on the verge of major breakthroughs in the criticism of narrative. Structuralism in the study of narrative has been followed by poststructuralism, by deconstruction, by narratology, by studies in material culture, and, quite recently, by claims that "neuro-aesthetics" will help understand what happens when we read a novel. Material culture studies have proliferated recently in research on the Victorian era, with great benefit to our historical understanding: studies of archives; of the history of book printing, design, advertising, and distribution; of reading practices; even of such matters as how garbage was collected and stored. Dickens's *Our Mutual Friend* is a novel about refuse or waste in the broadest sense. For a recent course at Beliot College on Victorian garbage, see www.beloit.edu/belmag/belmag_wp/?p=1004, accessed June 8, 2011. Each of these methodologies has tended to discount prior work and to claim that it has at last the right strategies for dealing with narratives of all kinds, though each methodology has gone on instigating new work. This work has been done by critics, by linguists, by rhetoricians, by humanistic sociologists, as I would call those who do material studies, and by those with a knowledge of recent developments in neuroscience. This multifarious development has all along been international in scope. The list of its distinguished practitioners would be long.[2]

At the same time new attention is being given to the role in human life generally of what may be called "fictions." "Fiction" is both a literary term and a term for those structures the individual and the community build for themselves in their interpretations of the world. The danger in the development of these modes of analyzing narrative is that the machinery of analysis may get in the way of authentic insight into what is going on in a given text. The lure of a pseudo-scientific certainty may lead to the coldness of detached schematic analysis, with its diagrams and barbarous "narratological" terms. No doubt Gerard Genette is right to see that a given passage in Proust is exceedingly complex stylistically, but one may doubt whether his multitudinous rhetorical terms ("prolepsis," "analepsis," and "metalepsis," for example) open themselves easily to wide adoption by readers and critics. Genette's work sometimes seems a slightly tongue-in-cheek attempt to carry the development of a refined terminology for analysis of narratives as far as it can go, or even a little further.[3] On the other hand, there is no doubt that some pre-structuralist interpretation of fiction is naive and impressionistic compared to the relative sophistication of criticism of poetry already in the "New Criticism."

One way around this problem may be a recognition that novels, like other works of literature, often contain hints and terms for their own reading. When this is so, the critic may not need to use a technical language brought in from the outside. A given novel may contain its own "critical language," it may raise its own questions about its status as fiction. Paul de Man held that texts deconstruct themselves. You do not need to deconstruct them from the outside. Just following their own fault lines is enough. In spite of the usefulness or even the necessity of a more universal terminology, especially the rhetorical and tropological terminology that has been used in recent decades so productively, it may be best to keep inside a given work, to try as much as possible to follow its own lines of self-interpretation or of self-contradiction. *Adam Bede* may be taken as an example by means of which to test the validity of this approach and its conceivable help in making George Eliot's novel something of use for reading today.

Adam Bede and Romanticism

The motto on the title page of *Adam Bede* is from Book Six of Wordsworth's *The Excursion*. In these lines the Pastor explains that in describing his parishioners he will omit the most violent or disastrous stories. This citation presents one self-interpretative element at the beginning of George Eliot's novel. Reading *Adam Bede* in the context of a passage from Wordsworth invites that reader to think of ways to justify the connection. Gordon Haight and U. C. Knoepflmacher have called attention to the way the story of *Adam Bede* recalls Wordsworth's narratives of sorrow, violence, loss, or betrayal, such as "The Thorn," "The Ruined Cottage," or "Michael," or to the way George Eliot, like Wordsworth, tells stories of rural life in a language without false poetic embellishment, the "real language of men in a state of vivid sensation."[4] Like Wordsworth, George Eliot claims to be a realist. She validates her story by appeal to its correspondence to things as they are. Like Wordsworth, she assumes throughout a continuity between man and nature. Language describing one can be used with unostentatious propriety to describe the other in such a way that its problematic metaphorical boldness hardly becomes an issue. Like Wordsworth, George Eliot wishes her stories to achieve universality through the simplicity and starkness of their outlines. This procedure is what William Empson calls a "version of pastoral,"[5] whereby the simple stands for the complex and makes the meaning of urban or cultured life, through a species of metonymy, more available. The putatively male narrator of *Adam Bede*, like the speaker of Wordsworth's poems, continually provides, on the basis of events in the story he?, she?, it? tells, generalizations that overtly express a claim to be universally valid for human life anywhere at any time.

To speak of Eliot's narrator as a "he" allows the reader to keep firmly in mind the distinction between the female author of the novel, Marian Evans (or Mary Ann or Mary Anne: even her real given name is variable), and the created role of the putatively male storyteller, George Eliot. I have considered using "Marian Evans" or "Marian Lewes" when I am speaking of the author, not the narrator, but this has seemed too awkward and too much against convention. "Marian Lewes" was the way she signed her letters after she began living with G. H. Lewes. Marian Evans became George Eliot, however, that is, went into drag, when she picked up her pen and began to write fiction. In *Adam Bede* Marian Evans seems self-consciously to have tried to "write like a man," whatever, exactly, *that* means. The pen name she chose is not entirely random or unmotivated, though it may be difficult to crack its code. It may echo "George Sand," the pseudonym Amantine Lucile Aurore Dupin chose for her works. Sand, notoriously, wore men's clothing in public. "George" is also of course the first name of her partner, George Henry Lewes. Eliot herself said she chose the name because "George was

Mr. Lewes's Christian name, and Eliot was a good mouth-filling, easily pronounced word."[6] Eliot's phrasing seems to be more than a little odd, even disingenuous. Pronouncing "Eliot" is not so much mouth-filling as mouth-opening and mouth-emptying. Saying it requires an expiration followed by the dental "click" of tongue against teeth of that final "t." Even saying "t" requires a mouth-emptying expiration.

After Mary Anne Evans published *Adam Bede* to great acclaim, under the *nom de plume* George Eliot, a certain Joseph Liggins, an obscure person from Nuneaton, where Marian Evans started boarding school in 1828, came forward and claimed to have written it, as well as Eliot's earlier *Scenes from Clerical Life*.[7] Many people for a good while believed his claim. I have decided to refer throughout this book to the narrators of *Adam Bede* and *Middlemarch* for the most part as "he," since she maintained the masculine pen name of George Eliot for all her work, long after everyone knew who the author was. Even that scrupulosity is a considerable over-simplification, as my figure of metaphorically going in drag already suggests. I have remained uneasy about which pronoun to use, as the way I keep returning to this issue will indicate, but saying he? she? it? over and over has seemed too awkward. I have found myself, nevertheless, often doing that anyway, to show I still see the problem. I am aware, however, that no choice in this case is innocent. I can well understand how some people might want Mary Anne Evans and her narrators always to be given female designations, in order to keep evident the fact that she is a great English woman writer. I think it is better, however, to recognize that gender distinctions are problematic in her life and work. She felt she had to take a male pseudonym in order to get a fair reading at that time and place for her fiction, especially since she was known to be living with a man to whom she was not married. Calling her narrators "he" or "it" is one way to keep gender questions salient when making readings of her work. Such questions are certainly central in the stories she tells. Nicholas Royle speaks eloquently, apropos of the narrator of *Middlemarch*, of "this narrator-madness," of "this male-female-author-metafictional character-narrator phantasmagoric collage of narratorial positions."[8] The classic essay on the neutrality (in both senses of the word) of the narrative voice in fiction is Maurice Blanchot's "La voix narrative (le 'il', le neutre)" ("The Narrative Voice [the 'he,' the neutral]").[9] I should think "il" would be better translated in this case as "it," since Blanchot's point is that the narrative voice is neuter. French "il" can be either masculine or neuter.

All the similarities between Wordsworth and Eliot are made explicit by the epigraph in its invitation to set Wordsworth and *Adam Bede* side by side, reading each in terms of the other:

> So that ye may have
> Clear images before your gladdened eyes
> Of nature's unambitious underwood
> And flowers that prosper in the shade. And when
> I speak of such among the flock as swerved
> Or fell, those only shall be singled out
> Upon whose lapse, or error, something more
> Than brotherly forgiveness may attend.[10]

Another deeper, more problematical relation of *Adam Bede* to the Romantic tradition may be identified. Romanticism has in an influential twentieth-century tradition been interpreted as the humanization or demystifying of Romance, or as the internalization of Quest Romance, or as a bringing into the open of a tension fundamental in literature between "representational" and "allegorical" elements.[11] These are different ways in which the triumph of the Romantic poets has been defined as a rediscovery of the autonomy and dangerous strength of the human imagination as it expresses its dominion over things through the power of words, or as it discovers the interference of dominion by language. What, it may be asked, if the mind exercising this power is not Wordsworth or Blake but Dorothea Brooke or Adam Bede, Dinah Morris or Hetty Sorrel, Emma Bovary, Pip in *Great Expectations*, Clara Middleton in *The Egoist*, Lizzie Eustace or Ayala in Trollope's *The Eustace Diamonds* and *Ayala's Angel*, Eustacia Vye in *The Return of the Native*, Conrad's Jim, or the narrator of Henry James's *The Sacred Fount*? The humanizing of Romance becomes, it may be, quite a different thing when it is displaced from the sovereign poet creating with his mastery over language the supreme fictions by which others may live, as Wallace Stevens puts it, to the more prosaic hero or heroine of a "realistic" novel. Such a person is firmly placed within an imagined community, trammeled by it. Nevertheless, a thematic continuity exists between the poet of *The Prelude* and all these Victorian and modernist heroes and heroines. One useful definition of much nineteenth-century fiction is to say that it transfers to the life of ordinary people in rural or urban society themes dramatized by the Romantic poets as the solitary experience of someone with an extraordinarily gifted imagination.

Such transference calls for corresponding changes in the strategies of criticism. In reading lyric poetry the critic must often demystify critical presuppositions of a metaphysical kind, the assumption that the poetic text names, reveals, or is founded on some spiritual reality which exists independent of it. This can best be done by showing that the poem itself puts such metaphysical presuppositions in question. An example is the metaphorical use of religious terms in *The Prelude*. This is countered by Wordsworth's explicit recognition that "Though reared upon the base of outward things, / Structures like these the excited spirit mainly / Builds for herself."[12] The critic of fiction, on the other hand, must most often put in question the presuppositions of realism, the assumption that a given novel is validated by its exact correspondence to some social, natural, or historical reality, something extra-verbal that pre-exists the words. She must look for ways in which the text itself performs such a putting in question. Novels, like lyric poetry, tend to rest on an unresolvable tension between mimetic and "allegorical," intratextual elements.

This invitation to a realistic reading, that is nevertheless shown to be fallacious by the work itself, takes forms special to the conventions of the Western novel. These forms often arise from a novel's explicit commitment to what may seem a naively mimetic theory of fiction. Such commitment is, nevertheless, in one way or another challenged by the effort of storytelling. It is challenged not only by the novelists' practices, but also in the thematic and dramatic development of the stories told. Often a novel turns back on itself in such a way that themes dramatized within the narrative raise questions about the status of the novel as a text. One might transpose to the novel Walter Benjamin's assertion about Brecht's staging. Some novels, such a rewriting of Benjamin would assert, "give expression to the relationship between the story being told and everything that is involved in the act of storytelling *per se*."[13] This turning back of the story told on the question of what it means to tell a story often constitutes one of the best avenues to understanding a given novel and to identifying the uses reading it might have today.

Adam Bede as Paradigmatic Realist Novel

At first sight, or perhaps even after a careful reading, *Adam Bede* may seem to raise no such problems. Few novels, in explicit theory and in triumphantly successful practice, have so admirably fulfilled the conventions of realism. Moreover, critics from George Eliot's day to the present have for the most part interpreted *Adam Bede* as straightforward realism. Chapter 17, "In Which the Story Pauses a Little," presents a classic definition of realism as "the faithful representing of commonplace things" (17: 159–67).[14] I discuss this chapter in detail in Chapter 3 below, in the course of my reading of *Middlemarch*. That discussion fits in better later on with the sequence of my argument. The definition of realism in chapter 17 of *Adam Bede* is reinforced, however, in many other statements by George Eliot, for example in her letters or in the important article of 1856 on Wilhelm Heinrich von Riehl, "The Natural

History of German Life."[15] In all these places she associates herself with a sociological fidelity in the description of rural life and customs. "[M]y strongest effort," says the narrator in the crucial passage in *Adam Bede*, "is . . . to give a faithful account of men and things as they have mirrored themselves in my mind. The mirror is doubtless defective; the outlines will sometimes be disturbed, the reflection faint or confused; but I feel as much bound to tell you as precisely as I can what that reflection is, as if I were in the witness-box narrating my experience on oath" (17: 159).

The justification for this resolute exactness of imitation follows: "These fellow-mortals, every one, must be accepted as they are: you can neither straighten their noses, nor brighten their wit, nor rectify their dispositions; and it is these people—amongst whom your life is passed—that it is needful you should tolerate, pity, and love: it is these more or less ugly, stupid, inconsistent people, whose movements of goodness you should be able to admire—for whom you should cherish all possible hopes, all possible patience" (17: 160). This avowed intention is magnificently accomplished in the circumstantial descriptions of rural culture in Warwickshire at the turn of the century: the picture of the carpenter shop of Jonathan Burge which opens the novel, the picture of the Hall Farm, or the details of dairying there, or of the Church in Hayslope, or of the harvest supper, and so on. I shall return in my section on *Middlemarch* to what is at stake in Eliot's assumption that most ordinary people are "more or less ugly, stupid, inconsistent." The assumption, I may say now, however, is false, at least false to my experience of rural people on Deer Isle, Maine, or in Sedgwick, Maine, where I now live during different times of the year.

This claim of a fidelity to what is real is like that of the Dutch genre paintings George Eliot so much admired and to which she implicitly refers in chapter 17 (17: 162).[16] This fidelity is confirmed by the use throughout *Adam Bede* of a narrator who is a kind of camera eye, therefore an "it" rather than a "he" or "she," though this "it" speaks of itself as an "I." This narrator is a "licensed trespasser" who speaks in the present tense of events sixty years past and who moves invisibly from one house or farm to another, inviting the reader to share his power to look in windows or to enter houses unannounced and unseen: "I will show you the roomy workshop of Jonathan Burge . . ." (1: 5); "Let me take you into that dining-room, and show you the Rev. Adolphus Irwine . . . We will enter very softly, and stand still in the open doorway without awaking the glossy-brown setter who is stretched across the hearth . . ." (5: 49); "Yes, the house must be inhabited, and we will see by whom; for imagination is a licensed trespasser: it has no fear of dogs, but may climb over walls and peep in at windows with impunity. Put your face to one of the glass panes in the right-hand window: what do you see?" (6: 65).

This narrator has also a constantly used power of withdrawal and of generalizing comment. He (please remember my reasons stated above for using "he" rather than "she") possesses a loving intimacy of knowledge, but also a detached perspective on history. From this distance he can make connections between one part of the story and another. He can provide comments on all the parts, comments that draw them together so that they form a unified system. This system is a unified whole that is validly, even scientifically, analyzed and explained. It is seen as though it were a patterned fabric. The fabric is made of recurring designs that may be subsumed under universal laws. Such a process of analysis is analogous in a fictive mode to the work of an anthropologist who reduces a primitive culture to an interpreted structure that may be assimilated into the universal enterprise of scientific comprehension.

The characters in the novel, it may be noted, are for the most part unaware of the meanings the narrator finds in the story he tells. They do not know all that the narrator and the reader know about what sustains their community. They do not know that a clairvoyant or telepathic licensed trespasser is spying on their every thought and feeling, as well as on their behavior and speech. I borrow the word "telepathic" from Nicholas Royle's remarkable essay arguing persuasively that it would be better to call the characteristic narrators of nineteenth-century English novels "telepathic" rather than to employ the more usual word, "omniscient."[17] George Eliot, for example, by the time she wrote *Adam Bede* apparently no longer believed in a personified, ubiquitous, all-knowing deity, however nostalgic she may have been for the comforts of such belief. However, the morning hymn by the seventeenth-century bishop of Bath and Wells, Thomas Ken, which Adam Bede sings in the first chapter of the novel, indicates that Adam, at least, believes an omniscient God knows his every thought: "For God's all-seeing eye surveys / Thy secret thoughts, thy works and ways" (1: 12). Some readers may at this point reflect that the narrator is just such an unseen all-seeing eye, a licensed trespasser and spy, a telepathist. Think what that would be like! Someone knows my every thought and feeling at all times. I cannot find any hiding place.

The ultimate purpose of the narrator's interpretation in *Adam Bede* is to confirm certain moral laws, most notably the evil of egoism as the source of human suffering and the good of self-denying sympathy. The central action of *Adam Bede*, the action that justifies its title, dramatizes this opposition. It follows the change in Adam from a hard clarity of vision leading him to judge others too harshly to a sympathy for others born of suffering. This softening makes him a new Adam worthy to marry Dinah.

The structuring principles of the interpretation offered by the narrator may be identified. A large number of metaphors drawn from the natural world, from animate or inanimate nature, both biological and mechanical realms, runs through the novel. Here are several examples from a great many: Rector Irwine is compared to a dog in his fondness for classical literature: "if you feed your young setter on raw flesh, how can you wonder at its retaining a relish for uncooked partridge in after life?" (5: 63). Hetty's beauty is compared to that "of kittens, or very small downy ducks," and then to a whole "descriptive catalogue" of other natural things (7: 76–7). The narrator says of Hetty and Arthur: "Such young unfurrowed souls roll to meet each other like two velvet peaches that touch softly and are at rest; they mingle as easily as two brooklets that ask for nothing but to entwine themselves and ripple with ever-interlacing curves in the leafiest hiding-places" (12: 120). Arthur in his yielding to the temptation to seduce Hetty is compared to those apparently seaworthy vessels which "are liable to casualties, which sometimes make terribly evident some flaw in their construction, that would never have been discoverable in smooth water" (12: 114). The narrator comments on the intertwining of Adam's love for Hetty and his eager interest in the technicalities of house-building that "our love is inwrought in our enthusiasm as electricity is inwrought in the air, exalting its power by a subtle presence" (33: 320). The narrator observes of Hetty's coldness toward Adam: "he could no more stir in her the emotions that make the sweet intoxication of young love, than the mere picture of a sun can stir the spring sap in the subtle fibres of the plant" (9: 90). So pervasive are such figures, both in the narrator's discourse and in the characters' speeches, that the inextricable intertwining of human beings and nature can be said to be nothing less than the basic ideological doctrine of *Adam Bede*. It is, one might believe, assumed throughout, never put in question.

Such tropes solve one big problem that exists for both narrators and characters, though in a different way for each. Thoughts and feelings in the sense of a global state of mind are, notoriously, difficult to express in language. No agreed-upon literal language exists for anger or love. In spite of Eliot's praise of sympathy, "feeling with," as the basis of morality, she did not, the evidence of her novels suggests, have much confidence that people (as opposed to telepathic narrators) have spontaneous insight into what another person is thinking or feeling. I shall return to this issue in my reading of *Middlemarch*. It is true that in *Adam Bede* the narrator sometimes makes observations that seem to indicate we can read other people's minds, at least the mind of some other people. Dinah Morris, exceptionally, is remarkably candid and transparent. The narrator speaks of Dinah's "calm pitying face, with its open glance which told that her heart lived in no cherished secrets of its own, but in feelings which it longed to share with the world" (14: 128). Dinah's feelings, however, are mediated by her face, which "tells" of her thoughts and feelings. Eliot elsewhere in the novel emphasizes the way faces may lie as well as tell the truth. Dinah, moreover, is bending her pitying glance on Hetty, who at that moment is lost in her dreams of being loved by Arthur Donnithorne. She pays little attention to Dinah's open face and loving speech. The narrator stresses a few sentences later that "Dinah was a riddle to her; . . . but she did not care to solve such riddles" (14: 128). A few pages after his assertion that Dinah's face is a veracious index to her mind and feelings, the narrator ironically asserts the stark counter-truth, apropos of men's propensity to misread the inner natures of the women they love: "Every man under such circumstances is conscious of being a great physiognomist. Nature, he knows, has a language of her own, which she uses with strict veracity, and he considers himself an adept in the language. Nature has written out his bride's character for him in those exquisite lines of cheek and lip and chin, in those eyelids delicate as petals, in those long lashes curled like the stamen of a flower, in the dark liquid depths of those wonderful eyes" (15: 138).

For Eliot, even in this early novel, we have at most indirect guesses at what is going on in other minds. Edmund Husserl called this "analogical apperception," that is, the assumption that the other person's thoughts and feeling must be analogous to my own.[18] Almost everyone, however, has seen a small brook, or a sunset, or a flower opening, or has touched a velvet-skinned peach. I can perhaps convey to you my state of mind by comparing it metaphorically to some natural phenomenon we both have experienced, as when Dinah tells Mr. Irwine that she sometimes feels "as if I could sit silent all day long with the thought of God overflowing my soul—as the pebbles lie bathed in the Willow Brook" (8: 82). The problem for the narrator is different because he is granted telepathic or omniscient knowledge of what all the characters are thinking and feeling. The narrator's challenge is to find ways to communicate that knowledge to readers. Comparisons of human beings' subjective secrecies to natural phenomena are an indispensable tool for doing this.

Such tropes are versions of that Wordsworthian assimilation of man and nature promised by the novel's epigraph. George Eliot's narrator, however, uses a more technical language than Wordsworth in his comparisons. The narrator has in mind specific models drawn from physics, from mechanics, or from biology. Such metaphors indicate that people, like natural or organic things, apparently have fixed natures, Hetty's hard egoism or Dinah's innate power of sympathy. "[T]hings take no more hold on [Hetty]," says Mrs. Poyser, "than if she was a dried pea," and she's "no better nor a cherry wi' a hard stone inside it" (31: 305, 306).

This scientism is reinforced by an overt commitment to a universal law of causality. The novel affirms a materialistic doctrine of time in which each event is caused by preceding events and may be fully explained by them. Change occurs in the human as in the natural realm according to regular and predictable laws. Time forms a causal chain of "links," to use a word from the titles of chapters 16 and 33. The world of *Adam Bede* is apparently one in which the human realm is conceived according to a strict analogy with the physical or biological world as it was seen by mid-nineteenth-century science, the science of the time just before Darwin. *Adam Bede* was published in 1859, the year of *The Origin of Species*, so Eliot could not yet have known that work, only its precursors. In such a scientistic world there is no discontinuity between men and things. The law for both is a rigid determinism. "Men's lives," says Mr. Irwine, "are as thoroughly blended with each other as the air they breathe: evil spreads as necessarily as disease" (41: 380). In such a world, there are no hiatuses, no spaces allowing for discontinuity or unpredictability. Every event can be explained by its cause. This cause has directly and intimately touched it to bring it about.

This way of assimilating the social realm to the current conception of the physical world leads directly to the "doctrine of consequences" that is so important a part of the fabric of moral judgment in *Adam Bede*. A human action, such as Hetty's seduction by Arthur, enters into an irreversible all-embracing stream of cause and effect. Once done it can never be undone. Hetty's deflowering and pregnancy is a physical fact. Its effects will proliferate onward indefinitely in ever widening circles of influence as "the bitter waters spread" (40: 369). "[T]hat's the deepest curse of all . . . ," cries Adam, "that's what makes the blackness of it . . . *it can never be undone.* My poor Hetty . . . she can never be my sweet Hetty again" (41: 379).

The interpretation of the story proposed by the narrator matches perfectly the mimetic theory of fiction he (she? it?) defends and practices. A novel is not an invention or a construction, not a "fiction" in the Nietzschean or Borgesean sense. It is a mirror, and the cool reflection of the narrator who observes the action from a distance both spatial and temporal allows him to move from particular witnessed events to scientific generalizations about the laws governing those events, laws valid for all men at all times. These laws superimpose on the linear sequence of the narrative an encompassing network of connections, relations, and abstractions. The narrative thereby becomes one example validating George Eliot's early version of what in the twentieth century was to be called "the human sciences." Aesthetic theory corresponds to moral message. The traditional interpretations of George Eliot's work according to this self-confirming reciprocity seem unassailable, wholly correct.

This would still be true even though it might be agreed that George Eliot does not mean the reader to believe that the story really did happen in history in just the way the narrator says it did. A fictional dimension is present even though Eliot asserted that the novel was based on a real event, what she called her "aunt's story" of a girl who killed her illegitimate baby, and even though Adam Bede is based on Eliot's father. These historical facts were reshaped by the narrative to create what Wolfgang Iser calls the "pragmatization" of the diffuse human power of conceiving an imaginary world.[19] Though it is a fictional construct, however, the story is still validated by its truth of correspondence to historical, social, and human reality. This reality is assumed to exist outside language. Even if the narrator and the story he tells are fictions they are implicitly affirmed to correspond rigorously to similar verbalized mirroring, for example those of Riehl, which might be performed for the "real" historical world. Riehl did this for German rural life. He called this the *Naturgeschichte des Volks*, translated by Eliot in her review of Riehl's work as "The Natural History of German Life."[20] If the story had happened in exactly this way it could have been truly told and truly interpreted in just the way George Eliot's narrator does tell and interpret the story of *Adam Bede*.

Challenges to the Paradigm of Realism in *Adam Bede*

There are, however, other details of the language of *Adam Bede*, puzzling passages that do not seem easily assimilated to the explanation. I have just given. To follow the implications of such passages is to discover that *Adam Bede*, like Dickens's *Bleak House* or his *Sketches by Boz*, like Meredith's *The Ordeal of Richard Feverel*, or like Hardy's *Tess of the d'Urbervilles*, puts in question its own apparent assumptions and has, as a consequence, a meaning far different from its manifest one.

One such passage comes in the opening sentences of the novel: "With a single drop of ink for a mirror, the Egyptian sorcerer undertakes to reveal to any chance comer far-reaching visions of the past. This is what I undertake to do for you, reader. With this drop of ink at the end of my pen, I will show you the roomy workshop of Mr Jonathan Burge, carpenter and builder, in the village of Hayslope, as it appeared on the eighteenth of June, in the year of our Lord 1799" (1: 5). Part of this has already been cited as an example of the narrator's ability to "show" the reader. The remainder of that sentence is the initial example in *Adam Bede* of the circumstantiality as to names, dates, places, and occupations which, as Ian Watt long ago demonstrated, is so important a part of realistic fiction's tradition.[21] This opening metaphor, however, must not be too easily passed over. It contains the first example in the novel of the mirror motif. This metaphor is of course a frequent figure for the relation between imitation and imitated in the tradition of realism, as in George Eliot's defense of realism in chapter 17 of *Adam Bede*. Mirrors, moreover, are used in a subtle way in this novel, as later in *Middlemarch*. They objectify self-regarding egotism, as when the vain Hetty Sorrel is shown in *Adam Bede* admiring her reflection in her aunt's polished furniture or dressing secretly in her tawdry finery before the mirror in her room.

This initial mirror is, however, an unusual one. It is made of a drop of ink. Though a drop of ink has a shiny reflecting surface and so might conceivably be used, in some odd emergency, as a mirror, this is a magic drop of ink. It reveals not what is immediately around it but "far-reaching visions of the past," such as telepathic mediums can see in their crystal balls or such as Egyptian sorcerers can see in magic drops of ink. Eliot's context here is the Victorian vogue of mediumistic séances, table rappings, and the like, as well as her reading of Edward W. Lane's Book, *An Account of the Manners and Customs of Modern Egyptians*.[22] The metaphor of the mirroring drop of ink calls attention, in the opening sentences of the novel, to puzzling aspects of mimetic theories of language. This ink drop is a mirror that is no mirror. It is a magical inscription that calls the past back into the present. It spreads out in the following paragraphs to form the written words bringing before the reader's imagination the carpenter shop of Jonathan Burge. A mirror that is an inscription is a transformation of the material world into another realm, the realm of performative writing that creates what it seemingly only describes. In that realm one encounters something outside the optic laws of reflection. One encounters, that is, some of the problematic aspects of language.

One of these is the way the same kinds of signs, articulated sounds or black marks inscribed on white, must do service for the names of physical objects like a door or a hammer, as well as for the names of things of a different sort: love, feeling, music, or religious emotion. Other examples are the way language is irreducibly temporal and the way every detail of grammar, syntax, or diction in a text, not to speak of each use of figurative language, is not a neutral reflection of something "out there." It is an interpretation or a transposition into language according to innumerable question-begging assumptions about language, grammar, and syntax. These are woven into the fabric of the language used and are different from language to language. Chinese, for example, has no pronouns and no verb tenses. Imposition of the grid of a given language is impossible to avoid by any means, not even by the most extravagant torsion of language back on itself. "[W]e all of us, grave or light," says George Eliot in a passage in *Middlemarch* I shall cite more than once, "get our thoughts entangled in metaphors, and act fatally on the strength of them" (10: 93).[23] If the complexity of meaning in *Adam Bede* is present, in part, in an unresolved conflict between a mimetic theory of fictional language and a counter-insight into the way language generates its own meanings through its relations to anterior linguistic conventions, this conflict is already present in the opening paradox of the mirroring drop of ink. The strategy of *Adam Bede* might be defined as the presentation in the story of one example of the implications of this initial metaphor. The words of the novel are the spreading out of that drop of ink to show the reader all the story of Hetty, Adam, and Dinah, in an expansion of narrative and interpretation of that narrative which, as it is produced, more and more makes it impossible to accept at face value any mirroring theory of fiction.

Four Passages Challenging Mimetic Realism

The problematic of language, to which I have just alluded, is one of the elements entangled among a recurring set of other themes in four important passages spaced throughout *Adam Bede*. The exploration of these will bring more clearly into the open the way *Adam Bede* puts its own overt assumptions in question. The reader will note that in these segments, Eliot's inveterate penchant for making universal generalizations on the basis of unique particulars is already in full operation. However much value Eliot gives to "the faithful representing of commonplace things" (17: 162), she seems to value almost as much the general laws that may be drawn from such things. The implication is that a universal human nature exists, the same in all places, times, cultures, and for all classes of people. A small example: apropos of the exceptional joy the love-smitten Adam Bede has in carpentry work, the narrator observes: "All passion becomes strength when it has an outlet from the narrow limits of our personal lot in the labor of our right arm, the cunning of our right hand, or the still, creative activity of our thought" (19: 191).

I shall return to this issue in my analysis of *Middlemarch*. Here are the longish passages I want to look at more closely:

> He was but three-and-twenty, and had only just learned what it is to love—to love with that adoration which a young man gives to a woman whom he feels to be greater and better than himself. Love of this sort is hardly distinguishable from religious feeling. What deep and worthy love is so? whether of woman or child, or art or music. Our caresses, our tender words, our still rapture under the influence of autumn sunsets, or pillared vistas, or calm majestic statues, or Beethoven symphonies, all bring with them the consciousness that they are mere waves and ripples in an unfathomable ocean of love and beauty; our emotion in its keenest moment passes from expression into silence, our love at its highest flood rushes beyond its object, and loses itself in the sense of divine mystery. (3: 34)

> It was to Adam the time that a man can least forget in after-life—the time when he believes that the first woman he has ever loved betrays by a slight something, a word, a tone, a glance, the quivering of a lip or an eyelid, that she is at least beginning to love him in return. The sign is so slight, it is scarcely perceptible to the ear or eye—he could describe it to no one—it is a mere feather-touch, yet it seems to have changed his whole being, to have merged an uneasy yearning into a delicious unconsciousness of everything but the present moment. So much of our early gladness vanishes utterly from our memory: we can never recall the joy with which we laid our heads on our mother's bosom or rode on our father's back in childhood; doubtless that joy is wrought up into our nature, as the sunlight of long-past mornings is wrought up in the soft mellowness of the apricot; but it is gone forever from our imagination, and we can only *believe* in the joy of childhood. But the first glad moment in our first love is a vision which returns to us to the last, and brings with it a thrill of feeling intense and special as the recurrent sensation of a sweet odour breathed in a far-off hour of happiness. (20: 199)

> Possibly you think that Adam was not at all sagacious in his interpretations, and that it was altogether extremely unbecoming in a sensible man to behave as he did—falling in love with a girl who really had nothing more than her beauty to recommend her, attributing imaginary virtues to her, and even condescending to cleave to her after she had fallen in love with another man, waiting for her kind looks as a patient trembling dog waits for his master's eye to be turned upon him . . . For my own part, however, I respect him none the less: nay, I think the deep love he had for that sweet, rounded, blossom-like, dark-eyed Hetty, of whose inward self he was really very ignorant, came out of the very strength of his nature, and not out of any inconsistent weakness. Is it any weakness, pray, to be wrought on by exquisite music?—to feel its wondrous harmonies searching the subtlest windings of your soul, the delicate fibres of life where no memory can penetrate, and binding together your whole being past and present in one unspeakable vibration: melting you in one moment with all the tenderness, all the love that has been scattered through the toilsome years, concentrating in one emotion of heroic courage or resignation all the hard-learnt lessons of self-renouncing sympathy, blending

your present joy with past sorrow, and your present sorrow with all your past joy? If not, then neither is it a weakness to be so wrought upon by the exquisite curves of a woman's cheek and neck and arms, by the liquid depths of her beseeching eyes, or the sweet childish pout of her lips. For the beauty of a lovely woman is like music: what can one say more? Beauty has an expression beyond and far above the one woman's soul that it clothes, as the words of genius have a wider meaning than the thought that prompted them: it is more than a woman's love that moves us in a woman's eyes—it seems to be a far-off mighty love that has come near to us, and made speech for itself there; the rounded neck, the dimpled arm, move us by something more than their prettiness—by their close kinship with all we have known of tenderness and peace. The noblest nature sees the most of this *impersonal* expression in beauty (it is needless to say that there are gentlemen with whiskers dyed and undyed who see none of it whatever), and for this reason, the noblest nature is often the most blinded to the character of the one woman's soul that the beauty clothes. Whence, I fear, the tragedy of human life is likely to continue for a long time to come, in spite of mental philosophers who are ready with the best receipts [recipes] for avoiding all mistakes of the kind.

Our good Adam had no fine words into which he could put his feeling for Hetty; he could not disguise mystery in this way with the appearance of knowledge; he called his love frankly a mystery, as you have heard him . . . How could he imagine narrowness, selfishness, hardness in her? He created the mind he believed in out of his own, which was large, unselfish, tender. (33: 318–19)

That is a simple scene, reader. But it is almost certain that you, too, have been in love—perhaps, even, more than once, though you may not choose to say so to all your feminine friends. If so, you will no more think the slight words, the timid looks, the tremulous touches, by which two human souls approach each other gradually, like two little quivering rain-streams, before they mingle into one—you will no more think these things trivial than you will think the first-detected signs of coming spring trivial, though they be but a faint, indescribable something in the air and in the song of the birds, and the tiniest perceptible budding on the hedgerow branches. Those slight words and looks and touches are part of the soul's language; and the finest language, I believe, is chiefly made up of unimposing words, such as "light," "sound," "stars," "music,"—words really not worth looking at, or hearing, in them-selves, any more than "chips" or "sawdust:" it is only that they happen to be the signs of something unspeakably great and beautiful. I am of opinion that love is a great and beautiful thing too; and if you agree with me, the smallest signs of it will not be chips and sawdust to you: they will rather be like those little words, "light" and "music," stirring the long-winding fibres of your memory, and enriching your present with your most precious past. (50: 441)

Most of the important interpretative motifs in *Adam Bede* are inter-woven in these texts, for example the assimilation of human psychology to natural fact. The secret presence in a man's "nature" of the forgot-ten joy of early childhood is like the indwelling of past sunlight in "the soft mellowness of the apricot." Lovers come together like two little quivering rain-streams. These passages radiate outward to connect with everything else in *Adam Bede*, both on the level of dramatic action and on the level of the narrator's sustained *continuo* of commentary on that action. Moreover, the four passages clearly echo one another. Though they are spaced at wide distances within the story, they resonate. They are like the return of a melody in a Beethoven sonata. Vibrations within the reader's memory as she reads invite her to interpret each text in terms of the others and to superimpose all four as radiant nodes of self-commentary repeated with a difference at intervals within the novel, each spreading outward to suggest an interpretation of the whole. To explicate these texts fully would be in fact to interpret the entire novel. Though that completeness will not be attempted here, and may in principle be impossible in any case, a beginning can be made.

The doctrine these texts propose seems clear enough. Certain fundamental human experiences—falling in love, religious feeling, strong responses to nature or to works of art—are structurally and qualitatively similar.[24] All are strongly emotive. All involve the loss of self-possession in a powerful sense of sympathy for someone or something outside oneself. All involve an interpretation of signs that differs in important ways from the ordinary understanding of words or other tokens. The usual sign is commensurate with its referent in the sense that it corresponds to it in a one-to-one matching in which there seems to be no mystery. This kind of sign seems consistent with the rational, scientific interpretation of human culture proposed throughout *Adam Bede* by the narrator. It also corresponds to the novel's theoretical realism. A mimetic novel must employ straightforwardly mimetic words. A referential theory of signs is also consistent with the hard-headed realism, a resolute determination to call a hammer a hammer, that is associated especially with Adam. This realism exists in his nature alongside his sensitivity to the "mystery" in religious or loving feeling. "[T]he natur o' things doesn't change," says Adam, "though it seems as if one's own life was nothing but change. The square o' four is sixteen, and you must lengthen your lever in proportion to your weight, is as true when a man's miserable as when he's happy; and the best o' working is, it gives you a grip hold o' things outside your own lot" (11: 105). The apparently casual examples the narrator gives of unproblematically mimetic words are "chips" and "sawdust." These names are associated with carpentry, that prime example in the novel of a realistic, measuring, constructive, calculating involvement with the world.

Side by side with such language is another different kind of sign, words like "light," "sound," "stars," "music." These words are associated with art and with the beautiful aspects of nature, the sources of two of the emotive experiences recurring in these passages. Other such signs are the first tiny indications that the woman a man loves is coming to love him in return, or "the first-detected signs of coming spring," or the subtle implications of "the words of genius." Such signs are incommensurate with what they name in the sense that though they name things of deep significance they are in themselves slight or trivial physical indications, no different from straightforwardly referential words like "chips" and "sawdust." Though words like "light," "sound," "stars," and "music" are in this like other signs, they are nevertheless the names of transcendent qualities or values. Such entities can never be weighed or measured. They come into existence, for us, only in the strength of our emotional response to the more or less trivial signs for them. This response links the present to the past just as any case of what Marcel Proust calls a *signe memoratif* does, the taste of Madeleine cake dipped in tea for Proust, the repetition of a sweet odor breathed in long ago for Eliot. "The secret of our emotions," says the narrator, "never lies in the bare object, but in its subtle relations to our own past" (18: 180). Those relations are to a past that is punctuated with intimations of what seems to be "an unfathomable ocean of love and beauty."

The referential theory of language that is adequate for "chips" and "sawdust" will not do for this other kind of sign. By implication such words also put in question the realistic theory of fiction on which the novel seems to be based. Non-mimetic signs are not valid indices of what they seem to point to in the physical world, as Hetty's beauty is not the index of her soul. They point rather to something that exists beyond the reach of referential language. The notion of a failure of emotive language as it passes beyond expression into silence recurs in these citations. "[O]ur emotion in its keenest moment," says the narrator, "passes from expression into silence" (3: 34). Words like "stars" and "music" are said to be "the signs of something unspeakably great and beautiful" (50: 441). The word "unspeakably" must be taken literally here. It indicates the paradoxical power of certain signs to indicate something beyond signification in the usual sense, something impossible to see and name in the way chips and sawdust can be seen and named. Wolfgang Iser might call it "the imaginary."[25]

The "something unspeakably great and beautiful"—quality, value, or power—is given a consistent metaphorical description in these passages. It is an "ocean" of love and beauty, a fathomless reservoir of feeling sustaining human good. It transcends time and any spatially limited objects. It may therefore be reached by many avenues and at any time—by love, by religious feeling, by a beautiful sunset, a statue, or a symphony by

Beethoven. It is "an unfathomable ocean of love and beauty" (3: 34), "a far-off mighty love" which in any of the various signs for it seems to have "come near to us, and made speech for itself there" (33: 319). To respond to a woman, a sunset, or a work of art with a spontaneous overflow of powerful feelings is to escape from the scientific world of cause and effect where each thing is limited at any one moment to one spot in space and time. This escape reaches a sudden perception that all the times of one's life form an organic network of relations. "[A] certain consciousness of our entire past and our imagined future," says the narrator, "blends itself with all our moments of keen sensibility" (18: 180). Such a perception is an important motif in these passages. It appears in the notion in the second text, so Wordsworthian or even Proustian in its resonance, of a binding together of two times in a man's life though a repetition of the same emotion triggered by a *signe memoratif*. The affective remembering of first love produces "a thrill of feeling as intense and special as the recurrent sensation of a sweet odour breathed in a far-off hour of happiness" (20: 199). In the third and fourth citations an emotive response to something present in the present is said to be sometimes so intense that it resurrects all a man's past as a present possession, in a unified fabric or melody transcending the ordinary detachment of one moment from another, "binding together your whole being past and present-in one unspeakable vibration" (33: 319), "stirring the long-winding fibres of your memory, and enriching your present with your most precious past" (50: 441). This transcendence of temporal limitation goes along with the experience of reaching the "unfathomable ocean" of love. In fact the two forms of transcendence are the same. The doctrine about time and the transcendent the narrator proposes in these passages is a more or less Christian form of what Jacques Derrida was to call "logocentrism." I shall have more to say about this in my reading of *Middlemarch*.

Of all the examples of strong feeling in these passages, falling in love is clearly the most important. The other examples are introduced as metaphors of loving: "For the beauty of a lovely woman is like music: what can one say more?" (33: 319). Falling in love is the most important case of what is meant by the key-word "sympathy" in *Adam Bede*. The reaching out of one person toward another in self-forgetful yearning, "the life in another life which is the essence of real human love" (43: 387), is for George Eliot the generative origin of any community. The love of a man for a woman is a synecdochic miniature of the relations that must bind the members of any living community together. This act must be repeated, renewed again and again, if the community is to be sustained, for the community exists only in concrete acts of "self-renouncing sympathy" (33: 319). *Adam Bede* ends with a marriage that is another synecdoche, part for whole. The marriage of Adam and Dinah stands for the re-establishment of the community of Hayslope after the illicit love of Arthur and Hetty has nearly destroyed it. Seth's love for Dinah, in the first passage I have cited, is in the following paragraph said to be analogous to the collective religious feeling of the early Methodists. Methodism is described in the same language as that used to describe individual acts of love. No wonder Blackwood was alarmed! The narrator presents a "picture" of Methodism as "an amphitheatre of green hills, or the deep shade of broad-leaved sycamores, where a crowd of rough men and weary-hearted women drank in a faith which was a rudimentary culture, which linked their thoughts with the past, lifted their imagination above the sordid details of their own narrow lives, and suffused their souls with the sense of a pitying, loving, infinite Presence, sweet as summer to the houseless needy" (3: 34–5).

My preliminary interpretation of these four passages has moved well beyond the scientism identified initially in George Eliot's theory of realism and in the implications of the materialist, quasi-scientific strand of the novel's metaphorical texture. Alongside the clear-headed, rationalistic vision that sees things as they are and calls them by their most exact names, there exists for the individual and for the community a power of sympathy that transcends such vision. Such sympathy relates people to a boundless source of love sustaining the community and giving it authenticity. *Adam Bede* seems to pivot on the tension between these two ways of looking at things. It seems to balance between the scientific rigor that George Eliot had learned from Mill, Spencer, Lewes, Comte, and others, and her desire to maintain some vestige of the religious faith and securely founded moral judgment she had apparently left behind for good with her childhood in Warwickshire. This maintaining may perhaps depend covertly on Spinozistic images, as in the notion of individual experiences of strong feeling as "mere waves and ripples" in the "unfathomable ocean of love and beauty." George Eliot translated not only Spinoza's *Ethics*, but also his *Tractatus Theologico-Politicus*. She may have been especially interested in Spinoza's theory of interpretation in the *Tractatus*. Spinoza, as she knew, was the forefather of the Higher Biblical Criticism of Eliot's day. That criticism was crucially important to her intellectual development. Spinoza believed that religious and political interpretations, such as Jewish readings of the Torah, were projections of unfounded presuppositions. They were errors in a way analogous to Eliot's presentation of her characters' love for another person as a misinterpretation. I shall discuss this in detail in my analysis of *Middlemarch*. Eliot was probably also influenced in her early work, especially in *Adam Bede*, by Spinoza's special form of pantheism, that is, by his identification of an impersonal, ubiquitous God with a material universe governed by cause and effect. Spinoza's famous formulation for this was *Deus sive Natura* ("God or Nature"), identifying the two. Human love, for Eliot, in the quasi-Spinozistic formulations she makes in *Adam Bede*, is said to be grounded on a divine love that apparently precedes it and is incarnated in it, for, as Dinah believes, "God . . . manifest[s] himself by our silent feeling, and make[s] his love felt through ours" (45: 402). You can read this in two ways, either as affirming God's existence as transcendent ground, or as saying our (fallacious) sense that God exists is created in our silent feeling and in our love.

What Do These Passages Really Say?

I have, however, so far ignored problematic aspects of the four passages. These must now be interrogated. Though the same pattern of themes occurs in all four and though love seems to be praised unequivocally in all four as the source of human good, three of the four, oddly enough, describe unsuccessful or foolish love, only the last a love destined to be fulfilled in marriage and in the assimilation of the couple into the community. One passage analyzes Seth Bede's hopeless love for Dinah, the next two Adam's mistaken belief that Hetty is returning his love, and only one the love of Dinah and Adam which makes possible the happy ending. This fact deserves a double emphasis. The strong feeling for another person in question in two of the passages is based on a fiction, a mistaken reading of signs. This implies that the same value can apparently be ascribed to such false interpretations as to those that seem to be true in the sense that the community confirms them. Adam is "not at all sagacious in his interpretations." Hetty is not what he thinks she is. He has "created the mind he believe[s] in out of his own, which [is] large, unselfish, tender" (33: 318, 319). "[I]t is possible, thank Heaven!" as the narrator says in another place, "to have very erroneous theories and very sublime feelings" (3: 35).

Once the theme of false interpretation, the human propensity to invent fictions on the basis of strong feeling and to live by them as if they were true, has been detected in these passages it proliferates outward to undermine the apparent meaning of all four. It also emerges as a constant theme in the novel, as when "Adam went to bed comforted, having woven for himself an ingenious web of probabilities—the surest screen a wise man can place between himself and the truth" (26: 261), or as when Hetty in her love for Arthur is said again and again in the novel, in language that picks up once more, but in a finely ironic way, the language of the "ocean" of feeling, to live "alone on her little island of dreams" (30: 288): "she was no more conscious of her limbs than if her childish soul had passed into a water-lily, resting on a liquid bed, and warmed by the midsummer sunbeams" (12: 118); "It was as if she had been wooed by a river-god, who might any time take her to his wondrous halls below a watery heaven" (13: 123).[26]

I note in passing that many conservative politicians and voters in the United States are these days, as at more or less any time, beguiled by fictions and act fatally on their basis, for example the repeatedly disconfirmed belief that billions in tax cuts for the rich will somehow trickle down into prosperity for the rest of us. Reading *Adam Bede*, however, is, I fear, not at all likely to teach that lesson to those Senators, Representatives, and voting citizens who are bamboozled by this dangerous fiction, even if we could imagine these good people sitting down one evening to perform a thoughtful reading of Eliot's novel. We human beings in our collective social life seem doomed by what Jacques Derrida calls a self-destructive "auto-co-immunity" that parallels the autoimmunity that can cause a human body's immune system to kill that body.[27]

Love, religious feeling, human beings' responses to a sunset or to a symphony by Beethoven—all are fictions in the sense that they are based on a mistaken interpretation of the data of sensation. They are a projection into external objects and events of values they do not have in themselves. They are an imposition on these objects and events of a web of connections and similarities not objectively there. All four of the long passages I have cited can be read in two radically different ways, in an invitation to double reading entirely characteristic of George Eliot's writing. The texts oscillate before the reader's eyes between these two interpretations, coming and going like a mirage or like those Gestaltist diagrams that vibrate between duck and rabbit or between inside out and inside in. Alongside the straightforwardly metaphysical interpretation I at first proposed, an interpretation ascribing actual and independent existence to the divine ocean of feeling, there is an interpretation that sees that divine ocean as a human construction, a projection. The texts contain their own covert demystification. They may be read in one way by the credulous, in another way by those who, like George Eliot herself, have lost their illusions, though retaining much nostalgia for them.

The Irony of Mistaken Interpretation in *Adam Bede*

This pervasive form of double meaning, running all through *Adam Bede*, and also through George Eliot's other novels in different ways, constitutes her special version of the irony that is fundamental to the novel as a genre. Eliot's translation of Ludwig Feuerbach's *Das Wesen des Christenthums* (*The Essence of Christianity*), that halfway station between Hegel and Marx or Nietzsche, was published in 1854, five years before *Adam Bede*. My four passages and *Adam Bede* as a whole are consonant in meaning with the peculiar Feuerbachian position that says, in effect: "Christianity is valid, but not as the believers have believed. To find its essence it must be turned inside out, man seen as the creator of God rather than the other way around." "Theology long ago became anthropology," as Feuerbach puts it, and therefore "Man and man, the unity of I and Thou, is God," or as he says more comprehensively, in his craggy Hegelian language, "God as the epitome of all realities or perfections is nothing other than a compendious summary devised for the benefit of the limited individual, an epitome of the generic human qualities distributed among men, in the self-realization of the species in the course of world history."[28]

In the four passages from *Adam Bede* a human being's "rapture" before sunset, statue, or symphony is accompanied by "a *consciousness* that these feelings are mere waves and ripples in an unfathomable ocean of love and beauty." The rural Methodists have "a *sense* of a pitying, loving, infinite Presence" (my italics). This consciousness and this sense, however, are projected illusions. Adam's interpretation of the "slight" signs Hetty makes is wholly mistaken. She is really falling in love with Arthur. The presence in a woman's eyes "*seems* to be a far-off mighty love that has come near to us," but only "seems" such. The "something unspeakably great and beautiful," the reader understands by the time he reaches the last passage, is created in the signs for it. It is not something objectively there to be referred to constatively in language. God manifests himself in our silent feeling because he comes into existence in that feeling, or, as this is put by Wallace Stevens, that inheritor of the tradition to which Wordsworth, Feuerbach, George Eliot, Nietzsche, and even Spinoza too in his own way, belong: "This happy creature—It is he that invented the Gods. It is he that put into their mouths the only words they have ever spoken!" and: "God is in me or else is not at all (does not exist)."[29]

Moreover, all these fictional projections are shown to be based on a group of linguistic errors, the error of taking a figurative analogy or association born of intense feeling as if it were literally true, the error, that is, of taking similarities as if they were identities. This is the error of hypostatizing metaphorical transfers and of believing that there really is a transcendent ocean of love because my feeling for a pretty woman or for a work of art is oceanic. To see through this error would imply a rejection of the apparently firm distinction between two kinds of language: chips and sawdust, on the one hand, light, music, stars, love, on the other. If all language is figurative, as Rousseau long ago argued, then apparently referential, mimetic, literal words like "chips" and "sawdust" are no less metaphorical than words like "light," "love," "stars," "music." To put this another way, Adam's world of measurement and scientific prediction, within which he knows a building constructed crookedly will fall and within which he judges with unforgiving harshness those who err in spite of foreseen consequences, is no less a fictional construction, cut off from any absolute "truth," than is the illusory world he enters when he allows his emotions to interpret the gestures Hetty makes as signs she is falling in love with him. His scientism has as much an emotive driving energy behind it, a desire to control and understand the world, as does his mistaken interpretation of the signs Hetty makes.

If fiction is a projection outward from the mind, a false interpretation, language is the instrument of this misinterpretation. Its source is the irreducible penchant of language toward metaphor, or, more broadly, toward figure, toward naming one thing with the name of another. There is no "proper" God-given name for a thing, whatever the Bible says about Adam's naming of all God's creatures. Therefore there is no metaphor, since the existence of a given metaphor depends by definition on the existence of a proper word for which it substitutes. All language is in one way or another a fictional interpretation. "Sawdust" subsumes under one word something that is as variable as those different kinds of snow for which Inuits are said to have so many different words.

We are all the ironic victims of such linguistic mistakes. The admirable analysis in *Middlemarch* of the linguistic bases of man's propensity to create false fictions is already performed, though less explicitly, in *Adam Bede*. Examples are the irony underlying the metaphors used to describe Hetty's dreams: "It was as if she had been wooed by a river-god," or the narrator's double-edged remark about Dinah's belief that some spiritual impetus tells her when to speak and when to keep silent: "And do we not all agree to call rapid thought and noble impulse by the name of inspiration?" (10: 104), or the description of love as parallel to our projection of meanings on the world around us: "We look at the one little woman's face we love, as we look at the face of our mother earth, and see all sorts of answers to our own yearnings" (19: 188), or the narrator's remark that "Love has a way of cheating itself consciously, like a child who plays at solitary hide-and-seek" (11: 107), or his statement that "Nature has her language, and she is not unveracious; but we don't know all the intricacies of her syntax just yet, and in a hasty reading we may happen to extract the very opposite of her real meaning" (15: 139). It would not be extravagant to say that the narrator of *Adam Bede* performs a rigorous act of deconstructive reading *avant la lettre*. Her sources for this procedure of what today we would call "rhetorical reading" were most likely the Higher Biblical Criticism, or Feuerbach, or Spinoza, or the work of such a German rhetorical theorist among her contemporaries as Philip August Böckh, whose work we know she had read.[30]

The metaphorical juxtaposition of human language and the language of nature, nature, that is, taken as a collection of ambiguous signs, recurs in *Adam Bede*. In relation to language, to other people, and to nature, man is in the position of the reader of a difficult text. He is forced to make interpretations that often turn out to be false. When Adam sees Arthur and Hetty in the wood and finally understands the relation between them, his understanding is compared to an act of reading: "He understood it all now—the locket, and everything else that had been doubtful to him: a terrible scorching light showed him the hidden letters that changed the meaning of the past" (27: 268). In another place nature is said to express itself in signs whose referents are hidden, just as a human language has meanings woven into it which its users may be unable to interpret correctly: "There are faces which nature charges with a meaning and pathos not belonging to the single human soul that flutters beneath them, but speaking the joys and sorrows of foregone generations—eyes that tell of deep love which doubtless has been and is somewhere, but not paired with these eyes—perhaps paired with pale eyes that can say nothing: just as a national language may be instinct with poetry unfelt by the lips that use it" (26: 258). This is a powerful, but terrifying wisdom. The face of the woman we love looks as if she must be gentle and loving, but that face actually expresses the gentle loving kindness of her grandmother or great-grandmother.

Hetty Sorrel as Sophist Figure

On the basis of this stern theory of mistaken interpretation, the function of Hetty Sorrel in the dramatic structure of *Adam Bede* may be identified. She plays the same role in this novel as the sophist does in Plato's *The Sophist* in relation to Socrates, the true sage. Hetty is the false double, the simulacrum, the mirror image of the true that puts in question that assumed truth. Just as, in Plato's dialogue, the final definition of the sophist, after all the labyrinth of deceptively branching trails has been threaded, cannot be distinguished from the definition of Socrates, the true sage,[31] so Hetty seems to be the opposite of Dinah, egotistic falseness and hardness set against Dinah's altruistic sympathy. Dinah, however, is as much a dreamer as Hetty is. The same language is used to describe the dreams of both. When the "new influence" of Hetty's growing love for Arthur comes over her, it is said to be "vague, atmospheric, shaping itself into no self-confessed hopes or prospects, but producing a pleasant narcotic effect, making her tread the ground and go about her work in a sort of dream, unconscious of weight or effort, and showing her all things through a soft, liquid veil, as if she were living not in this solid world of brick and stone, but in a beatified world, such the sun lights up for us in the waters" (9: 91). Dinah too lives within an analogous illusion. Her dreams also take a liquid form, a form similar to Hetty's dreams: "[I]t seems," Dinah tells Mr. Irwine, in a passage I have already cited in part, "as if I could sit silent all day long with the thought of God overflowing my soul—as the pebbles lie bathed in the Willow Brook. For thoughts are so great—aren't they, sir? They seem to lie upon us like a deep flood; and it's my besetment to forget where I am and everything about me, and lose myself in thoughts that I could give no account of, for I could neither make a beginning nor ending of them in words" (8: 82). The essential difference, of course, is that Hetty's dreams lead to ethically irresponsible actions, whereas Dinah's dreams support her good works. I shall return to this essential distinction in my discussion of Dorothea's two marriages in *Middlemarch*.

The energy George Eliot describes in the two passages just cited is her version of what Nietzsche calls the will to power, that is, the spontaneous urge to interpret, to distort, to make meaning, to find similarities in the disparate (like calling all those different substances "sawdust"), to connect the unlike, to make patterns, to simplify, to create fictions. Eliot's name for it is "feeling," the mighty river that flows out of human hearts alone or collectively to transform their surroundings and project meaning into them. This river is a resistless flow of emotion. "Sympathy," another name for "feeling," is for George Eliot the creator of culture, but it is a double strength, constructive and destructive at once. It is the source of all fictions, fictions both bad and good, those that are a mortal danger to the community as well as those that create and sustain it, Hetty's silly dreams as well as the noble ones of Dinah or Adam.

When the imagination of Hetty Sorrel, Adam Bede, or Dorothea Brooke is substituted for the imagination of Wordsworth, Blake, or

Stevens, the same insights are ultimately reached; the discovery that the excited mind builds its fictions mainly for itself, and the discovery that they are built on a misreading of signs. They are based on the fundamental figures of speech that pervade language use: metaphor, metonymy, synecdoche, prosopopoeia, catachresis. These figures are generated by emotion, for, as George Eliot says in *Middlemarch* of Peter Featherstone's pleasure in imagining the consternation the reading of his Testament will cause after he is dead, "images are the brood of desire," and "we are all of us imaginative in some form or other" (34: 48). Any putting together of the data of sensation, any linking of one moment with another, any interpretation of the world, any ascription of value, any judgment of good or bad, is a fiction, so Eliot's dark wisdom asserts. It is a network projected outward, the creation of a mirage of unity and meaning. For George Eliot the only distinction, it would seem, is between egotistical and collective fictions, Hetty's destructive dreams as against Dinah's power to bring people together through her sympathy for them. The truth-value of the two kinds of dreams is the same, though the difference for the living together of human beings is immense.

Adam Bede as a Story about the Reading of Signs and as a Text to be Read

What of the novel itself? Can it escape from the theory of fictions that emerges within the story as an analysis of the characters' penchant for misreading? The sweeping analysis in *Adam Bede* of the human propensity for making fictions and for living in terms of figures of speech, for taking figures literally, must necessarily turn back on the novel as a whole to put its status in question. The beauty of a lovely woman is like music. Calm majestic statues, Beethoven symphonies, and the words of genius, that have a wider meaning than the thought that prompted them, are inextricably entwined with the other motifs in the four passages I have discussed. Like religious feeling, love, and our response to nature, works of art are fictions too, as are the meanings that readers, listeners, or beholders import into them. *Adam Bede* is a literary work. It cannot be exempted from this indictment. It too is a fiction. It too is the creation of a systematic interpretation of reality based on figures of speech.

My interpretation, in establishing connections between widely separated passages and in proposing a global reading of the novel, must be defined, if we take George Eliot's analysis seriously, as another fiction in its turn. As George Eliot puts it in *Middlemarch*: "The text, whether of prophet or of poet, expands for whatever we can put into it, and even his bad grammar is sublime" (5: 55). To speak of a literary text at all is to interpret it, but the reader cannot properly enter into it or take possession of it without speaking or writing about it, without extending its writing with a rewriting of his or her own, even if that rewriting may remain implicit as part of the act of reading. The right response to this situation is not silence but refusal of the temptation to freeze a given novel into what is claimed to be a definitive explication, much as I am tempted, nevertheless, to say that I have in this book read *Adam Bede* and *Middlemarch* "right," once and for all. I know, however, that more and different interpretations will follow as long as these novels are read.

To follow out the implications of the narrator's commentary in *Adam Bede* is to recognize that the novel is not the mimetic mirroring it claims to be. In this novel George Eliot transposed the data of her own life, her memories of her father, her aunt's story of the original of Hetty, all she knew of life in Warwickshire and Staffordshire, into a fictional system governed by certain metaphorical and metonymic assumptions, for example the assumption that physical metaphors for human psychology have objective validity. She made a powerful imaginary world out of this verbalized material. The novel, however, in what is said about art and in the analysis it gives of the fiction-making power possessed even by the good characters (Adam's ability, for example, to create out of his own large soul a Hetty who does not exist), indirectly provides the reader with the knowledge necessary to read the novel as a self-contradicting "whole." Equipped with the insight provided by the novel, the reader of *Adam Bede* comes to see it as construction on George Eliot's part rather than the accurate mirroring she claims it to be in the chapter on realism. *Adam Bede* is, like *The Prelude*, the construction of a fictional self, the self of the narrator. The discourse of the narrator constructs a systematic interpretation of nineteenth-century Midland society as it has been transposed into an imaginary world. *Adam Bede*, read in a certain way, generates by means of words the illusion of a "divine" transcendence. That illusion is shown to be necessary to sustain the community within the novel's imaginary world. The novel, nevertheless, for those who read closely, reveals the illusion to be an illusion.

This narrator is a commenting spectator as invisible witness of the novel's imaginary community. The narrator is generated by the act of translation, displacement, and interpretation that makes out of language the world of *Adam Bede*. Marian Evans becomes George Eliot by means of the language, the words on the page, of *Adam Bede* and of George Eliot's other works. This speech act may be compared with what Phillipe Sollers says about Isadore Ducasse's decision to write under the pseudonym of Lautréamont: "Pleynet is therefore right to say: 'The pseudonym allowed the proper name to have a referent other than the paternal heritage. *Ducasse is henceforth the son of his works.*' This sentence is to be taken literally: as designating an engendering taking place in and by writing" (my trans.). When Marian Evans created George Eliot as the voice who speaks as the narrator of *Adam Bede* she changed her sex, took on the generative power of a father, in place of the derived and secondary role of the daughter of Robert Evans and, insofar as Adam Bede is a "portrait" of Robert Evans, she became as it were the father of her father.[32] The falsification in the narrator's declared realism is not that there were no historical realities to which the words of the novel "correspond," but in the claim that these can be reflected without being interpreted. Interpretation is persuasively analyzed in the case of the characters as false. This analysis necessarily turns back to undermine the apparent status of the novel itself. It constitutes a covert revelation of the fictional quality of the large patterns of recurrence, echo, and generalization that organize the novel. To say that in *Adam Bede* the narrator demystifies the characters' beliefs is not enough. A more complete formulation would say: in *Adam Bede* the story told and thereby demystified turns back to establish itself indirectly as a demystification of storytelling.

Repetition in *Adam Bede*

The working of this turning back of the novel onto itself may be more exactly identified by interrogating the function in *Adam Bede* of repetition. Repetition of various sorts is fundamental to the novel. *Adam Bede* is made up, like most works of fiction, of a sequence of repeated motifs, but the question of repetition is itself thematic. It is an issue in the novel. The authenticity of the novel as a text depends, the narrator tells the reader, on the way it is an accurate copy, a repetition in words of something extra-verbal. *Adam Bede* is claimed to be a duplication of something that pre-existed it and that is its measure, the source of its value. In a similar way, within the novel Dinah draws her value from the way she repeats the charity and saintly sympathy of Charles Wesley, her avowed· model in the sermon she gives, or of Christ himself, the model for any Christian to imitate. Hetty, the false imitator, challenges the validity of these repetitions. As Dinah imitates Wesley or Christ, so Hetty dresses up before her looking-glass to "make herself look like that picture of a lady in Miss Lydia Donnithorne's dressing-room" (15: 136). As I said earlier, like Dinah, Hetty is a dreamer. Like Dinah she feels that she is bathed in a warm ocean of love. The same metaphors as are used for the good people recur for her. Her near execution after being convicted of infanticide and her subsequent transportation are a sacrificial expulsion. She takes the sins of the community upon herself, the sin of Arthur in seducing her, the sin of the social structure that makes it impossible for him to marry her, the sin of the community's failure to satisfy her need for something more, for some grand satisfaction, for something like being wooed by a river-god, for something like the cheap ideals on which her silly little imagination is nurtured: "to sit in a carpeted parlor and always wear white stockings" (9: 90).

As the false imitation of the apparently true imitations, Hetty raises questions about whether there is an original, transcendent model to imitate. If there is no such model, if Dinah's belief that she is sustained by divine love is as much an illusion as Hetty's belief that she is wooed by a river-god, what then is the difference between the two? What is the difference between the illicit love of Hetty and Arthur and the good love of Adam and Dinah if both can be defined in the same metaphor, the image of the two little quivering rain-streams merging into one? (12: 120; 50: 441). What of the novelist's putative imitation of the real social world? Is that not also construction, interpretation according to certain preconceptions? Hetty's story brings into the open the way both the claim of the community to be modeled on objectively valid cultural forms and the pretense of the novel to be copy rather than construction are false.

By exposing this distressingly negative fact, however, the story of Hetty also demonstrates the need for illusion. A community needs the shared illusion that it is based on "eternal" values. The novelist, Marian Evans at least, needs the illusion that she is copying rather than fabricating. For George Eliot, as for Nietzsche, "we possess *art* lest we *perish of the truth*."[33] The "truth" is represented in the novel as the dark pool into which Hetty cannot bring herself to leap, the cold, extra-human reality that gives her such a vivid insight into the attractions of the community from which she has excluded herself. Or rather the dark pool is not so much the "truth" as it is the blank, the unapproachable, outside of human comprehension. Such a blankness is the only alternative to one form of fiction or another. One name for that blankness is "death." Neither Adam's hard-headed seeing of the "facts" nor the narrator's realistic representation is the truth, the naked, unveiled thing in itself, what is "really there." Each is merely one interpretation more.

The same thing may be said of the dark pool in which Hetty cannot bring herself to drown herself. The pool is not the truth but a figure for the empty or inhuman vacancy that appears when an illusion has been removed and not yet replaced by another one. The collapsing of fictional constructions, that illusionary world in which we live, produces not insight into the truth, but a confrontation without confrontation of death, the thing about which nothing can be said except figuratively. Death is the thing that is therefore not open to narration in realistic fiction. It remains a blank place in the narrative space, a missing moment in the narrative line. The dead body, that of Adam's father or of Hetty's baby, is always found after a blank space of time that can never be filled by truth-telling narrative language. The ultimate wisdom of *Adam Bede* is the recognition that fictions are necessary to life.

The essence of culture, in George Eliot's view, is human beings' will to power over brute nature, their ability to give nature meaning, to make it over into cultural forms like roads, buildings, institutions, marriages, laws, and customs. A community is therefore like a work of art. It is an escape from the ugliness of the underlying blank. *Adam Bede* shows this by describing a break in the continuity of a local culture in Hetty's foolish dreams. Her dreams are, one might say, a work of art shared by no one—except, unknown to her, the narrator. Her dreams are not embodied in community recognition, just as the individual reader's perhaps illicit enjoyment of the imaginary visions inspired by literature may remain private. Hetty's dreams are a terrible danger to the community, just as people used to think, in eighteenth- and nineteenth-century England, reading novels might endanger the community. Daydreams and reading may lead to actions that threaten to tear the community apart. Hetty's dreams also lead her to her confrontation with the dark water into which she cannot bring herself to plunge. The narrator's notation of this is a climactic example of the telepathic narrator's power to enter into the thoughts and feelings of an imaginary character even in an extreme situation and to speak for that character in words the character could probably have not herself summoned up. Compassionate, yes; sympathetic, yes, but this narrative voice is also a violator of secrets. The narrator is a disquieting, even, one might almost feel, a somewhat diabolical, intruder into the recesses of another person, unbeknownst to that person. The narrator is like Satan spying on Adam and Eve in *Paradise Lost*, in devilish parody of God's omniscience: "The horror of this cold, and darkness, and solitude—out of all human reach—became greater every long minute: it was almost as if she were dead already, and knew that she was dead, and longed to get back to life again" (37: 346).

Hetty's act, the sexual act forbidden by her society but motivated by her foolish dreams, her private lie, enters into the real physical world in the form of her pregnancy. It enters also into the already existing human world, the culture within which she lives. It takes such meaning there as the culture gives it. This, for Eliot, is not an absolute meaning. Hetty's pregnancy has no absolute meaning any more than does any other act or fact. Her child is illegitimate only in relation to the collective definition in her culture of the laws of marriage. This is suggested by various passages assimilating her to natural procreation in dogs and other animals. In a similar way, murder or suicide are valued by the culture rather than having an intrinsic value. They are taken into its system of definitions. Death is the darkness or solitude that lies behind all cultural forms, figured in the black pool into which Hetty looks and cannot jump, such is her passionate love of life. This love is her desire to belong to the collection of conventions that makes up the community within which she has lived. She sees these now, in an extraordinary moment of vision, recorded once more by the "clairvoyeuristic" narrator (see Royle reference below), in the perspective of the dark alternative that lies beneath that vision of everyday life. The narrator at this point seems to me more an impersonal "it" as linguistic medium than a "he" or a "she": "Oh how long the time was in that darkness! The bright hearth and the warmth and the voices of home—the secure uprising and lying down,—the familiar fields, the familiar people, the Sundays and holidays with their simple joys of dress and feasting,—all the sweets of her young life rushed before her now, and she seemed to be stretching her arms towards them across a great gulf" (37: 346).

The Community Restored

The rest of the novel, after the passage just cited, shows the community reacting to the destructive shock of discovering Hetty's act. It reacts by assimilating that act into its system of values and institutions, most overtly by trying and condemning Hetty in a court of law. The community closes the gap. It covers over the revelation of something outside that system that cannot be assimilated to it. According to a version of the paradox of the *felix culpa*, the happy sin, the community cements itself together more firmly than before through an implicit recognition that sympathy, shared human feeling, binds people together, as in Dinah's compassionate visit to Hetty in her jail cell. It binds together even those that have transgressed, and thereby makes the Hayslope community possible.

That community, however, never understands this as the narrator understands it, for example in his (her? its?) discussion of Adam's improvement by suffering: "Let us rather be thankful that our sorrow lives in us as an indestructible force, only changing its form, as forces do, and passing from pain into sympathy—the one poor word which includes all our best insight and our best love . . . He did not know that the power of loving was all the while gaining new force within him; that the new sensibilities brought by a deep experience were so many fibres by which it was possible, nay, necessary to him, that his nature should intertwine with another" (50: 436). Adam's suffering makes him a worthy husband for Dinah. At the end of the novel the breach in the collective fictions of the community has been repaired. The values of that community have been reaffirmed in the marriage of Adam and Dinah, the new Adam, baptized by suffering, marrying the new Eve.

The community is refounded on a transgression and on a death, Hetty's murder of her illegitimate child. Though this episode may be related to the traditional pattern of the fortunate fall, it has its own specific humanist meaning here. This meaning is difficult to identify, though I shall try to do so, in concluding my reading of *Adam Bede*. This humanist meaning is related to the theory of language in *Adam Bede*. A secure society, like that of Loamshire at the beginning of the novel, rests on a double illusion and is in a double jeopardy. It believes that its transcendental words and feelings name things that have an objective, extra-linguistic existence. It moves on the basis of that assumption toward a dangerous realism, a hardness of judgment like Adam's "the square o' four is sixteen." This hard commitment to facts is dangerous because it chokes off the sympathy that is the basis of social solidarity. Adam before his fall into suffering is guilty of this unforgiving sternness. He has "too little fellow-feeling with the weakness that errs in spite of foreseen consequences" (19: 190). Through Hetty's infanticide Adam and the community tacitly learn that they must yield to illusion. The orderly world of the community, secure in its judgments, needs periodical returns to the edge of what lies beneath it or outside it. In itself the community is appearance, false interpretation, but the necessity of these can be demonstrated only by a confrontation of the alternative. This is not "living in terms of the truth," but death, the death Hetty might have died and that her newborn baby dies. There is no living face to face with the truth.

Adam Bede not only demystifies ungrounded interpretation, that of Eliot's novel, that of the community, that of the individual characters, but also at the same time shows the necessity of illusion. Hence the double tone throughout. A culture is the false binding of moment with moment. It is misreading, fiction, but without fiction man has—nothing, or nothing but the unused and disembodied energy of feeling. A demonstration of the dangerous excess of the imagination, its tendency to go beyond benign construction and become destructive, is as fundamental in George Eliot's work as it is in Wordsworth's. This danger is presented in *Adam Bede* in the destructive power of Hetty's silly imagination. This leads her fatefully outside the safe bounds of the human community.

Seen from this perspective, *Adam Bede* shows itself to be a chain structure of fictions, link within link within link. Each link builds on the one behind, both destroying it by showing its fictionality and reconstituting it in a new form. Each fiction is based on figurative identifications. The strong feeling that creates systematic fictions motivates each stage. These fictions performatively create the ideals to which they refer. These ideals are made according to the projective process Feuerbach describes. They are magical pseudo-essences generated by men and women in their living together. The chief links in this chain are: the community of Hayslope as it is at the opening of the novel; Hetty within that community but endangering it by bringing into existence a subjective, imaginary world; the community re-establishing itself after it has been challenged and nearly destroyed; the narrator outside the story putting in question, by his manner of telling, the presumed grounding of the culture at all these levels, but in his turn constituting the story as a closed system, consistently interpreted in the narrator's double discourse; outside the narrator the novelist herself, Marian Evans, who is making it all up out of the drop of ink. She experiences in that making the transformation of her "real" sources in her early life. These were of course already fabricated through manifold acts of interpretation. The reader of *Adam Bede*, finally, is the last link in the chain. She threads her way through all the sequence and interprets that sequence in her turn. She participates in her way in that curious procedure of demystification whereby an illusion is shown for what it is and so suspended, only to be replaced not by the truth but by another illusion. We have art that we may not perish of the truth.

The value of Adam's Feuerbachian gesture of taking a little bread and a little wine before he goes to visit Hetty in prison lies not only in the way it repeats the Last Supper or the Christian Communion Service, but in the way it has the same kind of inaugurating and sustaining power within the community of Hayslope, about to be re-established after its fall, as Christ's last supper did in the inauguration of the myth (as Eliot saw it) of Christianity that held the community of Europe together for so long and that still has such power throughout the world. Just as Nietzsche's thought in Book Three of the posthumously constructed *The Will to Power* is at once the most sweeping demythologizing of everything on which Western culture has been based—God, causality, consciousness, science, and so on—and at the same time a demonstration that such ideologically motivated mistakes are necessary to continued human life, so *Adam Bede* shows that Hetty and Dinah are mirror images of one another. Dinah and the whole community she sustains are supported by dreams.

At the same time *Adam Bede* reveals the need for shared dreams if there is to be a community at all, by giving the reader a glimpse of the dread alternative to living within a fiction and also a glimpse of the dangerous complicity of dreaming, generator of illusions, in the process whereby illusions are destroyed (as Hetty is led to her confrontation with death by her dreaming). Dreaming is one form of what Wolfgang Iser calls "the imaginary." George Eliot both shows her readers something of the fragility of their assumptions and at the same time confirms them in their bondage to the imaginary. This oscillation is fundamental to Eliot's work. It constitutes her version of the relation among the real, the fictive, and the imaginary in literature generally. This is the way that in *Adam Bede* the story told turns back to put in question the apparent assumptions of the novelist's storytelling.

Chapter 2

Reading *Middlemarch* Right for Today

Totalization Affirmed and Undermined in *Middlemarch*

As I have shown in my interpretation of *Adam Bede*, a careful reading of that novel shows that even in this early Eliot work the story told puts storytelling in question. No reader of Eliot's novels can doubt, however, that the relation between human life and the act of narration is explored in greater depth in *Middlemarch* than in *Adam Bede*. *Middlemarch* is one of the most persuasive affirmations of the totalizing power of the realistic novel. At the same time it is one of the most compelling challenges to this power. This simultaneous affirmation and subversion is characteristic of the "mixed form" of Victorian fiction generally.[1] It is an aspect of the tradition of European fiction since *Don Quixote*. This doubleness takes special forms, however, among the Victorians. *Middlemarch* is an excellent example of those. It is a special case of great power both for affirmation and for denial. I shall follow out two related modes of simultaneous totalizing and fragmentation in *Middlemarch*: the analogy with historical narrative and the use of metaphorical models as a means of unification. First I shall define what is meant here by "totalization."

Versions of Totalization

> . . . this power of generalizing which gives men so much the superiority in mistake over the dumb animals . . . (*Middlemarch*, 58: 656)[2]

George Eliot's apparent aim in *Middlemarch* (1871–2) is to present a total imaginary picture of provincial Midlands society in England at the period just before the first Reform Bill of 1832. She also wants to interpret this picture totally. She wants in a fictional transposition both to show everything that is there and to show comprehensively how it works. She also wants to use the accomplished totalizing representation as a language of power to make her readers better by leading them to sympathize with their neighbors. She wants her novel to be both a totalizing representation and a performative text. She wants *Middlemarch* to be a long speech act that will make something happen in her readers.

An immense modern secondary literature, from Georg Lukács to Franco Moretti and beyond, has investigated the motif of totality as a feature of theoretical work from Kant and Schiller through Marx to later writers like Meyer Abrams and Theodor Adorno. Totality, as these writers show, has a double reference. On the one hand, it expresses the aesthetic idea that a good work of art will be a totality, an organic unity. On the other hand, it expresses the idea that society at a given time is a totality made up of complex relations of similarity and difference that might be reflected in an artwork such as a realist novel.

The enterprise of totalization in *Middlemarch* is shared with an important group of other masterworks of Victorian fiction. This group includes Thackeray's *Vanity Fair* (1847–8), Dickens's *Bleak House* (1852–3), *Little Dorrit* (1855–7), and *Our Mutual Friend* (1864–5), and Anthony Trollope's *The Way We Live Now* (1874–5). All these novels have many characters and employ multiple analogous plots. They cast a wide net and aim at inclusiveness, in part by a method of accumulation. Nevertheless, since the actual societies in question were unmanageably complex and multitudinous, some strategy of compression had to be devised in each case. As George Meredith puts this in the "Prelude" to *The Egoist*, "the inward mirror, the embracing and condensing spirit, is required to give us those interminable mile-post piles of matter . . . in essence, in chosen samples, digestibly."[3] The means of condensation vary considerably from novelist to novelist.

Dickens, for example, achieves inclusiveness by making the part stand for the whole. He emphasizes the synechdochic, representative, emblematic quality of his characters. Mr. Krook, the rag-and-bottle-shop keeper in *Bleak House*, stands for the Lord Chancellor, his shop for the Court of Chancery. The Court of Chancery, in turn, is a synecdoche for the "wiglomeration" of English society as a whole. In the same novel, Sir Leicester Dedlock is presented as an example of the whole class of aristocrats; Gridley, the Man from Shropshire, is an emblem for all the suitors who are destroyed by the delays of Chancery, and so on. The range of examples includes by this method implicitly all of England. Characters from the country and from the city, from the lowest level of society to the highest, are presented.

George Eliot is more straightforwardly "realistic" in her procedure, at least so it seems. *Middlemarch* presents a large group of the sort of people one would be likely to have found in a provincial town in the Midlands around 1830. Their representative or symbolic quality is not insisted upon. This would be the wrong track to follow in a search for her methods of totalization. George Eliot does not present examples from the whole range of English society, only for that local part of it she presents. The relation of the town called Middlemarch to English society is rather that of part to whole, or that of a sample to the whole cloth, according to a metaphor I shall be examining later. The relationship is once more synecdochic, but the kind of synecdoche in question is different from the one used by Dickens. George Eliot understood that synecdoche, part for whole, is an extremely problematic trope, since the example is always to some degree unique, *sui generis*. It is dangerous, she knew, to claim that the unique is at the same time "typical." In *Bleak House* the member of a class is implicitly presented as a "symbol" of the whole class. In *Middlemarch*, a fragment is examined as a "sample" of the larger whole of which it is a part. Nevertheless, the whole impinges on the part as the "medium" within which the part lives. National politics affect Middlemarch when there is a general election. The coming of the railroad upsets rural traditions. A symbol and a sample in works of fiction obey two different rhetorical laws. George Eliot's strategy of totalization is to present individual character or event in the context of their wider medium. She affirms universal laws of human behavior in terms of characters whose specificity and even uniqueness are indicated by the relative completeness of the psychological portraits of each, as well as by assertions by the narrator. Dorothea, Lydgate, Casaubon, Bulstrode, Fred Vincy, Mary Garth, and the rest are each unique. This fullness of characterization and the accompanying circumstantiality of social detail in *Middlemarch* have been deservedly admired. They make this novel perhaps the masterwork of Victorian realism.

The subtitle of *Middlemarch* is "A Study of Provincial Life." This may put the novel under the aegis of a kind of painting, a "study from life." The more powerful association of the word, however, is with a scientific "study." George Eliot is in *Middlemarch* attempting to fulfill for the life of an English provincial town that enterprise she had mapped out in her important early essay on the German sociologist of peasant life, Wilhem Heinrich von Riehl, already mentioned in my reading of *Adam Bede*. In that essay, "The Natural History of German Life" (*Westminster Review*, 1856), Eliot had implicitly proposed writing works of fiction that would do for English life what Riehl had done for the German peasant: "Art is the nearest thing to life: it is a mode of amplifying experience and extending our contact with our fellow-men beyond the bounds of our personal lot. All the more sacred is the task of the artist when he undertakes to paint the life of the People. Falsification here is far more pernicious than in the more artificial aspects of life."[4] Much of *Middlemarch* is modeled on the sociologist's respect for individual fact that George Eliot so praises in her essay on Riehl. (What more appropriate name could he have!) The experience of each character in *Middlemarch* is described in such detail that the reader is encouraged not to forget its differences from the experiences of the other characters, even ones superficially similar in social placement and gender.

Nevertheless, the narrator of *Middlemarch* assumes throughout that the behavior of these unique people, each of whom is other to the others, manifests universal laws. These laws may be formulated and *are* constantly formulated, as when the narrator says: "We are all of us born in moral stupidity, taking the world as an udder to feed our supreme selves" (21: 235). The special mode of totalization in *Middlemarch* is this combination of specificity and generalizing interpretation on the basis of this specificity. This generalizing is consistently proposed as valid not just for all people in the particular middle-class society of Middlemarch, and not just for all English society at a specific moment of its history, but for all people in all cultures at all times: "We are *all* of us born in moral stupidity . . ."

Middlemarch as Pseudo-History

Hegel: . . . "That history (that is, essentially world history [*Weltgeschichte*]) is founded upon a final purpose [*Endzweck*] in and of itself and that this purpose actually is realized and continues to be realized in it (the plan of Providence [*Vorsehung*]), that there is *reason* [*Vernunft*] in history, must be determined philosophically for itself and thereby determined to be necessary in and of itself." "History without such a purpose and without such judgment [*solche Beurtheilung*] would be only a senseless product of the imagination [*ein schwachsinniges Ergehen des Vorstellens*], not even a child's tale [*ein Kindermährchen*], for even children demand that their stories have some point, that is, at the very least, a purpose that can be divined and to which the events and actions can be related." Conclusion: every story must have a purpose [*Zweck*], hence also the history of a people, the history of the world. That is, since there is "world history," there must also be some purpose in the world process. That is, we demand only those stories that have a purpose: but we have demanded no stories at all about the world process, because we believe it to be a humbug [*Schwindel*] even to speak of such a thing. It already is apparent in the fortuitousness of my existence [*der Zufälligkeit seines Entstehens*: literally, "the fortuitousness of its origin or generation"] that my life has no purpose; that I am able to establish [*setzen*] some purpose for myself is something quite different. But a state has no purpose: it is only we who attribute to it this or that purpose. (Friedrich Nietzsche, notes of 1873)[5]

The nourishing fruit of the historically understood contains time as a precious but tasteless seed. (*Die nahrhafte Frucht des historisch Begriffenen hat die Zeit als den kostbaren aber des Geschmacks entratenen Samen in ihren Innern.*) (Walter Benjamin, "Theses on the Philosophy of History," 1940)[6]

One mode of *Middlemarch*'s totalizing claim is the explicit analogy George Eliot draws between her work and that of historians. "Historian" would include a sociologist like Riehl. She thought of the historian's work in the nineteenth-century way, that is, not solely as the identifying of fact, but also as the establishment on facts' basis of universal laws inherent in the world-historical sequence. Another mode of Eliot's totalizing, to be investigated subsequently, is the use of certain encompassing metaphors. These are not only claimed to integrate all the multitudinous details of this vast, multi-plotted novel but are also claimed to apply, like the moral or conceptual generalizations, to all human life at all times. In the end these two forms of totalizing are seen as the same, or, rather, history is seen as a special case of metaphorical totalizing. The historian's assumptions turn out to be a system of metaphors about origin, end, and ground. Jacques Derrida famously called this system "logocentrism." I shall dare occasionally to use this shorthand term to avoid repeating too often, like a mantra, "origin, end, and ground." The Greek word *logos* is a complex noun, like its German semi-equivalent, *Grund*. *Logos* means reason, ground, ratio, proportion, rhythm, and word, all at once. Christ, for example, the second person of the Trinity, is, in John's Gospel and in Christian theology, the *Logos*. Christ pervades the creation as Word, ground, and universal proportionality guaranteeing figurative analogies.

History is in *Middlemarch* one metaphorical model for human life along with others. The "same" place is reached by the critic who approaches the novel from the perspective of its use of history as metaphor and from the perspective of its use of metaphor itself. The differences within this "same," however, can only be shown by retracing the paths to be followed by those approaches, as I shall now try to do.

A novel is in various ways a chain of displacements—displacement of its author into the invented role of the narrator, further displacement of the narrator into the lives of imaginary characters whose thoughts and feelings are presented in that odd kind of ventriloquism or telepathic clairvoyance called "indirect discourse,"[7] displacements of the putative "origin" of the story (in historical events or in the life experience of the author) into the fictitious events of the narrative. *Middlemarch* is full of textually visible displacements, for example in quotations within the text, or in the epigraphs for each chapter that are such a conspicuous (and rather strange) feature of *Middlemarch*. I said the following in a comment on these epigraphs in *Reading Narrative*. I hope I may be permitted to graft my comments in this new place:

[C]omplications of the narrative line arise from all its doublings: doublings of narrators and narrators within narrators; the enigmatic doublings of indirect discourse; repetitions in multiple plots; displacements effected by citations, epigraphs, prefaces, inserted letters, quoted signs (in the literal sense of signboards), inscriptions, gravestone markings—all that interpolated language in novels that in different ways is not at the same level of discourse as the basic narration. My interrogation of these is organized around a cascade of questions. These are not rhetorical questions. I am really puzzled by the question of how these interpolations work and by the question of how they are to be differentiated from one another in their working.

What is the general effect of these graftings? They are aeroliths from some other planet, as one might call them, intruding into the enclosed atmosphere of the primary narrative language. Who speaks a given example of these, from what time or place? Are they inside or outside the story proper? How do they interact with that primary story-telling language to produce meaning? What is the effect, for example, in Anthony Trollope's *The Prime Minister*, when, after a prolonged immersion in the troubled inner consciousness of Plantagenet Palliser, the narrator shifts abruptly, in the gap between chapter and chapter, to the differently tormented mind of Ferdinand Lopez? What is the effect of George Eliot's citation, in Spanish and in English, as an epigraph to chapter two of *Middlemarch*, of the passage from *Don Quixote* about the washpan that is taken by Don Quixote as Mambrino's helmet? (2: 17). Is that effect different from the effect of the epigraph to chapter seventy-two, apparently composed by George Eliot herself: "Full souls are double mirrors making still / The endless vista of fair things before, / Repeating things behind"? (72: 813). A long study could be made of the epigraphs in *Middlemarch*, not to speak of all the other sorts of interpolations.

Who is to be imagined as speaking, writing, citing, or signing these epigraphs? The author, Marian Evans? Or the narrator, George Eliot, the fictive persona of Marian Evans? What are the epigraphs' relations to the main body of the chapters on which they comment? Are they ironical? Straightforwardly interpretative? Superior in knowledge to the narrator, or equal, or inferior? Located just where in the psychic and scriptive space of the novel? Is the effect of such epigraphs different from that of citations inside the main body of the narration, as when Septimus Harding, in Anthony Trollope's *The Warden*, says to his daughter: "There is an old saying, Nelly: 'Everyone knows where his own shoe pinches'"?[8] Do citations made by characters in novels differ in function from those made by the narrator, as when Hardy cites Shakespeare in a title to place his rustics "under the greenwood tree," while those rustics presumably do not know Shakespeare?[9]

One of the ways in which a sideways movement into the void of fiction is effaced and at the same time surreptitiously revealed is the curious tradition, present in the modern middle-class novel from its sixteenth-century beginnings on, whereby a work of fiction is conventionally presented not as a work of fiction but as some other form of language. This other form is almost always some representational discourse rooted in history and claiming to be the direct report of real human experience. It seems as if works of fiction are ashamed to present themselves as what they are. They must therefore always present themselves as what they are not. They must claim to be some non-fictional form of language. A novel must pretend to be a kind of language validated by its one-to-one correspondence to psychological or historical reality.

This suppression of the displacement involved in writing a work of fiction takes several common forms. A novel may present itself as a collection of letters (*Clarissa*, *Les Liaisons dangereuses*), as memoirs or edited documents (*The Posthumous Papers of the Pickwick Club*), as an old manuscript found in a trunk or bottle (Poe's "Manuscript Found in a Bottle"), as an autobiography (*Robinson Crusoe*, *David Copperfield*, *Henry Esmond*), as a legal deposition (as in the last section of Melville's *Benito Cereno*), as journalism (Dickens's *Sketches by Boz*), as a travel book (Melville's *Typee*), or even as a realistic painting: the subtitle of Thomas Hardy's *Under the Greenwood Tree or The Mellstock Quire* is "A Rural Painting of the Dutch School," as the subtitle of *Middlemarch* is "A Study of Provincial Life," though the word "study" here, as I have said, may refer as much to a sociological or scientific treatise as to a form of painting. Pretending to be sociology would add another form of displacement to my list.

Perhaps the most important form of this masking is the presentation of a novel as a species of history. The term "history" tends to contaminate other forms of displacement and to displace them. The full title of *Henry Esmond*, a fictional autobiography in form, is *The History of Henry Esmond, Esq., A Colonel in the Service of Her Majesty Q. Anne, Written by Himself*. The full title of Dickens's autobiographical novel is *The Personal History of David Copperfield*. Perhaps the most famous example of the use of the term "history" in the title of a novel is *The History of Tom Jones, A Foundling*. Abundant examples may be found from one end of the modern tradition of the novel to the other. The final one of Trollope's Barset novels is called *The Last Chronicle of Barset* (though the distinction between a "chronicle" and a "history" is important), and H. G. Wells published in 1910 *The History of Mr. Polly*.

The reasons for the predominance of this particular displacement are evident. By calling a novel a history its author at one stroke covers over the implications of gratuitousness, of baseless creativity and lie, implicit in the word "fiction." At the same time he or she affirms for the novel in question the solid basis in pre-existing fact that is associated with the idea of history. A particularly striking example of this anxiety to obscure the way a work of fiction is a work of fiction, along with an eagerness to enroll it under the banner of history, is a passage in Henry James's essay on Trollope (1883). It seems as if the fictional imagination, for James at least, can only be liberated as long as it hides from itself what it actually is. It seems as if a novel, in James's sense of it, can only be taken seriously by its readers if it pretends to be what it is not. James deplores Trollope's "wanton" "violation" of "that illusion dear to the intending novelist," the illusion that the events recounted actually happened in the real world. He much exaggerates, by the way, the degree to which Trollope commits this "pernicious trick." It occurs much less frequently in Trollope's later fiction than in his earlier novels. Moreover, a present-day critic would find these examples of the "anti-novel" in Trollope much more defensible and significant, much more part of the traditional technique of the novel from *Don Quixote* on, than does James. Trollope, says James, "took a suicidal satisfaction in reminding the reader that the story he was telling was only, after all, a make-believe. He habitually referred to the work in hand (in the course of that work) as a novel, and to himself as a novelist, and was fond of letting the reader know that this novelist could direct the course of events according to his pleasure." Against this James affirms his strong commitment to the idea that a work of fiction depends for its validity and power on claiming that it is history:

It is impossible to imagine what a novelist takes himself to be unless he regard himself as an historian and his narrative as a history. It is only as an historian that he has the smallest *locus standi*. As a narrator of fictitious events he is nowhere; to insert into his attempt a backbone of logic, he must relate events that are assumed to be real. This assumption permeates, animates all the work of the most solid story-tellers; we need only mention (to select a single instance), the magnificent historical tone of Balzac, who would as soon have thought of admitting to the reader that he was deceiving him, as Garrick or John Kemble would have thought of pulling off his disguise in front of the foot-lights. Therefore, when Trollope suddenly winks at us and reminds us that he is telling us an arbitrary thing, we are startled and shocked in quite the same way as if Macaulay or Motley [distinguished nineteenth-century historians] were to drop the historic mask and intimate that William of Orange was a myth or the Duke of Alva an invention.[10]

An admirably suggestive passage! Here the rationale of the traditional calling a novel a history is brought to the surface, not least in the metaphors James uses, in the hyperbolic "heat" (his term) of his tone, and in his oblique confession that it is just because a work of fiction is not history that it must maintain so carefully the fiction that it is. Though William of Orange and the Duke of Alva were real persons and the characters of Balzac unreal, as much a lie as the play-acting of Garrick or Kemble, the novelist must maintain the fiction that his characters have historical reality or else he is "nowhere." This means, I take it, that a fiction confessing to being a fiction vanishes into airy vapor or falls into a fathomless abyss, like a man who loses his footing, the ground he stands on, his *locus standi*, his *logos*. The substantiality of "the most solid story-tellers" depends on having a "somewhere," an assumed historical reality as ground or scene. Such a context, by the species of metonymic transfer that is the basis of all narrative, will give solidity to the story narrated on the basis of that *locus* and to the interpretation of the story performed by its narrator.

The assumption that his narrative is history gives more than simply a foundation to the novelist's work. It also "insert[s] into his attempt a backbone of logic" (another *logos* word there!). Without the assumption of a historical basis, a work of fiction would, it seems, disintegrate into unconnected fragments, or become a "large loose baggy monster," in James's famous phrase,[11] an invertebrate, a jellyfish or Medusa. Only if it is assumed to be history will a novel have a beginning, middle, and end, so forming a coherent whole, with a single meaning or individuality, like a vertebrate animal. In his use of the word "logic," with its accompanying metaphors of *"locus"* and "backbone," James exposes the connection between the notion of organic form in the novel and the system of assumptions that is associated with the idea of history in Western culture. James's formulations are "logocentric" through and through. The traditional notions of form in fiction, James implicitly recognizes, are displaced versions of ideas about history. The system of assumptions about organic form and meaning in the novel (whose master expression is James's own admirable prefaces to his works), stands or falls with the metaphor defining a work of fiction as a species of history.

I note in passing that James conspicuously fails to reck his own rede. To say that *The Golden Bowl*, or *The Wings of the Dove*, or even the early *The Portrait of a Lady* reads like Macaulay or Motley is a manifest absurdity. James makes extravagant use of novelistic devices—a fictional hyperbolically telepathic narrator, not to be identified with Henry James, that uses indirect discourse to report on what goes on "secretly" in the minds and feelings of the imaginary characters; elaborate figures of speech and word play, such as puns and stress on the strangeness of ordinary words; conspicuously problematic speech acts.[12] These can be, and are, used, sparingly, in history writing, but if Macaulay had written his *The History of England* in the style of *The Golden Bowl*, people would have thought he had lost his mind. George Eliot, however, was already using versions, almost as extravagant as James's, of the narrative devices whose systematic use distinguish fiction from history, as I shall show.

The presuppositions about history that have been transferred to the traditional conception of fiction's desired form may be identified. They include the notions of origin and end ("archeology" and "teleology"); of unity and totality; of underlying "reason" or "ground"; of self-hood, consciousness, or "human nature"; of the homogeneity, linearity, and continuity of time; of necessary progress; of "fate," "destiny," or "Providence"; of causality; of gradually emerging "meaning"; of representational truth—in short, all those presuppositions about world history challenged so peremptorily by Nietzsche as they are exemplified in the citations from Hegel that Nietzsche makes in the epigraph cited above.

Certain metaphors, such as those of flowing water, of woven cloth, or of a living organism, tend to recur in expressions of this system of assumptions, as I shall show for *Middlemarch*. The regular appearance of these overt metaphors whenever the system is being expressed reveals the fact that the system is itself a metaphor, a figure whose originally metaphorical or fictive character has been effaced. "History is like flowing water, or woven cloth, or a living organism," we are encouraged to think. As Hegel, you will remember, says, using in reverse the metaphorical equation I am exploring, "even children demand that their stories have some point, that is, at the very least, a purpose that can be divined and to which the events and actions can be related." A story without such an aim and the subservience of all its parts to that aim would be "a senseless product of the imagination."

The set of assumptions common to both Western ideas of history and Western ideas of fiction is not—it is a point of importance—a collection of separate attributes, detached from one another, the distinctive features that happen to be there. They are on the contrary a true system, in the sense that each implies all the others. No one of them may be withdrawn, shaken, or solicited without a simultaneous putting in question of all the others. All the elements of these integrated assumptions about history may be transferred without distortion to the customary notion of fiction's form. The formal structure of the novel is usually conceived of as the gradual emergence of its meaning. This coincides with its end, the fulfillment of the teleology of the work. The end is the retrospective revelation of the unity of the whole, its "organic unity." The last page is the goal toward which the whole novel has been moving, inhabited as it has been throughout by "the sense of an ending." Usually, for Victorian novels, this is the expected "happy ending." The sense of an immanent ending articulates all the parts as the backbone of the narrative. At the same time the image of a progressive revelation of meaning is to be applied to the idea of the "destinies" of the characters. Their lives make "sense" as the gradual revelation of a whole, the "meaning of their lives." The end of the novel is the final exposing of the fates of the characters as well as of the formal unity of the text. These notions of narrative, of character, and of formal unity in fiction are congruent with the system of concepts making up the Western idea of history.

No doubt historians have not waited for writers of fiction to perform the act of interrogation that would make this system of assumptions tremble or perhaps vanish like a spider-web blown away by the wind. Nor has the putting in question of this system had to wait for the deconstructive rigor of a Jacques Derrida or a Roland Barthes.[13] As Leo Braudy in *Narrative Form in History and Fiction: Hume, Fielding, and Gibbon* and Hayden White in *Metahistory*[14] long ago showed, the writing of history was already a problematic enterprise for eighteenth- and nineteenth-century historians, or indeed for modern historians since Vico. No doubt it already seemed problematic to Thucydides, Plutarch, and Herodotus.

As James's revealing final metaphor indicates, all historians have consciously worn "the historic mask," much as an actor wears his costume and makeup. This is true not in the sense that historians have believed that William of Orange was a myth or the Duke of Alva an invention, but in the sense that they have often been aware that the narrating of an historical sequence in one way or another involves a constructive, interpretative, fiction-making act. Historians have always known that history and the narrative of history never wholly coincide. Nevertheless, the system of assumptions about history I have briefly described has had great coercive power to bewitch not only historians and philosophers of history, but also writers of fiction who model their enterprise on that of the narrative historian. The system has also had great power over critics and theorists who interpret novels. The system tends magically to weave itself in a new form even when it has been deliberately abolished, like a spider-web spun again out of the entrails of our Western languages, or like Penelope's web woven anew each morning after its nightly destruction, or like that living labyrinth traced out on the bare ground over the maze laid out by Daedalus in the ancient dance of Theseus.[15] I shall demonstrate later how a reference to Theseus is justified in a reading of *Middlemarch*.

Demystification of the Connection of Narrative and History

One of the most persistent forms of this endlessly renewed, endlessly defeated, unweaving has been enacted by works of fiction. A putting in question of its own enterprise has been an intrinsic part of the practice of prose fiction in its modern form from *Don Quixote* on through *Tristram Shandy* and the nineteenth-century novelists down to John Barth and J. L. Borges, Thomas Pynchon and E. L. Doctorow in the twentieth century. This unraveling has also been a dismantling of the basic metaphor by means of which prose fiction has defined itself, that is, a certain idea of history and history writing. Insofar as a novel raises questions about the key assumptions of storytelling, for example about the notions of origin and end, about consciousness or selfhood, about causality, or about gradually emerging unified meaning, this putting in question of narrative form becomes also obliquely a putting in question of history or of the writing of history. What seemed to be the *locus standi* by analogy with which the novel was written turns out to be itself undermined by the activity of storytelling. Insofar as a novel "deconstructs" the assumptions of realism in fiction, it also turns out to dismantle naive notions about history or about the writing of history.

One admirable example of this is George Eliot's *Middlemarch*. *Middlemarch* is not in any obvious way part of that tradition of the anti-novel to which I alluded above in invoking the names of Cervantes, Sterne, Borges, and Pynchon. It is solidly within the tradition of realistic fiction. *Middlemarch* explicitly places its events in a particular historical time and place, English provincial life in the period just before the first Reform Bill. It builds up carefully the historical background of this time and place. In that sense it is a "historical novel." It presents its narrator explicitly as a "historian" and is overtly based on certain historical assumptions. These include the assumption that each historical period is unique and the assumption that "historical forces" determine the life that can be lived at a certain time. Dorothea Brooke's life, for example, was disabled by the lack of any "coherent social faith and order which could perform the function of knowledge for the ardently willing soul" (Prelude: 3–4). The "determining acts of her life" were "the mixed result of young and noble impulse struggling amidst the conditions of an imperfect social state" (Finale: 924). As George Eliot says, "there is no creature whose inward being is so strong that it is not greatly determined by what lies outside it" (Finale: 924).

The word "history" is a key term in the opening sentence of *Middlemarch*. Here Dorothea, in a famous analogy, is presented as the repetition with a difference of St. Theresa, a St. Theresa born out of her time: "Who that cares much to know the history of man, and how the mysterious mixtures behaves under the varying experiments of Time, has not dwelt, at least briefly, on the life of Saint Theresa . . ." (Prelude: 3). In *Middlemarch*, moreover, history is a theme within the story itself. It appears in the historical researches of Casaubon, and in the relation of art to history as that relation is put in question in the discussions between Will Ladislaw and his German friend Naumann. History is also constantly kept before the reader as the basic analogy for the narrator's own enterprise.

One example of a place where history is an overt issue is a masterly passage in chapter 11 describing the "shifting . . . boundaries," the "subtle movement," of "old provincial society" (11: 104). Here George Eliot's presentation of a model of social interdependence and gradual change in *Middlemarch* is put explicitly under the aegis of the similar enterprise of Herodotus: "In fact, much the same sort of movement and mixture went on in old England as we find in older Herodotus, who also, in telling what had been, thought it well to take a woman's lot for his starting-point" (11: 105). Another example is the splendid passage in chapter 20 describing Dorothea's response to the "stupendous fragmentariness," the "unintelligible" "weight," of Rome:

> To those who have looked at Rome with the quickening power of a knowledge which breathes a growing soul into all historic shapes, and traces out the suppressed transitions which unite all contrasts, Rome may still be the spiritual centre and interpreter of the world. But let them conceive one more historical contrast: the gigantic broken revelations of that Imperial and Papal city thrust abruptly on the notions of a girl who had been brought up in English and Swiss Puritanism, fed on meagre Protestant histories and on art chiefly of the hand-screen sort; a girl whose ardent nature turned all her small allowance of knowledge into principles, fusing her actions into their mould, and whose quick emotions gave the most abstract things the quality of a pleasure or a pain. (20: 215)

Another example is the opening of chapter 15, in which George Eliot explicitly defines her strategy as a novelist in contrast to that of "a great historian, as he insisted on calling himself," Henry Fielding:

> But Fielding lived when the days were longer (for time, like money, is measured by our needs), when summer afternoons were spacious, and the clock ticked slowly in the winter evenings. We belated historians must not linger after his example; and if we did so, it is probable that our chat would be thin and eager, as if delivered from a camp-stool in a parrot-house. I at least have so much to do in unraveling certain human lots, and seeing how they were woven and interwoven, that all the light I can command must be

concentrated on this particular web, and not dispersed over that tempting range of relevancies called the universe. (15: 158)

I shall return later to examine the rhetoric of this passage. History, however, as you can see, takes its place in *Middlemarch* as one theme parallel to a chain of other themes. Among these themes are religion (dramatized in Bulstrode's story), love (in the three love stories), science (Lydgate), art (Naumann and Ladislaw), and superstition (Fred Vincy). The treatment of each of these themes falls into the same pattern. In each case the narrator shows the character to be mystified by a belief that all the details she or he confronts make a whole governed by a single center, origin, and end—logocentrism, in short. In each case the narrator demystifies the illusion and shows it to be based on an error, the fundamental linguistic error of taking a figure of speech literally. This error assumes that because two things are similar they are equivalent, sprung from the same source, or bound for the same end, explicable by the same grounding principle. As the narrator famously says, in a passage already cited that might be taken as a diagnosis of the mental illness from which all of the characters in *Middlemarch* suffer, "we all of us, grave or light, get our thoughts entangled in metaphors, and act fatally on the strength of them" (10: 93). "Act fatally"—that is a strong formulation. Getting your thoughts entangled in metaphors is lethal. Casaubon is beguiled into wandering endlessly and fruitlessly in the labyrinthine complexity of ancient myth by his false assumption that there is a "Key to all Mythologies," namely Christian revelation. He believes "that all the mythical systems or erratic mythical fragments in the world were corruptions of a tradition originally revealed" (3: 26). Lydgate searches for the "primitive tissue" of which all the bodily organs will be differentiations: "have not these structures some common basis from which they have all started, as your sarsnet, gauze, net, satin and velvet from the raw cocoon?" (15: 165–6). Bulstrode thinks that Providence justifies his deceptions and that his worldly success is proof that God is guiding his life toward his salvation. Fred Vincy believes that because he is a good fellow luck will be on his side, "keeping up a joyous imaginative activity which fashions events according to desire" (23: 262). He believes that "the universal order of things would necessarily be agreeable to an agreeable young gentleman" (23: 257). "What can the fitness of things mean," he assumes, "if not their fitness to a man's expectations? Failing this, absurdity and atheism gape behind him" (14: 150). This analysis of Fred Vincy's folly is a good example of the not altogether sympathetic irony that characterizes the narrator's discourse in *Middlemarch*. I shall return to Eliot's irony as a mode of somewhat condescending superiority.

Rosamond's spinning of the "gossamer web" of love (36: 385) in her courtship by Lydgate falls into the same pattern. Her fantasy too is the construction of a fiction governed by an illusory beginning and end. In her case the model is literary. Like Emma Bovary she has read too many bad novels. "Rosamond," says the narrator, "had registered every look and word, and estimated them as the opening incidents of a preconceived romance—incidents which gather value from the foreseen development and climax" (16: 185). Though the "basis for her structure had the usual airy slightness" and is, so to speak, a groundless ground, nevertheless she "was of remarkably detailed and realistic imagination when the foundation had been once presupposed (12: 130). "Foundation"—this is another name for James's *locus standi*.

Dorothea's nearly fatal mistake in marrying Casaubon is only the most elaborately described version of this universal error. She is both "ardent" and "theoretic." Her ardor takes the form of seeking some guide who will transfigure the details of her everyday life by justifying them in terms of some ideal end. Her error is generated by her "exalted enthusiasm about the ends of life, an enthusiasm which was lit chiefly by its own fire" (3: 30). It is an error of interpretation, once again the error of taking a figurative similarity as an identity. Dorothea thinks that because Casaubon reminds her of St. Augustine, of Pascal, of Bossuet, of Oberlin, of his seventeenth-century namesake, Isaac Casaubon (alluded to in the novel [1: 11]), of Milton, and of "the judicious Hooker" (1: 11) (quite an ironic parade of precursors!), he must be the equivalent of those spiritual geniuses, "a guide who would take her along the grandest path" (3: 31).[16] "The really delightful marriage must be that where your husband was a sort of father" (1: 11). Casaubon is a text, a collection of signs that Dorothea misreads, according to that universal propensity for misinterpretation that infects all the characters in *Middlemarch*.

Parallel to these forms of mystification is the belief that history is progressive, teleological. This illusion is deconstructed along with the rest, perhaps even more explicitly. The way this happens is for my purposes especially apt, since the example George Eliot gives is the Hegelian theory that art cooperates in the world process and assists in the self-development of the world spirit. Will Ladislaw is the spokesperson for George Eliot's undoing of this particular version of the association between history and narrative. Unlike the other characters, Ladislaw has no desire to find out origins. Casaubon acidly reports him to have "said he should prefer not to know the sources of the Nile, and that there should be some unknown regions preserved as hunting-grounds for the poetic imagination" (9: 89). Will makes fun of Naumann's Hegelian or "Nazarene" theory of art: "the divinity passing into higher completeness and all but exhausted in the act of covering your bit of canvas. I am amateurish if you like: I do *not* think that all the universe is straining towards the obscure significance of your pictures" (19: 212).

The effort of demythologizing in *Middlemarch* can be defined as a dismantling of various versions of the metaphysical system on which the traditional idea of history depends. In spite of its recourse to the conventional *locus standi* of defining itself as a displaced form of history, the novel pulls the rug out from under itself and deprives itself of that solid ground without which, if Henry James is right, it is "nowhere." George Eliot's fiction deprives itself of its ground in history by demonstrating that ground to be a fiction too, a figure, a myth, a lie, like Dorothea's interpretation of Casaubon or like Bulstrode's reading of his religious destiny.

Totalizing Metaphors in *Middlemarch*

> *text* ... from Medieval Latin *textus*, (Scriptural) text, from Latin, literary composition, "woven thing," from the past participle of *texere*, to weave.[17]

If *Middlemarch* deprives itself of its apparently solid ground in an analogy with history, it allows itself another form of totalizing ground. This form seems more appropriately fictional. It is the habitual use by the narrator (and sometimes by the characters) of certain all-encompassing metaphorical models inviting the reader to see the persons and events of the novel as a whole. Such metaphors are put forward as a means of thinking of all the people in Middlemarch in their interrelations through time. Each metaphor is an interpretative net that the reader is invited to cast over Middlemarch society. She can use it as a paradigm by means of which to think of the whole as a totality.

There are three such families of metaphors. Each group is related to the others, fulfilling them, but at the same time contradicting them, cancelling them out, undermining their validity. The reader must be warned beforehand, however, not to be beguiled, as so many characters in *Middlemarch* are, by the assumptions that these metaphors are displaced names for some literal referent. Though many historical realities, such as the then new railroad system and the Reform Bill of 1832, are referred to in *Middlemarch*, those references are transposed into an imaginary realm. They enter a heterocosm that is generated out of exchanges of language that are like self-generating monetary exchanges in the modern capitalist world. The metaphors I am about to discuss are figures for what is already figurative, imaginary, not literal or extra-linguistic. They

are that odd sort of locution, metaphors for something already a tropological displacement or a linguistic fiction. Dorothea, Bulstrode, and the
rest of the characters can be met with only in the pages of *Middlemarch*,
and the reader must never forget that all-too-forgettable fact.

Before identifying and exemplifying these metaphors, however, let
me say a word about the basic narrative conventions of *Middlemarch*.
Much of the novel is made up of the discourse of the narrator, often
speaking telepathically for the characters in indirect discourse and
then interpreting that in sovereign superiority. Most of the rest of the
novel is the give and take of conversation between two or more of the
characters, with accompanying commentary by the narrator. The basic
presupposition of *Middlemarch* is that the characters do not understand
one another intuitively, far from it, while the narrator has telepathic
clairvoyance about what is going on in the minds and feelings of all the
characters. Nicholas Royle calls this, in a witty neologism, "clairvoyeurism."[18] Think of it! The (fictive or imaginary) characters are subject,
everywhere and at all times, without their knowledge, to a penetrating,
analytical, judgmental, mediumistic inhabitation by the (fictive or imaginary) narrator. The narrator sees without being seen. One might call the
narrator a "host," a mediumistic host, that is, of all those ghosts he, she,
or it calls up: Dorothea, Casaubon, Will Ladislaw, Lydgate, Rosamond,
and the rest. The narrator's power as spirit medium can enter into every
corner of the characters' minds and hearts to report what it finds there.
I mean "medium" both in the sense of spiritualist medium and in the
sense of the narrator's language as medium. The whole imaginary heterocosm depends on the latter. I repeat the words "fictive" and "imaginary" to remind the reader that neither the characters nor the narrator
have any existence outside language. The words on the page generate
them.[19] I say "telepathic" rather than "omniscient" because I follow
Nicholas Royle in thinking that the theological implications of "omniscient" are inappropriate for the kind of insight Eliot's narrator has.[20]
That insight is much more accurately described as the sort of clairvoyance or "second sight" nineteenth-century mediums claimed to have.[21]
Nevertheless, George Eliot's clairvoyeurism has its parallel in what I
was taught in Sunday School about how I must watch my every thought
because God is "overlooking," with total insight, what I think and feel.
Frightening thought! By the time Marian Evans wrote *Middlemarch*,
she had long since come to see the notion of an omniscient, omnipresent, self-conscious, paternal deity as yet another illusion, perhaps as the
greatest illusion, perhaps as the father of ideology, as it was for Marx.
Even so, like most lapsed Christians, she cultivated the nostalgias, not
least in displacing theology into the "as if" of fictional conventions.

The narrator reports his (her? its?)[22] insight in indirect discourse, of which George Eliot was a master. In his indirect discourse the narrator speaks in the third person past tense for what was first person present tense for the character, or perhaps for what was an inarticulate "feeling/thinking" to which the narrator gives eloquently appropriate, but also ironically undermining, words. The characters, on the contrary, have no natural insight into their fellows. Of the opacity others have for each character, one can generalize what the narrator says about Lydgate and Rosamond: "Poor Lydgate! or shall I say, Poor Rosamond? Each lived in a world of which the other knew nothing" (16: 185). This observation comes just after a long section in which the narrator enters by mediumistic telepathy into Lydgate's mind and feelings, and just before a section devoted to telepathic reporting of Rosamond's anticipations of marrying Lydgate. Her thoughts are something of which Lydgate has no inkling.

The reader might think that this law of non-intuition of the other is abrogated when the narrator says of Fred Vincy's insight into old Peter Featherstone's mind: "Fred fancied that he saw to the bottom of his uncle Featherstone's soul, though in reality half what he saw there was no more than the reflex of his own inclinations" (12: 132). The other half, however, the correct half, is not the result of telepathic insight, but, as many passages in the novel make clear, the result of a lucky reading of signs, a reading that just happens to be right.

Critics have made much of the high value Eliot gives to "sympathy," etymologically "feeling with," as the basis of morality. Such feeling with one another and understanding of one another as the characters of *Middlemarch* have are gained with great difficulty. They remain a matter of guesswork, not of direct intuition. Each character remains living, often disastrously living, in a world of which others know nothing. Much emphasis is put on radical misreading of others as a possible source of great sorrow, as in Dorothea's misreading of Casaubon. Dorothea is intelligent, sensitive, and has warm good will, but these do not save her from taking Casaubon for someone radically other than who he is. Nor is it the whole story to over-emphasize the narrator's compassionate sympathy for the characters. Much of the narrator's clairvoyant analysis of this or that character is ironically and even comically critical, as in the narrator's report that Mr. Casaubon thinks that his long celibacy means that he has stored up for himself a great reservoir of passion and is "surprised to find what an exceedingly shallow rill it [is]" (7: 69). I shall return later to this passage. In the figure of the shallow rill, this comic formulation is a not entirely delicate hint at Casaubon's probable impotence.

The narrative voice in *Middlemarch* expresses devastating insight into a given character's foolishness, self-deception, and egoism. The narrator says we should sympathize, but does not give good grounds for that. Rather the reverse. The narrative discourse gives grounds rather for the delicious pleasure of Eliotic irony at the expense of the characters. The narrator's clairvoyeurism is shared with the reader by way of the words on the page. We are made complicit in this elaborate exercise in Peeping-Tomism, frequently by direct appeals by the narrator to the reader to share in his telepathic insight: "pardon these details for once—you would have learned to love them if you had known Caleb Garth" (23: 259). Royle calls this particular appeal a "patently mad assertion" ("On Second Sight," 89). I suppose this is because the reader knows Caleb Garth is an invention, an imaginary personage in a novel. It is crazy to say otherwise. No way exists for the reader to "know" Garth in the real world.

Several recent brilliant essays on Eliot's strangest and most troubling story, *The Lifted Veil*,[23] have recognized this paradox. Latimer, the hero of *The Lifted Veil*, is suddenly one day granted telepathic insight into the follies, selfishness, and malicious badness of those around him:

> . . . the rational talk, the graceful attentions, the wittily-turned phrases, and the kindly deeds, which used to make the web of their characters, were seen as if thrust asunder by a microscopic vision, that showed all the intermediate frivolities, all the suppressed egoism, all the struggling chaos of puerilities, meanness, vague capricious memories, and indolent make-shift thoughts, from which human words and deeds emerge like leaflets covering a ferment-ing heap.[24]

"Fermenting heap!" That is strong language for what human interior-ities are really like. It is no wonder that Eliot postponed the publication of *The Lifted Veil* until near the end of her life, though it was written early in her career, when she was at work on *The Mill on the Floss*. I shall return later, in a discussion of the celebrated chapter 17 of *Adam Bede*, to the implications of Eliot's somewhat cynical and uncharitable view of ordinary human nature. Such insight as Latimer and Eliot's narrators have has its dangers. Latimer's clairvoyance and its accom-panying foreknowledge more or less destroy him. He foresees even the time and miserable circumstances of his own death. Eliot's great novels, however, grant Latimer-like insight to their narrators and, by way of the narrator's reports of the characters, to the reader. We are supposed to be made better people, more loving and tolerant of our neighbors, by the same kind of penetrating understanding that has such a devastating effect on Latimer. George Eliot's novels remained poised in the face of this aporia.

The totalizing metaphors I am about to identify and demonstrate are woven into the fabric of the narrator's discourse of remorseless insight. I am abstracting them from their contexts in order to classify and understand them. In their contexts they often come within a few sentences of one another. An example of this is two pages in the long analysis of Lydgate's personality and ambitions for himself. (Lydgate's name, by the way, combining as it does two words for blockage, does not inspire confidence in his future, whatever gifts he may have.) Lydgate wants to be a medical scientist who will be a good provincial doctor and at the same time identify in the laboratory researches of his spare time the "primitive tissue" that is the origin of all the body's organs. The narrator speaks of the way Bichat's work is "already vibrating along many currents of the European mind," of Lydgate's search for "the primitive tissue," of a man's life as the way he "swims and makes his point or else is carried headlong," of the way any one of us flawed human beings, Lydgate included, is someone "whose better energies are liable to lapse down the wrong channel under the influence of transient solicitations," and of the way "all conceit is not the same conceit, but varies in correspondence with the minutiae of mental make in which each of us differs from another" (15: 166–7). "Tissue"; "current"; "minutiae": I shall return to each of the metaphors used in these two pages in my categorization and rhetorical reading of each family of metaphors in *Middlemarch*. The reader who happens to notice the ostentatiously metaphorical texture of the novel may happen to wonder whether the narrator's dictum applies to the narrator also, or whether he, she, or it is somehow exempt from the somber generalization, already twice cited: "we all of us, grave or light, get our thoughts entangled in metaphors and act fatally on the strength of them." Uttering this wisdom, the narrator, in using the metaphor "entangled," commits again the sin he condemns.

The recurrence of totalizing metaphors throughout *Middlemarch* and their assumed validity affirms one of the most important presuppositions of the novel. The unique life of each character is presented as part of a single system of complex interaction in time and space. No man, for George Eliot, lives alone. Each exists in "the same embroiled medium, the same troublous fitfully-illuminated life" (30: 323). The narrator comments throughout on the nature of this "medium" (a third meaning for the word, along with spirit medium and means of communication) and on the interaction of character with character. The voice of the narrator is sympathetic certainly, but also deliciously ironic, mocking, and clairvoyant in his (her, or its) insight into human folly. That irony is often present in the form of a repetition in indirect discourse of what a given character thinks and feels at a certain moment, as when the narrator reports that Fred Vincy believes, according to a passage already cited, that "the universal order of things would necessarily be agreeable to an agreeable young gentleman" (23: 257). The narrative voice is in *Middlemarch*, as in Victorian novels generally, the most immediate presence for the reader, along with reported speech of the characters as overheard by the narrator and commented on. The narrator's language is the chief generating force behind the stylistic texture of the novel.

Middlemarch as Fractal Pattern

Perhaps the most salient totalizing metaphor presented as a model for the community of Middlemarch is actually a family of related metaphors. Each member of this family compares Middlemarch society or some part of it to a spatially or temporally deployed material complex— a labyrinth, or flowing water, or woven cloth. Two important implications of these metaphors as they are used in the novel may be identified. The first is the assumption that a society is in some way like a material field and therefore is open to the sort of objective scientific investigation that may be applied to any such field, for example to flowing water. The other is the assumption, reinforced by many passages in the novel, that the pattern of small-scale pieces of the whole is the same as the pattern of the whole and so may be validly described with the same figures. This is the assumption of the validity of one kind of synecdoche. Or one could compare it to fractal similarity. The part is in configuration like the whole. An investigation of a sample will lead to valid conclusions about the whole. If Middlemarch society as a whole is like flowing water or like woven cloth, the mental life of each of its inhabitants may also be validly described in the same metaphors. In the same way, when the reader or the narrator focuses on the relation between two of the characters out of the whole lot, the same metaphors will be found to be valid on that scale too. In the other direction, as I have suggested, it is implied that what is true in Middlemarch is also true for English society as a whole, or even for human life anywhere and at any time.

Middlemarch is full of such shifts in perspective from close up to far away and back to close up again, according to the law of scientific method that Lydgate admirably formulates: "there must be a systole and diastole in all inquiry," he says at a sad moment in his life, and "a man's mind must be continually expanding and shrinking between the whole human horizon and the horizon of an object-glass" (63: 710). Eliot's assumption is that, in the social world at least, such changes in scale reveal a strict homogeneity between the large-scale and small-scale grain of things. As Will Ladislaw phrases it, "the little waves make the large ones and are of the same pattern" (46: 513).

Middlemarch as Web

The most persistent of these structural metaphors, as has often been noticed by critics, is the figure of the web. One explicit application of the web image to the whole range of social relationships in the novel comes in a famous passage where the narrator distinguishes his-her-its enterprise from that of Fielding. Whereas Fielding lived in more spacious times and could allow himself the luxury of "copious remarks and digressions," "I at least," says the narrator, "have so much to do in unraveling certain human lots, and seeing how they were woven and interwoven, that all the light I can command must be concentrated on this particular web, and not dispersed over that tempting range of relevancies called the universe" (15: 158). The narrator's effort is not just that of observation. He must, like a good scientist, take apart the specimen being analyzed, unravel all its fibers to see how it has been woven and interwoven. That the texture of Middlemarch society may be accurately represented in a metaphor of woven cloth is taken for granted throughout the novel. It appears in many apparently casual phrases as a reinforcement of more elaborate analyses by inviting the reader to keep the paradigm of the web before her or his mind. Lydgate, to give one example from early in the novel, finds himself for the first time "feeling the hampering threadlike pressure of small social conditions, and their frustrating complexity" (18: 200–1). An allusion to Gulliver tied down by the Lilliputians with their tiny ropes may probably be detected here.

The metaphor of a web is also used repeatedly in *Middlemarch* to describe the texture of smaller-scale entities within the larger tissue of the social fabric. The love-making of Rosamond and Lydgate, for example, is called the collective weaving of an intersubjective tissue: "Young love-making—that gossamer web! Even the points it clings to—the things whence its subtle interlacings are swung—are scarcely perceptible; momentary touches of fingertips, meetings of rays from blue and dark orbs, unfinished phrases, lightest changes of cheek and lip, faintest tremors. The web itself is made of spontaneous beliefs and indefinable joys, yearnings of one life towards another, visions of completeness, indefinite trust. And Lydgate fell to spinning that web from his inward self with wonderful rapidity . . . As for Rosamond, she was in the water-lily's expanding wonderment at its own fuller life, and she too was spinning industriously at the mutual web" (36: 385).

Another important use of the web metaphor is made in the description of Lydgate's scientific researches. Lydgate's attempt to find the "primitive tissue" is based on the assumption that the metaphor of woven cloth applies in the organic as well as in the social realm. His use of the figure brings into the open the parallelism between George Eliot's aim as a sociologist of provincial life and the aims of some biologists of her time. Lydgate's research is based on the hypothesis that all the organs of the body are differentiations of "certain primary webs or tissues." The metaphor is crucial in the passage already quoted to indicate Lydgate's mystified belief in origin: "have not these structures some common basis from which they have all started, as your sarsnet, gauze, net, satin and velvet from the raw cocoon?" (15: 165–6). That Lydgate is wrong in his hypothesis, that he did not know about organic cells, much less about DNA, is part of the pathos of his failure as a scientist, even though his grasp of scientific method (empirical investigation of testable hypotheses on the basis of objective evidence) is admirably correct. A lot is taken for granted, however, even by scientists today, in the assumption that such a thing as objective evidence exists.

If Lydgate assumes that biological entities may be described as tissues, the narrator of *Middlemarch* makes the same assumptions about the subjective lives of the characters. Of Lydgate, for example, the narrator says that "momentary speculations as to all the possible grounds for Mrs Bulstrode's hints had managed to get woven like slight clinging hairs into the more substantial web of his thoughts" (31: 334). Much later in the novel, basing the generalization again on Lydgate's psychology, the narrator asks, somewhat acidly: "is it not rather what we expect in men, that they should have numerous strands of experience lying side by side and never compare them with each other?" (58: 652). This image of mental or intersubjective life as a reticulated pattern of threads is implicit when a few pages earlier the narrator says of Rosamond and Lydgate that, "Between him and her indeed there was that total missing of each other's mental track, which is too evidently possible even between persons who are continually thinking of each other" (58: 650). The image of mental or social life as travelling along tracks which may or may not intersect with others is also latent in an earlier remark about Will Ladislaw: "There are characters which are continually creating collisions and nodes for themselves in dramas which nobody is prepared to act with them" (19: 214).

Middlemarch as Stream

To the metaphor of a web must be added the metaphor of a stream. Collective or individual life in Middlemarch is not a fixed pattern like a carpet. The web is always in movement. The pervasive figure for this in the novel is flowing water. This figure is to some degree homogeneous with the figure of the web. Flowing water, for George Eliot, is made up of currents, filaments flowing side by side, intermingling and dividing. Flowing water is, so to speak, a temporalized web. Casaubon, for example, is said, in a fine series of phrases, to have possessed "that proud narrow sensitiveness which has not mass enough to spare for transformation into sympathy, and quivers thread-like in small currents of self-preoccupation or at best of an egoistic scrupulosity" (29: 311). Lydgate, after he has first met Rosamond, "had no sense that any new current had set into his life" (16: 182). Of his life when it is in the midst of being lived (in the middle of its march, as one might say), the narrator asserts that it has "the complicated probabilities of an arduous purpose, with all the possible thwartings and furtherings of circumstance, all the niceties of inward balance, by which a man swims and makes his point or else is carried headlong," for "character too is a process and an unfolding" (15: 166). The word "unfolding" adds both a textile and a textual figure to the one about swimming, as when we speak of an "unfolding drama." In another place, the narrator speaks of "the chief current" of Dorothea's anxiety (22: 245), and, as opposed to the egoistic scrupulosity of Casaubon's small soul, "in Dorothea's mind there was a current into which all thought and feeling were apt sooner or later to flow—the reaching forward of the whole consciousness towards the fullest truth, the least partial good" (20: 226). In the climactic scene of Dorothea's renunciation of her fortune to marry Will, "the flood of her young passion bear[s] down all the obstructions which had kept her silent" (83: 898).

Minutiae in Middlemarch

One final element will complete the description of the quasi-scientific model Eliot uses to describe the subjective life of the individual, the relations of two persons within the social "medium," and the nature of that medium as a whole. This element has already been anticipated in what has been said about the correspondence, in Eliot's view of things, between small and large-scale structures. This idea, however, is but one aspect of a larger assumption, the notion that any process in any of the three "scales" is made up of "minutiae" that may be endlessly subdivided. Any "unit" or single fact, in social or in mental life, is not single but multiple. A finer lens could always make smaller parts visible. The smaller parts, in turn, are made up of even smaller entities.

One corollary of this vision of things is the rejection of the concept of single causes that more or less straightforwardly characterizes, for example, *Adam Bede*. In *Middlemarch* George Eliot still believes in causality, but in the psychological and social realms causes are now seen as unimaginably multiple. No fact is in itself single. No fact is explicable by a single relationship to a single cause. Each fact is a kind of multitudinous node that exists only apparently as a single thing because we happen to have the microscope focused as we do. If the focus were finer, the apparently single fact would subdivide. It would reveal itself to be made of multiple minutiae. If the focus were coarser, the fact would disappear within the larger entity of which it is a part. A single momentary state of mind, for example, exists in relation to all its latent motives, the minutiae of mental life that underlie it. It exists in relation also to its own past and future. It exists in multiple relations to what is outside it, especially to all the other people to whom the person is socially related. The metaphor of the variable lens of a microscope is used by Eliot to make this point. The passage is one of many examples of the assumption, so important also in *Adam Bede*, that the social and natural worlds are analogous: "Even with a microscope directed on a water-drop we find ourselves making interpretations which turn out to be rather coarse; for whereas under a weak lens you may seem to see a creature exhibiting an active voracity into which other smaller creatures actively play as if they were so many animated tax-pennies, a stronger lens reveals to you certain tiniest hairlets which make vortices for these victims while the swallower waits passively at his receipt of custom" (6: 65).

One might ask, parenthetically, how and why the metaphor of the microscope has been contaminated here by another apparently unrelated metaphor, that of money, taxes, and "custom." This interpretation of one metaphor by another metaphor is characteristic of Eliot's use of figure. An attempt to explain fully this linguistic habit will come further on in this book, but I can say already that the displacement of one figure by another is asymmetrically parallel to the displacement of the weak lens by the strong lens of the microscope. In each case, a new vision of things replaces a previous one. The optical visions are apparently reconcilable, whereas when the money metaphor is superimposed on the microscope metaphor the two figures interfere with one another even if they are not wholly contradictory. The text of *Middlemarch* goes on to apply the metaphor of the double-lensed microscope to a particular case in the novel: "In this way, metaphorically speaking, a strong lens applied to Mrs Cadwallader's match-making will show a play of minute causes producing what may be called thought and speech vortices to bring her the sort of food she needed" (6: 65). Eliot's narrator, the reader can see, is extremely self-conscious about what is at stake in using metaphors to name things that, within the imaginary world of the novel, have objective, material existence.

The phrase "play of minute causes" is echoed throughout the novel by similar phrases that keep before the reader the idea that the mental and social events being described are extremely complex. This complexity is essential to their mode of existence. The narrator speaks, for example, of "a slow preparation of effects from one life on another" (11: 104), or of an ardor which cooled "imperceptibly," like other youthful loves ("Nothing in the world more subtle than the process of their gradual change!" [15: 161]), or, in a passage cited earlier, of "the minutiae of mental make in which one of us differs from another" (15: 167), or of Lydgate's "testing vision of details and relations" (16: 183), or of "the suppressed transitions which unite all contrasts" (20: 215), or of the "nice distinctions of rank in Middlemarch" (23: 258), or, in a chapter's epigraph, of "the living myriad of hidden suckers whereby the belief and the conduct are wrought into mutual sustainment" (53: 576), or of a "fact" which "was broken into little sequences" (61: 685), or of the way Bulstrode's "misdeeds were like the subtle muscular movements which are not taken account of in the consciousness" (68: 762). The reader will note that many of these passages stress the obscurity of minutiae. They exist and they are causally effective, but they are hard to see. It takes a strong microscope, so to speak, to detect them.

Triumph of Metaphorical Totalization

All this family of intertwined metaphors and motifs—the web, the current, the minutely subdivided entity—make up a single comprehensive model of Middlemarch society as being a complex moving medium, tightly interwoven into a single fabric, always in process, endlessly subdividable down to invisible minutiae. This medium can be seen and studied objectively, as if there could be an ideal observer who does not change what he observes and who sees the moving web as it were from all perspectives at once, from close up and from far away, with both gross and fine lenses, in a continual systole and diastole of inquiry. The storyteller in *Middlemarch* is in short that ideal observer of Victorian fiction, the "omniscient" or, as Nicholas Royle would prefer, "telepathic" narrator. That narrator's aim is to do full representative justice to the complexity of the human condition in its social medium. There are many admirable passages in *Middlemarch* giving examples of what the narrator sees, each a new application of the model I have been describing. None is perhaps so comprehensive an exploitation of the totalizing implications of this family of metaphors as an eloquent passage in chapter 11, already cited in part, describing "old provincial society." The passage, in its admirable exploitation of these objectivizing metaphors, primarily in this case that of flowing water, can speak for itself. It is a wonderfully powerful and compact formulation. The passage presents a model of society as an extremely complex physical entity in which each element is limitlessly subdividable into minutiae of minutiae. Each element is, moreover, constantly in movement, both in itself and in its relations to every other element in the closed system. That system, it is implied, can be seen and studied from the outside, by a scientific observer who can move closer to and further away, as well as around it, to see it from all perspectives:

> Old provincial society had its share of this subtle movement: had not only its striking downfalls, its brilliant young professional dandies who ended by living up an entry with a drab and six children for their establishment, but also those less marked vicissitudes which are constantly shifting the boundaries of social intercourse, and begetting new consciousness of interdependence. Some slipped a little downward, some got higher footing: people denied aspirates, gained wealth, and fastidious gentlemen stood for boroughs; some were caught in political currents, some in ecclesiastical, and perhaps found themselves surprisingly grouped in consequence; while a few personages or families that stood with rocky firmness amid all this fluctuation, were slowly presenting new aspects in spite of solidity, and altering with the double change of self and beholder. (11: 104–5)

The Optical Metaphor

> Therefore speak I to them in parables: because they seeing see not; and hearing they hear not, neither do they understand. (Matthew 13: 13)

> . . . he does not have eyes for seeing the unique; seeing similarities and making things alike (*die Aehnlichseherei und Gleichmacherei*) is the sign of weak eyes. (Friedrich Nietzsche)[25]

"Double change of self and beholder": I have said that my first family of metaphors in *Middlemarch* does not raise problems of perspective. It presupposes the possibility of an ideal observer such as that assumed in much nineteenth-century science, in the days before relativity and quantum mechanics. What I said is one aspect of Eliot's discourse, but an optical or perspectivist metaphor for epistemology has already introduced itself surreptitiously into many of my examples. The narrator must "cast all the light [he] can command" on his particular web in order to see clearly how it is woven. Study of the web requires constant changes of the lens in the systole and diastole of inquiry. Any conceivable observer in Middlemarch will be herself changing along with all the other changes and so will change what she sees.

A pervasive figure for the human situation in *Middlemarch* is that of the seer who must try to identify clearly what is present before him or her. This metaphor contaminates the apparently objectivist implications of the metaphor of the flowing web. As more and more examples of it accumulate, it struggles with an imperialistic will to power (if metaphors can by a prosopopoeia be said to "struggle for power") to replace that objectivism with a fully developed perspectivism. The clairvoyance of the narrator, according to this alternative model for the human condition, can be obtained only because he, she, or it is able to share the points of view of all the characters, thereby transcending the limited vision of any single person. "In watching effects," as the narrator says, "if only of an electric battery, it is often necessary to change our place and examine a particular mixture or group at some distance from the point where the movement we are interested in was set up" (40: 443). The narrator can move in imagination from one vantage point to another, or from close up to far away. He can, in Eliot's Miltonic allusion in the next chapter, be like the angel Uriel "watching the progress of planetary history from the Sun" (41: 458). At the same time he can share in that microscopic vision of invisible process, perceptible only to inward imaginative vision. This is splendidly described in a passage about Lydgate's method as a scientist. This passage also covertly describes the claims of George Eliot's own fictional imagination. Lydgate, the narrator says, is endowed "with the imagination that reveals subtle actions inaccessible by any sort of lens, but tracked in that outer darkness through long pathways of necessary sequence by the inward light which is the last refinement of Energy, capable of bathing even the ethereal atoms in its ideally illuminated space . . . [H]e was enamoured of that arduous invention which is the very eye of research, provisionally framing its object and correcting it to more and more exactness of relation; he wanted to pierce the obscurity of those minute processes which prepare human misery and joy . . ." (16: 183, 184). The processes in question exist objectively, but they cannot be seen as such, only reinvented in a subjective model that turns the world inside out in a spectacular act of invention. This mirroring invention makes the outward invisible darkness inwardly visible, for example as pathways of atoms bathed in light, though no one has ever seen an atom, an electron, a proton, much less a neutron, with the naked eye. Imaginative invention, aided by clever machines, makes them visible, that is, in a transposed, constructed model, like those models made by George Eliot's metaphors.

The metaphor of the complex moving web, the "embroiled medium," is, one can see, further complicated, or even contradicted, by this metaphor of inward vision. Each of those nodes in the social web that is a separate human being is endowed with a power to see the whole. This power is defined throughout the novel as essentially distorting. Each man or woman has a "centre of self, whence the lights and shadows must always fall with a certain difference" (21: 235). The "radiance" of Dorothea's "transfigured girlhood," as the narrator says, "fell on the first object that came within its level" (5: 48). Her mistakes, as her sister Celia tells her, are errors in seeing, of which Dorothea's literal myopia is a metonymy. "I thought it right to tell you," says Celia apropos of the fact that Sir James intends to propose to Dorothea, "because you went on as you always do, never looking just where you are, and treading in the wrong place. You always see what nobody else sees; it is impossible to satisfy you; yet you never see what is quite plain" (4: 39–40). Mr. Casaubon too, like all the other characters, is "the centre of his own world" (10: 92). From that central point of view he is "liable to think that others were providentially made for him, and especially to consider them in the light of their fitness for the author of a Key to all Mythologies" (ibid.). Of all the inhabitants of Middlemarch it can be said that each makes of what he or she sees something determined by her or his idiosyncratic perspective, for "Probabilities are as various as the faces to be seen at will in fretwork or paper-hangings; every form is there, from Jupiter to Judy, if you only look with creative inclination" (32: 337). Seeing is irreducibly figurative, tropological. It sees, "at will," faces in wallpaper or fretwork.

Creative Seeing as the Will to Power: The Parable of the Pier-Glass

Seeing is for George Eliot not a neutral, objective, automatic, dispassionate, or passive act. It is the creative projection of light from an egotistic center motivated by desire and need. This projected radiance orders the field of vision according to the presuppositions of the seer. The act of seeing is the spontaneous affirmation of a will to power over what is seen. This affirmation of order is based on the instinctive desire to believe that the world is providentially structured in a neat pattern of which one is oneself the center, for, as a passage already cited says, "we are all of us born in moral stupidity, taking the world as an udder to feed our supreme selves" (21: 235). Another striking metaphor there! This interpretation of the act of seeing is most fully presented in the admirable and frequently discussed parable of the pier-glass at the beginning of chapter 27:

> An eminent philosopher among my friends, who can dignify even your ugly furniture by lifting it into the serene light of science, has shown me this pregnant little fact. Your pier-glass or extensive surface of polished steel made to be rubbed by a housemaid, will be minutely and multitudinously scratched in all directions; but place now against it a lighted candle as a centre of illumination, and lo! the scratches will seem to arrange themselves in a fine series of concentric circles round that little sun. It is demonstrable that the scratches are going everywhere impartially, and it is only your candle which produces the flattering illusion of a concentric arrangement, its light falling with an exclusive optical selection. These things are a parable. The scratches are events, and the candle is the egoism of any person now absent—of Miss Vincy, for example. Rosamond had a Providence of her own who had kindly made her more charming than other girls, and who seemed to have arranged Fred's illness and Mr Wrench's mistake in order to bring her and Lydgate within effective proximity. (27: 294)[26]

This passage is more complicated than perhaps it at first appears. It begins with an example of what it describes. This example implicitly takes note of the fact that George Eliot's own "parabolic" method in this text, as in many other passages in *Middlemarch*, is a seeing of one thing in the "light" of another. The word "parable," like the word "allegory," the word "metaphor," or indeed all terms for figures of speech, is of course itself based on a figure. "Parable" means, etymologically, "thrown beside," from the Greek *para*, beside, and *ballein*, to throw. A parable is set or thrown at some distance from the meaning which controls it and to which it obliquely or parabolically refers, as, in its definition, a parabolic curve is controlled, across a space, by its parallelism to a line on the cone of which it is a section. The line and the cone may have only a virtual or imaginary existence, as in the case of a comet with a parabolic course. The parabola creates that line in the empty air, just as the parables of Jesus remedy a defect of vision, give sight to the blind, and make the invisible visible. In George Eliot's parable of the pier-glass the "eminent philosopher" transfigures "ugly furniture," a pier-glass, by "lifting it into the serene light of science." He makes an obscure scientific principle visible. In the same way, the candle makes the random scratches on the pier-glass appear to be concentric circles, thereby revealing the location of the candle flame. Similarly, Rosamond interprets what happens around her as being governed by her private Providence, thereby revealing her narcissistic viewpoint, just as George Eliot's narrator sees provincial society as like a woven web, or the ego of an individual person in the light of a comparison to a candle. The same projective, subjective, egotistic act, seeing one thing as thrown, parabolically, beside another, is involved in all four cases.

At this point the reader may remember that the narrator, in a passage I took earlier as a "key"[27] expression of George Eliot's use of a model of objective scientific observation, says "all the light I can command must be concentrated on this particular web." (Note that personifying "I." The narrator of *Middlemarch* can only with difficulty be thought of as a purely neutral or neuter narrative voice.) With a slight change of formulation "all the light I can command" could be seen as implying that the subjective source of light not only illuminates what is seen but also, as in the case of the candle held to the pier-glass, determines the structure of what is seen. Middlemarch society perhaps appears to be a web only because a certain kind of subjective light is concentrated on it. The passage taken in isolation does not say this, but its near congruence with the passage about the pier-glass, a slightly asymmetrical analogy based on the fact that the same metaphorical elements are present in each, allows the contradictory meaning to seep into the passage about the web when the two texts are set side by side. Each is seen as a modulation of the other. The same key would not open both, though a "master key" might. The meaning is not in either separately, but in the slightly dissonant resonances created in the space between them.

In spite of the disquieting possibilities generated by resonances between two similar but not quite congruent passages, the narrator in various ways throughout *Middlemarch* is clearly claiming to be able to transcend the limitations of the self-centered ego by seeing things impersonally, objectively, scientifically: "It is demonstrable that the scratches are going everywhere impartially." This objective vision, such is the logic of George Eliot's parable, shows that what is "really there" has no order whatsoever, but is merely random scratches without pattern or meaning. The pier-glass is "minutely and multitudinously scratched in all directions." The idea that reality is chaotic, without intrinsic order or form, and the corollary that any order it may appear to have is projected illicitly by some patterning ego, would seem to be contradicted by the series of apparently valid totalizing metaphors I have explored—web, flowing water, and so on—as well as by the generalizing, moralizing, rationalizing, order-finding, affirmative activity of the narrator throughout the book. It would seem hardly plausible, at this point at least, to say that reality for George Eliot is a chaotic disorder. It might seem more likely that this is an irrelevant implication of the parable. It is an implication that has by accident, as it were, slipped in along with implications that are "intended." A final decision about this must, however, be postponed.

Among the "intended" implications may be one arising from the fact that a pier-glass is a kind of mirror, while the examples of the "flattering illusion" George Eliot would have encountered in Herbert Spencer or in Ruskin involved different reflective surfaces. Ruskin, for example, speaks of the path of reflected moonlight seen across the surface of a lake by a spectator on the shore.[28] The pier-glass would, after all, reflect what was brought near it, as well as produce its own interfering illusion of concentric circles. The candle is a displacement or parable for Rosamond's ego or that of any man or woman. Rosamond would of course see her own image in the mirror, Narcissus-like. This implication of the parable links it with all those other passages, not only in *Middlemarch*, but also in *Adam Bede* or in *Daniel Deronda*, where egotism is symbolized by the admiration of one's image in a mirror, or where the work of representation is expressed in the traditional image of holding a mirror up to nature.

A passage in chapter 10, for example, apropos of the low opinion Mr. Casaubon's neighbors have of him, says that even "the greatest man of his age" could not escape "unfavourable reflections of himself in various small mirrors" (10: 92). This apparently uses the figure of the mirror in a way contradicting the parable of the pier-glass. The mirror is now the ego rather than the external world. Nevertheless, what is always in question when the mirror appears is narcissistic self-reflection. This may be thought of as our seeing our own reflection in the mirroring world outside because we have projected it there. Or it may be thought of as our distortion of the world outside in our reflecting ego, so that it takes on the configuration of our private vision of things. Any two subjectivities, according to this model, will face one another like two confronting mirrors. If Casaubon was "the centre of his own world," and had "an equivalent [to Dorothea's] centre of self, whence the lights and shadows must always fall with a certain difference" (10: 92; 22: 235), the people in whom he seeks the reflection of his own sense of himself are not innocent mirrors. They are themselves instruments of distortion: "even Milton, looking for his portrait in a spoon, must submit to have the facial angle of a bumpkin" (10: 92). The image of the mirror would imply that the projection of one's selfish needs or desires on reality orders that random set of events into a pattern. This pattern is a portrait of the ego itself. It is an objective embodiment of the ego's subjective configurations. The terrible isolation of each person, for George Eliot, lies in the way each goes through the world encountering only himself or herself. She or he can see only her or his own image reflected back by the world because she or he has put it there in the first place, in the illusory (mis)interpretation of the world the ego spontaneously makes.

The narrator of *Middlemarch*, it would seem, can escape from this fate only by using perspective to transcend perspective, by moving from the microscopic close-up to the panoramic distant view, and by shifting constantly from the point of view of one character to the point of view of another. Such shifts will give a full multi-dimensional picture of what is "really there," as when the narrator, after a prolonged immersion within the subjective experience of Dorothea, asks: "—but why always Dorothea? Was her point of view the only possible one with regard to this marriage? I protest against all our interest, all our effort at under-standing being given to the young skins that look blooming in spite of trouble . . . In spite of the blinking eyes and white moles objectionable to Celia, and the want of muscular curve which was morally painful to Sir James, Mr Casaubon had an intense consciousness within him, and was spiritually a-hungered like the rest of us" (29: 309–10).

Human Beings as False Interpreters

> [S]ouls live on in perpetual echoes, and to all fine expression there goes some-where an originating activity, if it be only that of an interpreter. (16: 179)

The word "interpretation," which I used above and have just cited from Eliot in a different context, will serve as a clue indicating the presence within the optical metaphors of an element so far not identified as such. This feature contaminates and ultimately subverts the optical model in the same way that the optical model contaminates and makes more problematic the images of the web or of the current. All the optical pas-sages contain elements showing that for George Eliot seeing is never just optical. Seeing is never simply a matter of identifying correctly what is seen, seeing that windmills are windmills and not giants, a wash-pan a wash-pan and not the helmet of Mambrino, to use the example from *Don Quixote* cited once already from the epigraph for chapter 2 of *Middlemarch*. Seeing is always interpretation. What is seen is always taken as a sign standing for something else, as an emblem, as a hiero-glyph or parable.

Superimposed on the models for the human situation of the objective scientist and the subjective perspectivist, interlaced with them, overlapping them in each of their expressions, is a model for the situations of the characters and of the narrator which says all human beings in all situations are like readers of a text. Moreover, if for George Eliot all seeing is falsified by the limitations of point of view, it is an even more inevitable law, for her, that we make things what they are for us by naming them in one way or another. This naming is the incorporation of empirical data into a conventional system of signs. A corollary of this law is the fact that all interpretation of signs is false interpretation. The original naming was an act of interpretation that falsified. The reading of things made into signs is necessarily a further falsification, an interpretation of an interpretation. An important sequence of passages running like Ariadne's thread through the labyrinthine verbal complexity of *Middlemarch* develops a subtle theory of signs and of interpretation. Along with this goes recognition of the irreducibly figurative nature of all language.

Chapter 3

Chapter Seventeen of *Adam Bede*: Truth-Telling Narration

Before retracing this thread, it is needful to return to what George Eliot says about the language of *Adam Bede* in chapter 17 of that novel. The narrative voice in that chapter, I note in passing, seems more to be the author speaking, Marian Evans or Marian Lewes wearing the pseudonymous mask of George Eliot, than an imaginary narrator created by Marian Evans out of words. Or one might say the two George Eliots are indistinguishably conflated: "So I am content to tell my simple story . . ." (17: 160). Who is this "I"? It seems, illogically or undecidably, to be both Eliots at once. *Adam Bede*, the reader will remember, was published in 1859, thirteen years before *Middlemarch*. I have already touched briefly on the chapter in question in the section on *Adam Bede* in this book, but need to read it more carefully now as a prelude to continuing my reading of *Middlemarch*. "The irreducibly figurative nature of all language"? Surely my formulation is a striking reversal, so it seems, of what is said about the language of realism in chapter 17 of *Adam Bede*. Though the notion of a referential language of truth-telling narration is challenged by the story told in *Adam Bede*, as I have shown, the itinerary of my interpretation of *Adam Bede* depends, at a certain moment, on taking George Eliot's theory of narrative language in chapter 17 as an unequivocal base on which the rest of the reading of the novel could rest. "The story," I said, "is . . . validated by its truth of correspondence to historical, social, and human reality. This reality is assumed to exist outside language." As preparation for following through the theory of interpretation in *Middlemarch* it is "needful," to use one of George Eliot's own words, to return to chapter 17 of the earlier novel in order to interrogate it closely. It is necessary to question it, as if, to modify another of George Eliot's own expressions in that chapter, it were in the witness box responding under oath to interrogation.

The theory of realism proposed in chapter 17 of *Adam Bede* depends on the notion that there can be a literal, non-figurative, truth-telling language of narration. "So I am content," says the narrator, "to tell my simple story, without trying to make things seem better than they were; dreading nothing, indeed, but falsity, which, in spite of one's best efforts, there is reason to dread. Falsehood is easy, truth so difficult . . . Examine your words well, and you will find that even when you have no motive to be false, it is a very hard thing to say the exact truth, even about your own immediate feelings—much harder than to say something fine about them which is *not* the exact truth" (17: 160–1). What, exactly, is this language, the words with which the novelist can say the exact truth about inner feeling or outer facts, without a fraction more or less, like a board cut by Adam Bede to perfect size and fit?

The theory of the *function* of such language in chapter 17 is clear. It is a version of the definition of mimesis that goes back to Aristotle. This theory is one of the constants of Occidental metaphysics. The theory is an economic one, in the broadest sense of that term. In George Eliot's case it is an economic theory heavily tinged with the language of Protestant ethics. In Aristotle's *Poetics* the function of mimesis is knowledge. Imitation is natural to man, and it is natural for him to take pleasure in it. He takes pleasure in it because he learns from it. He learns from it the nature of the things or persons imitated, which without that detour through mimesis would not be visible and knowable.

In chapter 17 of *Adam Bede* the argument is not so much that I should know my neighbor as that I should love him or her. This can be facilitated by a faithful copy:

> These fellow-mortals, every one, must be accepted as they are: you can neither straighten their noses, nor brighten their wit, nor rectify their dispositions; and it is these people—amongst whom your life is passed—that it is *needful* you should tolerate, pity and love: it is these more or less ugly, stupid, inconsistent people, whose movements of goodness you should be able to admire—(17: 160, my italics)

> It is more *needful* that I should have a fibre of sympathy connecting me with that vulgar citizen who weighs out my sugar in a vilely-assorted cravat and waistcoat, than with the handsomest rascal in red scarf and green feathers;—more *needful* that my heart should swell with loving admiration at some trait of gentle goodness in the faulty people who sit at the same hearth with me . . . (17: 162–3, my italics)

The reader will note how condescending Eliot is here to her ordinary fellow citizens. They are all more or less ugly, stupid, vulgar, and distressingly inconsistent, yet it is such people we must love and admire, since that is the way most people are. The defense of art here, like Aristotle's, depends on the notion that, paradoxically, things and people, in this case one's neighbors, cannot be loved and admired unless they make a detour through the mirroring of art in order to become visible and hence lovable. Robert Browning's Fra Lippo Lippi makes a parallel argument in his defense of a representational art:

> God's works—paint any one, and count it crime
> To let a truth slip. Don't object, "His works
> Are here already; nature is complete:
> Suppose you reproduce her—(which you can't)
> There's no advantage! you must beat her, then."
> For, don't you mark? we're made so that we love
> First when we see them painted, things we have passed
> Perhaps a hundred times nor cared to see;
> And so they are better, painted—better to us,
> Which is the same thing. Art was given for that;
> God uses us to help each other so,
> Lending our minds out.[1]

In George Eliot's case, in consonance with what Browning's Lippi asserts, the argument is that it is "needful," we have an ethical and even quasi-financial "obligation," not only to reflect things accurately in the mirror of our minds but to return that reflection with "interest," so to speak, that is, in a represented or mimetic form. The reflection must be turned into a genre painting or into a realistic novel. This must be done in such a way that what is reflected will be seen, understood, and loved. The obligation is economic, legal, and ethical, all at once. George Eliot's narrator, at the end of the chapter, says: "I herewith discharge my conscience" (17: 166). This is the fulfillment of a categorical moral imperative, the one thing needful. At the same time it is the fulfillment of a contract, as when one has borrowed money from the bank and must pay it back with interest, "discharge" the debt. It is also, finally, the fulfillment of a legal obligation, as when one must tell the truth under oath in the witness box.

An implicit relation to a fourth dimension, that of religious obligation, guarantees all three of these superimposed circuits of detour and return. I must, in conscience, love God first and then love my neighbor as myself, as Jesus said (Matt. 22: 37–40). The truth-telling of the witness is based on an oath sworn "before God," or "in God's name." The painter or novelist, in his return with interest of what his mind has reflected, imitates God in that productivity whereby all the creation emanated from God only to be returned to him with a plus value of that chorus of praise all nature raises in speaking back the name of God to God. This is stated in concentrated form in the simultaneously indicative, imperative, and performative last line of Gerard Manley Hopkins's "Pied Beauty": "He fathers-forth whose beauty is past change: / Praise him."[2] The syntax of this in the full grammar of the poem makes it mean at once: "All created things do praise him"; "Let all things praise him"; and "I here, in the poem, perform the speech act of praising him."

All three forms of the human circuit of detour and return, the economic, the ethical, and the legal, each grounded implicitly in the divine circuit of creation, and each functioning as a figure for the act of realistic representation, come together in George Eliot's initial profession of obligation:

> But it happens, on the contrary, that my strongest effort is to avoid any such arbitrary picture, and to give a faithful account of men and things as they have mirrored themselves in my mind. The mirror is doubtless defective; the outlines will sometimes be disturbed, the reflection faint or confused; but I feel as much bound to tell you as precisely as I can what that reflection is, as if I were in the witness-box narrating my experience on oath. (17: 159)

The reflection here is double. This is true of the Victorian theory of realism generally. A system of intertwined figures and concepts about art or literature tends to govern in one way or another all Victorian discourse about realist representation. Examples would include the abundant writings of Ruskin or, at the other end of a scale of complexity and sophistication, the multitude of fiction reviews in Victorian periodicals. All versions of this theory tend to be simultaneously subjective and objective in their notions about truth. They move uneasily back and forth between one and the other. The value of a novel, for George Eliot, as for her contemporaries generally, lies in its truth of correspondence to things as they are, objectively. On the other hand, what the words of the novel represent is not objective things as they are but those things as they have already been reflected, subjectivized, in the mirroring mind of the novelist. Any mirroring subjectivity, as George Eliot here explicitly affirms and as her contemporaries tended to agree, always distorts. Subjectivity is like a mirror in a funhouse, concave, convex, or wavy, so that, as she says in a passage in *Middlemarch* already cited in part: "I am not sure that the greatest man of his age, if ever that solitary superlative existed, could escape these unfavourable reflections of himself in various small mirrors; and even Milton, looking for his portrait in a spoon, must submit to have the facial angle of a bumpkin" (10: 92). Even so, the novelist must represent as accurately as possible the reflection he finds in the defective mirror of his or her mind. The truth of correspondence in realism is not to objective things, or only indirectly to objective things.

It is rather to things as they have already made a detour into necessarily distorted subjective reflections. George Eliot's obligation, as he or she says, is "to give a faithful account of men and things as they have mirrored themselves in my mind."

From things to mental images to verbal account—the words on the page in a realistic novel are the product of a double translation or transference. Their function, moreover, is performative, not merely descriptive. The obligation fulfilled in "the faithful representing of commonplace things" (17: 162) is to generate the right feelings in the reader or beholder of such representations. These feelings bring the people who feel them to do the right thing, for, as Adam Bede says, "It isn't notions sets people doing the right thing—it's feelings" (17: 163). The double mirroring of a realistic art makes something happen. It makes the right things happen by making people do the right thing. Commonplace things as they are must be returned, after their double detour, first into the mirroring mind, then into the words that give a faithful account of what is reflected in that mind, and then by way of those words back into the extra-linguistic world. Things as they are must be reintroduced into the culture that produced the art and which that art represents. They must be returned with the plus value of a power to generate good feelings and therefore good actions. Only then is the "account" fully made and closed, the obligation fulfilled, the note discharged, the mortgage on the house of fiction paid off, the divine commands of conscience obeyed.

Down with the Art of the Unreal!

In the context of this economic-ethical-religious-affective-performative theory of realism George Eliot mounts his or her attack on idealizing art, the art of irrealism. This attack runs as a crossways woof through all the fabric of chapter 17 of *Adam Bede*, counterpointing and supporting the positive argument. At first sight the attack on ideal beauty and goodness seems entirely reasonable. People are not like that, at least not those near to me, and therefore there can be no use, no obligation, nothing "needful," in representing people as they are not. Much more is at stake here, however, than might at first appear.

What George Eliot explicitly rejects in the counter-woven argument of the chapter is the theological underpinning that implicitly supports the economic theory of realism I have traced out. Though it is not a question here of direct influence, the best shorthand description of what Eliot rejects would be to give it the proper name "Immanuel Kant." It was by no means necessary to know Kant's works in order to be a Kantian or an anti-Kantian in the nineteenth century, nor is it so in our own day. Kant in *The Critique of Judgment* codified a set of notions about art that is one of the constants of the Western tradition. The genius, according to Kant, imitates nature not by copying it, but by duplicating its manner of production. As God spoke nature into existence by means of the divine word and by means of his Son, the Word, so the genius, by virtue of a power given him by nature, speaks into existence an imaginary heterocosm that adds something hitherto unheard-of to nature. It adds the plus value of a new beauty that is beyond price. This new beauty is beyond measure by any slavish standards of mirroring correspondence to things as they are. The novel beauty the genius creates is grounded in the analogy between his *logos* and the divine *logos*. This analogy is based in nature or goes by way of nature, though only because nature is the word of God, a voice made into substantial things. Analogy, as the word suggests, is always a similarity in voices or in words.[3]

This Kantism George Eliot rejects. He rejects it by removing its ground in the analogy between God's way of producing nature and the way the genius produces his works. Without this analogy the works of genius are simply unreal. They are a detour into the imaginary from which there is no return to the real world of ugly, stupid, inconsistent neighbors. Therefore such works of art are of no use. They fulfill no obligation. They are the reverse of "needful."

George Eliot's way of expressing this is in several ways odd. It is odd for one thing in its effacement of the problem of language by a shift from language to another art, painting. This sideways displacement occurs regularly throughout chapter 17, for example in the famous appeal to Dutch genre painting as a model for truth-telling in literature. One effect of this is to make the reader forget the problem of the medium in literary realism. The implication is that the language of realism is a literal, non-figurative language functioning like a photograph or like a scientific drawing. It goes by way of a one-to-one correspondence between the word and the thing to which it refers. This would mean, by the way, that nouns and adjectives, as in the phrase, "yellow wallpaper," are paradigmatic examples of words, not conjunctions, adverbs, articles, or even verbs.

That language is the medium of realism and that there are specific problems associated with this medium are issues intermittently confronted in chapter 17. An example of one such issue that George Eliot at least implicitly recognizes is the temporality of narration. "An account of men and things as they have mirrored themselves in my mind" is not a static spatial picture. It is a running narrative going from word to word, according to another meaning of "account" alongside the economic and ethical ones. An "account" is a telling over, an enumeration one by one of a series of items which are then added up to make a sum. Another place where linguistic problems are recognized occurs in a passage cited above. In this passage George Eliot reminds the reader of the difficulty of finding the right word even for what is closest at hand and most intimate, one's own emotions; "it is a very hard thing to say the exact truth, even about your own immediate feelings." The shift from language to painting or drawing invites the reader to forget all those problems that are specific to language. It invites her to think of narration in language as like making an exact atemporal drawing of something physically there before the artist's eyes, like a lion or a jug: "The pencil is conscious of a delightful facility in drawing a griffin—the longer the claws, and the larger the wings, the better; but that marvelous facility which we mistook for genius is apt to forsake us when we want to draw a real unexaggerated lion" (17: 160).

"The pencil is conscious"—it is an odd phrase. It seems as though the phallic-shaped instrument of writing must have its own impulse toward falsehood. This impulse toward falsehood is given an implicit male gender, the putative gender of the narrator himself, in this cross-dressing masquerade, whereas the faithful representing of commonplace things is perhaps implicitly female. This may seem an implausibly large issue to pin on an innocent metonymy assigning consciousness to the means of writing rather than to the writer, but readers of *Middlemarch* or of George Eliot's work generally will know that a contrast between male and female imaginations is a major feature of her work. Her work turns on a dismantling of the "phallogocentric" male system of metaphysics and its replacement by what one might call Ariadne's performative "yes" to life. This performative is dramatized in Dorothea's marriage to Will Ladislaw at the end of *Middlemarch*. I shall later show this in detail.

The facility of the conscious pencil that produces griffins is mistaken by the mind of the one holding the pencil for genius. It is taken in error as a God-given gift for generating works of art not copied from nature but nevertheless valid. The conscious pencil, however, produces nothing but nullities, empty fictions. This facility in falsehood is defined sardonically elsewhere in the chapter as "that lofty order of minds who pant after the ideal" (17: 166). The conscious pencil of the false genius produces by its lofty elevation those embodiments of religious, mythological, and heroic ideas that are so resolutely rejected throughout the chapter. They are rejected as "falsehoods" or at best as validated only in a Feuerbachian way as projections of purely human values. All those paintings of the

Madonna, for example, are for George Eliot, as for Ludwig Feuerbach, to be venerated not because Mary was the Mother of God but because a Madonna in art embodies the ideal of human motherhood. It is as if George Eliot were prepared to hurry with averted face through all the rooms in the Louvre marked "Renaissance Painting, Italy" in order to get to the room of Dutch genre paintings with all the relief of someone escaping the temptations of a false ideal in order to confront once more the real:

> I turn, without shrinking, from cloud-borne angels, from prophets, sibyls, and heroic warriors, to an old woman bending over her flower-pot, or eating her solitary dinner . . . (17: 161)

> Paint us an angel, if you can, with a floating violet robe, and a face paled by the celestial light; paint us yet oftener a Madonna, turning her mild face upward and opening her arms to welcome the divine glory; but do not impose on us any aesthetic rules which shall banish from the region of Art those old women scraping carrots with their work-worn hands, those heavy clowns taking holiday in a dingy pot-house, those rounded backs and stupid weather-beaten faces that have bent over the spade and done the rough work of the world . . . (17: 162)

> There are few prophets in the world; few sublimely beautiful women; few heroes. I can't afford to give all my love and reverence to such rarities: I want a great deal of those feelings for my everyday fellowmen, especially for the few in the foreground of the great multitude, whose faces I know, whose hands I touch, for whom I have to make way with kindly courtesy. (17: 162)

Rejecting an aesthetic of the sublime, the beautiful, the ideal, the rare, the distant, George Eliot affirms with great persuasive power a counter-aesthetic of the ugly, the stupid, the real, the frequent, the statistically likely, the near. It is the griffin replaced by the lion, or better, by the house cat (though I by no means find my three cats stupid or ugly). Once again the economic metaphor is essential. I have only so much love and reverence banked in my account of emotional savings, and I "can't afford" to squander it on ideal rarities, if indeed they exist at all. All my emotion is needed for those who are near at hand, those "more or less ugly, stupid, inconsistent people," my neighbors. Once more Eliot's question-begging and condescending assumption about "my everyday fellowmen" is crucial. As I have already said, I do not find my lobster-fishing and clam-digging neighbors here in Deer Isle, Maine, ugly, stupid, or inconsistent. George Eliot, however, needs to assert this dubious assumption in order to make the argument about realistic representation plausible, as I shall show.

The Language of Realism

What I have said so far about chapter 17 seems clear enough. It is consistent in its rejection not so much of the Kantian sublime as of a Kantism deprived of the analogy between the artist's creative voice with its power of production, on the one hand, and the divine *logos*, or "Word," with its power to make all by fiat, on the other.

What exactly is the mode of language by which the novelist produces in literature something analogous to the adherence to the real of Dutch genre paintings? It would seem that the answer to this question would be easy to give. Surely the realistic novelist works primarily with referential, non-figurative language, language validated by its truth of correspondence to things as they are. This is the sort of language that calls a spade a spade or an old woman scraping carrots an old woman scraping carrots.

In my reading of *Adam Bede* in the first section of this book I have argued that the theory of language elsewhere in this novel is considerably more problematic than the notion of referential literalism apparently espoused in chapter 17. This other theory, developed in relation to the characters, plays ironically, as I have shown, against the notion of referential language affirmed for the narrator's truth-telling in chapter 17. The theory of language in chapter 17 itself, however, is not so simple either. The question of realism's language is the missing link in the chain of George Eliot's argument. This link can be reconstructed from the implications of the figures and negations George Eliot uses to tell the reader what that language is like and what it is not like. This reading process might be compared, if I may use a figure of my own, to the archeologist's reconstruction of the missing limb of an ancient statue or to the paleontologist's making of a complete skeleton from a few fossil bones. In this case too a rather unexpected animal emerges when the pieces are put together. It is more a griffin than a lion or a house cat.

The question, the reader will remember, is what language will not only render a true account of things and men as they have mirrored themselves in the narrator's mind, but also will render that account in such a way as to add the interest of the one thing needful. The one thing needful is the creation of a fiber of sympathy tying the reader in love and reverence to her ugly, stupid, inconsistent neighbors. The narrator tells the reader that such language will be like genre paintings and unlike religious, mythological, or historical painting. Nothing is said about how one imitates in words the methods of those "Dutch paintings, which lofty-minded people despise" (17: 161). Exactly what linguistic procedures can the reader infer are involved? The reader is told, at least implicitly, first by the narrator and then by Adam Bede himself in a long speech cited verbatim by the narrator from a conversation he had with Adam "in his old age" (17: 163), that the proper language of storytelling will be like the sermons of Mr. Irwine and unlike the sermons of Mr. Ryde. This is an odd moment in the novel. The narrator elsewhere in the text has been anonymous, invisible, impersonal, omniscient, telepathic, and omnipresent, able to move freely and instantaneously in time and space, able to see without being seen, able to enter into the minds and hearts of the characters at will. Suddenly the narrator narrows down to focus on a single "real" person and becomes dependent on a speech by that person for his or her information. The informant, moreover, is most likely Mary Anne Evans's father, said to be the model for Adam Bede. It is as if a cut-out photographed figure were inserted by collage into a Dutch painting.

About this more must be said later. Now the question is the following: if the implicit comparison with two kinds of preaching gives a model for storytelling that is linguistic rather than graphic, what is the difference between Irwine's sermons and Ryde's? Again the reader is told little except negatively. Irwine, says Adam, "was [not] much of a preacher." "[H]e preached short moral sermons, and that was all" (17: 164, 165). Ryde, on the other hand, preached sermons full of "notions" and "doctrines," but these forms of language were ineffective in making his parishioners do the right thing and love their neighbors. This opposition is the context of a passage already quoted that distinguishes notions from feelings:

> "But," said Adam, "I've seen pretty clear ever since I was a young un, as religion's something else besides notions. It isn't notions sets people doing the right thing—it's feelings ... Mr Ryde was a deal thought on at a distance, I believe, and he wrote books; but as for math'matics and the natur o' things, he was as ignorant as a woman. [Note, by the way, the irony of the last phrase, when one thinks of it as written not by "George Eliot" but by Mary Anne Evans, daughter of Robert Evans, the "original" of Adam.] He was very knowing about doctrines, and used to call 'em the bulwarks of the Reformation; but I've always mistrusted that sort o' learning as leaves folks foolish and unreasonable about business. (17: 163, 164)

This seems to offer a clue to the proper language of storytelling in a double displacement, first to the question of the effective language of preaching and then from that to an apparent analogy between language causing "feelings" or "resolutions" and the language of mathematics, business, and "the natur o' things." This shift goes by way of a bifurcation between notions and doctrines, on the one hand, and some kind of language that will bring about "resolutions," on the other. A measuring, hard-headed, literally naming, referential language, dramatized in the novel in Adam's profession of carpentry, seems to give the reader a model for the proper language of narration. But no, somewhat surprisingly, both the language of mathematics and the language of literal naming are dismissed as of no account, as ineffective, as unable to generate feelings and the good actions that follow from them:

> It's the same with the notions in religion as it is with math'matics,—a man may be able to work problems straight off in's head as he sits by the fire and smokes his pipe; but if he has to make a machine or a building, he must have a will and a resolution, and love something else better than his own ease. (17: 163)

> I look at it as if the doctrines was like finding names for your feelings, so as you can talk of 'em when you've never known 'em, just as a man may talk o' tools when he knows their names, though he's never so much as seen 'em, still less handled 'em. (17: 165)

If it is not the language of mathematics and if it is not the language of literal naming, then what is it? It must be some form of language that corresponds not to doctrines in religion, nor to the abstract calculations of mathematics, nor to the naming of tools, but to doing something with those tools, to the performance of an action. Realistic fiction must make something happen in the pragmatic world of things and people. It must make the correct things happen. The search for the proper language of storytelling has eliminated one by one all the obvious candidates. The search has narrowed itself down into a corner where only one answer is possible. Realistic narration must depend, as this chapter conspicuously does, on figurative language. Even more narrowly, it can be said to depend on a special form of figurative language: catachresis, the use of terms borrowed from a visible, namable realm to name what has no literal language of its own. Only such language can perform into existence, by a speech act, feelings, a will, a resolution. The operation of such catachreses is itself necessarily described in figure in the chapter, as like this or as like that, since it cannot be literally described in itself.

Such a language will make a break in the remorseless chain of cause and effect that ordinarily operates, for George Eliot, both in the physical or social worlds and in the internal world of the self. Only such a break, a fissure dividing before and after, can effect a redirection of feeling's power in the self. This produces a consequent redirection of the power to do something good in the outer world of that self's neighbors. The renaming of things by the figure called catachresis is genuinely performative. It brings something altogether new into the world, something not explicable by its causes. Even though, like all performatives, it must use words already there in the language, it redirects those words to unheard-of meanings. It makes something happen in the "real world" that would not otherwise have happened. This happening has no "basis" other than the fictive, figurative, re-evaluation performed by the catachreses renaming one's ugly, stupid, inconsistent neighbors as lovable. George Eliot's language for this, or rather the language he borrows from Adam Bede, is borrowed from scripture, which borrows it from the natural world, in a multiple displacement, each realm of language supplementing a lack in the one of which it comes in aid. Just as the language of realism is catachresis, so it can only be spoken of as like this or like that, as like religious experience, or as like violent changes in nature, which in turn are like religious experience. Realism is catachresis, and it can be named only in catachresis:

> "I know [says Adam] there's a deal in a man's inward life as you can't measure by the square, and say, 'Do this and that'll follow,' and, 'do that and this'll follow.' There's things go on in the soul, and times when feelings come into you like a rushing mighty wind, as the Scripture says, and part your life in two a'most, so as you look back on yourself as if you was somebody else." (17: 164)

> "If we've got a resolution to do right, He gave it us, I reckon, first or last; but I see plain enough we shall never do it without a resolution, and that's enough for me." (17: 166)

In the context of what George Eliot says elsewhere in this chapter about the fictive status of religious ideals, angels, Madonnas, and so on, the word "He" here, naming God as the base of sudden discontinuous changes in human feelings and actions, is another catachresis, perhaps the most extravagant of all. It gives the name of the personified deity to what is actually, according to George Eliot at this point in her life and according to her master-source, Ludwig Feuerbach, only human feeling. To Adam it seems that God gives feelings that give proper resolutions. George Eliot and the careful reader see plain enough, as Adam does not, that God is, for Eliot at least, a name for human feelings. Eliot and the reader see that such performative catachreses function as that force of change parting a man's life in two almost. An example of such a catachresis is religious language identifying God as the source of the rushing mighty wind in the soul.

Even though chapter 17 is strongly committed, in its overt affirmations, to realism as exact reproduction, the covert argument is for a certain use of figurative language. Such language does not say directly what it means. The language of realistic fiction is not based solidly on any extra-linguistic entities. It transforms such entities into something other than themselves. Your ugly, stupid, neighbor is made lovable when he or she has passed through the circuit of representation in a "realistic" novel.

One example of figurative language stares the reader in the face in this chapter, so close at hand and so pervasive as to be almost invisible. In this it is like the big name written all across a map, and therefore undetectable, in Dupin's figure for the invisibility of the obvious in Edgar Allan Poe's "The Purloined Letter." In chapter 17 of *Adam Bede*, as in the novel as a whole, the example of this invisible/visible force is the voice of the fictitious narrator concocted by Marian Evans. This narrator speaks as a male "I." "He" speaks as if all these things had really happened in history just as they are told. He bases his defense of realism on the purported conversation of another fictitious character, Adam Bede, and on Adam's analysis of religious experience. This kind of experience is shown elsewhere in the novel to be a response to the "ideal" in the sense of the unreal. Religious experience is a human projection, a fiction.

The response of the reader who knows the "source" of Adam in Mary Anne Evans's own life is to become subject to an uneasy oscillation. This is Mary Anne Evans reporting accurately the speech and opinions of her father, thereby giving a faithful account of men and things as they have mirrored themselves in her mind. No, it is Marian Lewes pretending to be a male narrator reporting the speech of another invented character, "based" perhaps on her father, but transposed into the realm of the imaginary where it has performative force. The transposition of the author to the narrator, her father to Adam, corresponds, on the larger scale of the creation of character, to that smaller-scale creation of figures of speech whereby a literal word is carried over not to substitute for another literal word but to name something which has no name other than the figurative one, as strong feelings, notoriously difficult to name literally, are like a rushing mighty wind. Such nomination does not so much name something that already exists as make something happen in the "real" world, something that would not otherwise have happened.

Performative Undecidability

Like all performatives, this one is ultimately ambiguous. Its "undecidability" is characterized by the way it is impossible to know whether anything really happens as a result of its force, or whether it only happens fictively, so does not "really" happen at all. Can one hold to the distinction between a real event and a fictive one? Does something really happen when a marriage is performed, a ship christened, or does it only happen in imagination or as a social fiction? This is precisely the issue in George Eliot's Feuerbachian treatment of religious experience and religious practices. Moreover, even if it can be decided that performatives do make something happen, it can never be decided exactly what that something is and whether that something is good or bad. All performatives are unpredictable and immeasurable, as J. L. Austin, Paul de Man, and Jacques Derrida, in their different ways, knew.[4] A performative can never be successfully controlled, defined, or have a decisive line put around its effects.

The peculiar final paragraph of chapter 17 of *Adam Bede* uneasily recognizes this. In the attempt to discriminate his own good performative evaluations from the other bad ones, George Eliot inadvertently reveals the structural kinship of all three. He is like a man who confesses to a criminal act by compulsively making a point of denying that he has committed it. In this final paragraph something odd about the initial idea of a contractual debt almost comes to the surface as George Eliot, as "he" says, "discharge[s] [his] conscience." He pays this debt by confessing that he has had "quite enthusiastic movements of admiration" for "more or less commonplace and vulgar" people, people "who spoke the worst English" (17: 166). Eliot's argument has been that the realistic novelist has an obligation to return what has been given to him in social experience by making an exact copy that will pay the debt with interest. This interest is an added power to generate enthusiastic movements of admiration for the ugly and the commonplace. The word "enthusiastic" in its context rings with the irony of its etymology. It plays back and forth among the religious, aesthetic, and sentimental uses of the word. George Eliot's form of inflation, of being filled with a god (the etymological meaning of "enthusiastic"), is not any of these. It is a sideways transposition of them all, as realism is a mirror image of something that is not, strictly speaking, there. To put this in another way, realism is like the act of coinage. It is like that sort of performative that stamps an image on paper or metal and so makes it pass current, makes it worth so much as currency. I shall discuss later George Eliot's extensive use of monetary tropes in *Middlemarch*.

No way exists to use literal, conceptual, notional, or doctrinal languages for this mirroring with a difference. Only the performative catachresis of a figurative language that comes like a mighty rushing wind in upon the soul and breaks it in two almost will work. The impact of such language is like religious experience, or like falling in love, or like a force of nature, according to the quadruple equation linking art, nature, love, and religion throughout *Adam Bede*. The ground of the "like" in this analogical series running "A is like B is like C is like D" is no solid ontological *logos*. The ground is analogy or figuration itself. The base of these analogies is analogy. This means, in spite of the claim to a solid ground in "reality," that realistic fiction brings groundless novelty into the social world. That is not necessarily a bad thing. So-called realism brings, for example, my power to love my ugly, stupid neighbor. Realism inserts an infinite zero as multiplier or divisor into the circuit of the equation moving away from reality and back to it. This zero is something without ground or substance that nevertheless has power to make something happen. Its efficacy makes it dangerous, a force perhaps for good, perhaps for ill. In this it is analogous to the way the same unpredictable energy of human emotion and human dreaming, in the story proper, motivates Hetty Sorrel's badness as well as Dinah Morris's goodness.

The danger in performative figures almost surfaces, however, in the attempt, in the final paragraph of chapter 17, to discriminate among three emotive attitudes: baseless idealism, cynical nihilism, and George Eliot's realism. The attempt to discriminate reveals, in spite of itself, a similarity among the three. To try to erect barriers allowing a compartmentalization brings into the open an impossibility of deciding what difference exists among these three modes of valuing. A secret equivalence in measuring circulates among them. This might be defined by saying that any number multiplied by zero is zero, any number divided by zero is infinity. I shall return to Eliot's use of zero's strange properties when I return to *Middlemarch*.

The final paragraph is of great "interest." It seems at first a rather casual afterthought added to the main argument in defense of realism made earlier. In fact, it is of great importance as a revelation of the ground, or rather groundlessness, the zero base, of that argument. It asserts an equivalence in the low valuation given to the ugly real by "the select natures who pant after the ideal," on the one hand, and by mean, narrow, selfish natures, on the other. Both idealists and cynics join in finding "real" people of no account: "For I have observed this remarkable coincidence, that the select natures who pant after the ideal, and find nothing in pantaloons or petticoats great enough to command their reverence and love, are curiously in unison with the narrowest and pettiest" (17: 166–7). These two kinds of under-valuers are in turn opposed to George Eliot himself, who finds his neighbor of infinite account. Nevertheless, this comes to the same thing, as the paragraph covertly reveals. It makes the same sum, in the sense that both the low valuation and the high are figurative measures of what, as the chapter tells the reader over and over, are "in fact" ugly, stupid, inconsistent people. To love such people is just as baseless as to call them, as Mr. Gedge the innkeeper did, "a poor lot" (17: 167). In fact Mr. Gedge may be closer to an exact mirroring of people as Marian Evans actually sees them. Gedge's cynicism is a baseless valuing as much as is George Eliot's loving reverence for commonplace people. The difference, all-important for George Eliot, like a plus or minus sign before a zero, is that the positive evaluation is life-enhancing, however imaginary it may be. The positive evaluation creates and sustains the human community on the base of those baseless fictions that are absolutely "needful" if there is to be a human community at all: "It is more needful that I should have a fibre of sympathy connecting me with that vulgar citizen . . ."

All emotive evaluation is performative. It makes something happen that has no cause beyond the words that express it. Since my neighbor is "really" ugly, stupid, inconsistent, to view a woman as not worth loving unless she dies before you possess her (French cynical idealism, the cynicism of those who reject the real and pant after the ideal); to measure everything by the norm of a mean and narrow mind, like Mr. Gedge, and find it wanting ("a poor lot, sir, big and little, and them as comes for a go o' gin are no better than them as comes for a pint o' twopenny—a poor lot" [17: 167]); to love one's ugly neighbor, knowing he or she is ugly, like George Eliot—all three are strangely similar. They are in unison. They make the same sum in the sense that they give measures that are analogies lacking a solid base in any *logos*. More than a simple opposition exists in the relation between the closed-circuit economy of realism, on the one hand, the ugly mirroring the ugly and returning the ugly to the ugly with love for it added in, and, on the other hand, the infinite economy of genius's beautiful works (angels and Madonnas, prophets, sibyls) mirroring nothing but the inventive soul of its creator, flying off into the inane ideal without possibility of return. Realism also adds a fictive plus value. Madonnas or angels also make us admire human motherhood and self-denying aspiration.

George Eliot discharges his conscience, pays off his obligation, by covertly admitting his kinship with the positions he rejects. Extremes meet in their common lack of transcendent ground. The cynicism which measures all people by a zero and finds them all equally poor comes to the same thing, from the perspective of their imaginary nature, as the positive measure which gives my neighbor an infinite value, so generating a resolution to do good, to love him or her.

It comes to the same thing and yet it comes to a very different thing in its effects. That makes all the difference. Even the most charitable performative, however, has its dangers. The oscillation generated by the impossibility of distinguishing categorically between these two attitudes, the selfish and the unselfish, the cynical and the charitable, is the pervasive rhythm of thought and feeling in *Adam Bede* as a whole. It is dramatized in the secret identity and yet infinite difference between Hetty and Dinah. It is dramatized in the impossibility of deciding whether Adam's deluded love for Hetty is a good thing or a bad thing; "He created the mind he believed in out of his own, which was large, unselfish, tender" (33: 319). It is mimed, finally, in the impossibility of deciding whether the "I" who speaks in chapter 17 is Marian Evans (Lewes) talking of the real, historical, autobiographical world of her father, her home county, and her childhood experience, or whether, as it must also be, it is those realities transposed into the fictive voice of an invented male narrator speaking of fictive events and valuing them in gratuitous figurative exchanges moving back and forth from love to nature to art to religion. It is both and so neither.

Chapter 4

Returning to *Middlemarch*: Interpretation as Naming and (Mis) Reading

If I had put the full discussion of chapter 17 of *Adam Bede* in my reading of *Adam Bede*, it might have exploded that essay. It would have distorted that essay's margins and sequential argument, as a virus distorts and ultimately destroys the cell it enters by reprogramming its DNA. What effect it has on my rhetorical reading of *Middlemarch* the reader must judge. It may be "incalculably diffusive," as George Eliot says of Dorothea Brooke's effect on those around her. After this detour into an interpolation discussing *Adam Bede* again, "in which [my own] story pauses a little," it is possible now to return to *Middlemarch* with, I hope, additional understanding of George Eliot's narrative procedures. I return to pick up again the dropped thread of the theme of interpretation in *Middlemarch*. This thread is woven of smaller threads that appear and reappear in the larger thread, according to that law of subdivision already identified. The smaller threads woven together to form the paradigm of text and interpretation in *Middlemarch* may be briefly identified.

One such fiber is George Eliot's recognition in *Middlemarch* that the act of nomination is never innocent. Even the most apparently literal act of naming incorporates what is named into a pre-existing system of interpretation and so gives it a value and a relative weight. As Fred Vincy says in a breakfast-table discussion with Rosamond and his mother, "All choice of words is slang. It marks a class ... [C]orrect English is the slang of prigs who write history and essays. And the strongest slang of all is the slang of poets" (11: 199). Any conceivable dialect or idolect is slang of some sort.

Much later in the novel, Mrs. Cadwallader, after the disaster of Dorothea's marriage and the death of Casaubon, diagnoses Dorothea's problem as a linguistic one. Mrs. Cadwallader defines madness as not calling things by the names our neighbors use. "We have all got to exert ourselves a little to keep sane," she says, "and call things by the same names as other people call them by." To which Dorothea answers: "I never called everything by the same name that all the people about me did." "But I suppose you have found out your mistake, my dear," returns Mrs. Cadwallader, "and that is a proof of sanity" (54: 595). At the end of the novel, Mary Garth somewhat ironically justifies her fidelity to Fred Vincy, in spite of her clear awareness of his shortcomings, by saying, "I don't think either of us could spare the other, or like any one else better, however much we might admire them. It would make too great a difference to us—like seeing all the old places altered, and changing the name for everything" (86: 914). To change the names of things would alter the things themselves as they exist for those who use the old names. What they are for us depends not so much on the way they are seen as on the way they are named. Naming determines seeing. Naming is an arbitrary fidelity, like our love for the person nearest to us.

If this is so, it is also the case, for Eliot, that the physical and social worlds, as each individual encounters them, are not neutral and objective. They have already been named, and thereby interpreted, by all the previous generations. Those generations lived within the physical world and made it over into a human one. They embodied their ideals and readings of the world in buildings, in roads, in utensils, as well as in institutions and customs, in ways of production, distribution, and consumption, in their currency system. All these are now embedded in the ordinary names for things. History is not something abstract, stored up in archives and books. It confronts the individual at every moment of her life. It surrounds her and permeates her, as every United States citizen today, in 2011, is steeped in the fact that we are still in the midst of the Great Recession, with catastrophic unemployment, are experiencing probably irreversible human-caused climate change, are still in prolonged wars with two Middle Eastern countries, and are living in a period of amazingly rapid teletechnological transformation (computers, the Internet, cell-phones, iPads, Facebook, Twitter).

The most dramatic expression in *Middlemarch* of being embedded in history is Dorothea's encounter with the "stupendous fragmentariness" of Rome, its "vast wreck of ambitious ideals" (20: 215, 216). Rome makes visible the fact that a civilization is an interpretation of the world. It does so by displaying, layer upon layer, a long sequence of incompatible interpretations as they are embodied in material constructions. Each interpretation has been superseded. Each exists now as ruins. This shows that even the most homogeneous community exists objectively not as a neutral collection of objects. It is the transformation of those objects into a system of signs. If this is the case, then the world is not a set of objects for seeing. It is like a text that is already an interpretation.

It must therefore be interpreted in its turn, since all reading is interpretation.

Passages adding up to a surprisingly sophisticated theory of interpretation are distributed here and there throughout *Middlemarch*. They often appear in apparently casual asides that draw their full meaning from their echoing of other passages. This theory involves a system of hermeneutical presuppositions. Any text, George Eliot assumes, is open to a variety of interpretations. No one of these can be proved to be the correct one. Each interpretation is in one way or another in excess of the signs given. The causes of this penchant for false interpretation are two linguistic errors. One is the habit of seeing similarities as identities, that is, the habit of taking metaphors literally. The other is the habit of interpreting any large body of signs as governed by some origin, end, or center. This penchant for mistaken reading is related to the egotistic needs of the interpreter. The putative origin or end, it seems, organizes the whole body of signs into an organic whole. Such a whole seems to have an ideal meaning. The penchant for false interpretation leads to just that error dramatized in the analogous stories of Dorothea's misreading of Casaubon, of Casaubon's search for the "Key to all Mythologies," and of Lydgate's search for the primitive tissue.

Such misreading is universal. It is not a remediable fault. A member of the community, Lydgate for example, "may be puffed and belauded, envied, ridiculed, counted upon as a tool and fallen in love with, or at least selected as a future husband, and yet remain virtually unknown—known merely as a cluster of signs for his neighbours' false suppositions" (15: 158). These suppositions are inevitably false, in part because we make our interpretations by thinking in terms of analogies. Celia has a "marvellous quickness in observing a certain order of signs" (5: 51). Nevertheless she misunderstands her sister because she makes the error of interpreting Dorothea's interest in Casaubon as parallel to Dorothea's earlier interest in old Monsieur Liret, their teacher at Lausanne. In a similar way—but please note that in saying that I am doing the thing I am trying to put in question with George Eliot's help. It seems that one cannot avoid thinking in analogies even when interrogating the act of thinking by way of analogies. "In a similar way," as I was saying, Casaubon's historical quest is governed by the search for analogies among the mythical fragments remaining from the various civilizations of the ancient world. Such thinking leads the thinker astray into the endless labyrinth of mistaken interpretation. The mistake is to some degree an inability to resist taking superficial similarities as substantial identities based on some ontological substratum. In Casaubon's case the assumed base is Christian revelation, of which all other non-Christian myths are confused glimpses. Such a substratum would confer an identical origin, meaning, or end on all the apparently analogous signs.

The assumption that such a base exists is what Eliot calls, in a passage already cited, that fatal "power of generalizing which gives men so much the superiority in mistake over the dumb animals" (58: 656). This mistake is based on a failure to understand figurative language. As I have already more than once echoed Eliot as saying, in what is for me a crucial generalization, "[W]e all of us, grave or light, get our thoughts entangled in metaphors, and act fatally on the strength of them" (10: 93). "Poor Mr Casaubon," for example, "had imagined that his long studious bachelorhood had stored up for him a compound interest of enjoyment, and that large drafts on his affections would not fail to be honoured" (10: 93). He thinks of emotions as like money in the bank, multiplying with time if they are not used, or as like water which may be stored indefinitely in some capacious reservoir. "Hence," says a passage referred to in part earlier, when "he determined to abandon himself to the stream of feeling," he "perhaps was surprised to find what an exceedingly shallow rill it was. As in droughty regions baptism by immersion could only be performed symbolically, so Mr Casaubon found that sprinkling was the utmost approach to a plunge which his stream would afford him" (7: 69). This is both devastatingly funny and at the same time sad. If you don't use it, you lose it.

The comic irony of these passages does not contradict their serious intent, nor the grave compassion with which the narrator watches the characters wander into their private labyrinths of false interpretation and act fatally on the strength of them. The irony lies partly in the uncertainty as to whether these metaphors are Casaubon's own or ascribed to him by the narrator. In the latter case, they would be a metaphorical interpretation of Casaubon's feelings or half-articulated thoughts. In principle no way exists to tell for sure about this, since Mr. Casaubon exists only as the narrator's language about him. Indirect discourse is indecipherably ambiguous. It is almost always impossible to divide the language of indirect discourse into one pile for the character, another for the narrator. Therefore it is impossible to tell here whether the thinking by analogy is entirely Casaubon's or is largely, as seems likely, the ironic use of figure by the narrator. In the latter case it would be the narrator, not Casaubon, who names the latter's folly as thinking unused emotions are like money in the bank invested at compound interest, or like a plunge into the stream of feelings. Or perhaps Casaubon himself half-consciously uses this figure about himself. It is impossible to know for certain one way or the other.

The metaphor of text and misinterpretation is also used for Dorothea's misreading of Casaubon. Here the emphasis is even more on the latitude of interpretation. Every reading is in excess of the signs given in the sense that it projects a large coherence on them that is not objectively present. Dorothea's reading fills in gaps by an unconscious act of interpolation. This is governed by her needs and assumptions, that "joyous imaginative activity which fashions events according to desire" (23: 262), as the narrator puts it apropos of Fred Vincy's belief that he has his own private providential good luck. The narrator, in turn, presents his interpretation of Dorothea's acts of interpretation in generalizations that implicitly claim universality. The disquieting notion (for a literary critic at least) that all interpretation is misinterpretation is in these passages affirmed with an all-inclusive sweep that rivals Nietzsche's more celebrated assertions about interpretation in *The Will to Power*:

> Against positivism, which halts at phenomena—"There are only *facts* [*nur Thatsachen*]"—I would say: No, facts is precisely what there is not, only interpretations [*Interpretationen*]. We cannot establish any fact "in itself": perhaps it is folly [*Unsinn*] to want to do such a thing.
>
> "Everything is subjective," you say; but even this is interpretation [*Auslegung*]. The "subject" ["*Subjekt*"] is not something given, it is something added and invented and projected behind [*Dahinter-Gestecktes*] what there is.—Finally, is it necessary to posit an interpreter behind the interpretation? Even that is invention, hypothesis.
>
> In so far as the word "knowledge" has any meaning, the world is knowable; but it is *interpretable* [*deutbar*] otherwise, it has no meaning [*Sinn*] behind it, but countless meanings.—"Perspectivism [*Perspektivismus*]."
>
> It is our needs that interpret the world; our drives and their For and Against. Every drive is a kind of lust to rule [*Herrschsucht*]; each one has its perspective that it would like to compel all the other drives to accept as a norm.[1]

For Eliot, as for Nietzsche, the only true generalization seems to be the double statement that it is human to make generalizations and that all generalizations are in error. They are all the false finding of similarities in the dissimilar. They are the casting of an illicit net of unity over dispersed signs, the filling in of gaps in ways not justified by the signs themselves.

Of Dorothea's early encounters with Casaubon, for example, the narrator says: "Signs are small measurable things, but interpretations are illimitable, and in girls of sweet, ardent nature, every sign is apt to conjure up wonder, hope, belief, vast as a sky, and coloured by a diffused thimbleful of matter in the shape of knowledge" (3: 27). That he goes on to qualify this by saying that young girls "are not always too grossly deceived" undercuts the absoluteness of the generalization in a way compatible with George Eliot's rejection of generalization elsewhere. In another context he says: "I protest against any absolute conclusion" (10: 92). This qualification, however, only ironically modifies the claim that "interpretations are illimitable." It suggests that among the many ways in which we may commit the universal mistake of misreading signs is one that may lead us by accident to a "proper" goal by a sequence of false reasoning: "for Sinbad himself may have fallen by good-luck on a true description, and wrong reasoning sometimes lands poor mortals in right conclusions: starting a long way off the true point, and proceeding by loops and zigzags, we now and then arrive just where we ought to be" (3: 27). The sudden appearance of Sinbad the Sailor here is an example of the way deviation, being off course, may provide a figure that makes it possible to circle by loops and zigzags to the right conclusion. The conclusion, in this case, ironically, is that human beings have a fatal propensity to get their thoughts entangled in metaphors, such as this abrupt appearance of Sinbad. If Casaubon is a text to be read, he has a susceptibility to be the victim of multiple interpretations, like the Bible or like *Hamlet*, or perhaps even like *Middlemarch* itself, for "the text, whether of prophet or of poet, expands for whatever we can put into it, and even his bad grammar is sublime" (5: 55).

In another place, Dorothea's interpretation of Casaubon is said to be like the reading of history by those theologians who see it as God's providential writing. For such interpreters, actual events are as coherent a text as the synoptic gospels seem to believers: "His efforts at exact courtesy and formal tenderness had no defect for her. She filled up all blanks with unmanifested perfections, interpreting him as she interpreted the works of Providence, and accounting for seeming discords by her own deafness to the high harmonies. And there are many blanks left in the weeks of courtship, which a loving faith fills with happy assurance" (9: 81). Once more, that emotion is the motive force behind misinterpretation is evident in this passage. Dorothea loves Casaubon, and that leads her to misread him. This is the dark side of Adam Bede's dictum that "It isn't notions sets people doing the right thing—it's feelings . . ." Dorothea's feelings are good, but they lead her to do the wrong thing. The words of *Middlemarch* turn from this side to that, zigzagging in the face of this aporia.

Behind the narrator's analysis of Dorothea's disastrous limitations as a reader is a shrewd assimilation by the author of some of the disquieting implications of German Biblical criticism. These Marian Evans had encountered more through her work in translating Strauss's *Leben Jesu* than in her translation of Feuerbach, but, as Avrom Fleishman has shown, she had read much other work in this area.[2] Her use of the vocabulary of German hermeneutic theory in the narrator's reading of Dorothea's reading of Casaubon indicates her awareness that perhaps the most disquieting implication of this theory lies in the possibility of transposing it to the realm of human intercourse. If I misread a book, nothing may happen, though of course it would be a mistake to count on that too confidently, as the results of what to many appear to be misreadings of the Bible or of the Koran are showing at the present time (2011). If I misread my neighbor, however, I risk bringing the deepest life-long sorrow on myself or on others, as the sad stories of Dorothea's first marriage to Casaubon and of Lydgate's marriage to Rosamond show. Nevertheless, *Middlemarch* argues that such misreading is inevitable and irremediable. Dorothea does not move from blindness to insight but from one disastrous blindness, her infatuation with Casaubon, to another blindness, her love for Will Ladislaw. The latter is luckily more benign, but it is no less an interpretation generated by emotion and in excess of the data. For George Eliot, there are only different forms of blindness. Genuine insight into the roar on the other side of silence would be deadly even for the narrator, and deadly also for "you and me," readers and critics. That, however, still remains to be shown.

Interpretation as the Creation of Totalizing Emblems

To speak of "showing" or of blindness is to return to metaphors of seeing. The latter, it appears, cannot be put in a pigeon-hole entirely separate from the metaphors of reading. The optical metaphors and the metaphors that see other people as texts to interpret overlap rather than wholly excluding one another. The figure of interpretation functions as an analysis of what happens in seeing. Even in perception we are readers of a text, decipherers of signs. For George Eliot, this does not mean we should undertake an objective search for the true meaning of the signs. Rather, the activity of reading casts a web of interpretation over what is really there, the "small measurable things" making up the substance of signs. This web of interpretation is always in excess of the given. It always takes each small measurable thing as something other than what it is. A sign by definition stands for something other than itself. It is the present vicar or vehicle of something absent. The act of interpretation, for George Eliot, by choosing a reference is therefore generative of meaning, rather than a revelation of some meaning already there but hidden. There is no correct interpretation of a sign except within the "key" of a received code, for the meaning of a sign depends on what one brings to it. All things are spontaneously and originally perceived not as objects to be identified, but as emblems, as parables.

This fact is kept before the reader by an important sequence of scenes which threads through the novel, knitting one part to another. Each of these shows Dorothea making what she beholds into an emblem of her spiritual situation. Often she is looking through a window. Usually she is alone, but in the last scene she stands beside Will Ladislaw, and they look out a window together. These scenes include Dorothea's visionary response to the "stupendous fragmentariness" of Rome (20: 215), already cited; all those times when she looks out her boudoir window at Lowick, her home after marrying Casaubon, toward the long avenue of limes; her vision from the same window of Featherstone's funeral; the scene in which, after her night of grief over Will's supposed betrayal of her, she looks out her window to see a "man with a bundle on his back and a woman carrying her baby" (80: 873). She interprets this last scene as an emblem of "the largeness of the world and the manifold waking of men to labour and endurance" (ibid.). It is also read by Dorothea as evidence of her involuntary participation in that activity. This participation cannot be escaped, only performed well or badly. For George Eliot, "reading" the world is not passive and withdrawn. It is an activity, a "doing" that makes something happen, for good or for ill: "She was a part of that involuntary, palpitating life, and could neither look out on it from her luxurious shelter as a mere spectator, nor hide her eyes in selfish complaining" (ibid.).

The final scene in this series is the climactic one in which Will and Dorothea stand together looking out the window at Lowick at a thunderstorm, prepared to separate forever. The storm outside is finally answered by Dorothea's tears inside the room and by "the flood of her young passion hearing down all the obstructions which had kept her silent" (83: 898). This passion precipitates her into Will's arms, another Ariadne accepting her rescuing Dionysus. I shall return to this scene and to the presence in the novel of the Ariadne myth.

All these episodes show the passing of vision in the limited sense of seeing into vision in the wider sense of emblematic interpretation. All exemplify Adam Bede's paternal wisdom that it isn't notions but feelings that lead to action, sometimes bad action, sometimes good. Dorothea's experience of Rome, for example, becomes a permanent emblem of all her moods of "dull forlornness":

Forms both pale and glowing took possession of her young sense, and fixed themselves in her memory even when she was not thinking of them, preparing strange associations which remained through her after-years. Our moods are apt to bring with them images which succeed each other like the magic-lantern pictures of a doze; and in certain states of dull forlornness Dorothea all her life continued to see the vastness of St. Peter's, the huge bronze canopy, the excited intention in the attitudes and garments of the prophets and evangelists in the mosaics above, and the red drapery which was being hung for Christmas spreading itself everywhere like a disease of the retina. (20: 216)

The concluding figure here admirably transfers the outside to the inside, as do Dorothea's tears in the scene at the end of the novel. What is external and visible, the red drapery, becomes a limitation on seeing projected outward, like a disease of the retina. Dorothea's dull forlornness, like such a disease, conditions what is seen and makes it into an emblem of her inner state. In the same way, when Dorothea returns from her wedding journey, her new vision of her boudoir at Lowick and the view from her window there is shown to transfigure what is seen into a sign of her "moral imprisonment." The visible scene becomes a parabolic sign for her sense of her idealistic ardor's frustration. Outside becomes the emblem of inside. This experience paradoxically intensifies Dorothea's sense, at this moment of her life, of the distance of inside from outside and of her being kept from engaging herself in "claims that would have shaped her energies" (28: 305). In the failure of that engagement of inner energies in outer scene both inside and outside dissolve in the same "shrinking," the same "vanishing" into ghostly intangibility;

> . . . she saw the long avenue of limes lifting their trunks from a white earth, and spreading white branches against the dun and motionless sky. The distant flat shrank in uniform whiteness and low-hanging uniformity of cloud. The very furniture in the room seemed to have shrunk since she saw it before: the stag in the tapestry looked more like a ghost in his ghostly blue-green world; the volumes of polite literature in the bookcase looked more like immovable imitations of books . . . Her blooming full-pulsed youth stood there in a moral imprisonment which made itself one with the chill, colorless, narrowed landscape, with the shrunken furniture, the never-read books, and the ghostly stag in a pale fantastic world that seemed to be vanishing from the daylight. (28: 304, 306)

This admirably desolate passage can stand for the truly awful experience of all those Victorian middle- and upper-class wives and daughters who, when they ask what they can do, are answered as Casaubon answers Dorothea's question, "Whatever you please, my dear" (28: 305). The splendid sequence of passages I have cited, gravely compassionate but at the same time brilliantly and remorselessly analytic, product of the narrator's telepathic voyeurism, shows that for George Eliot the emblematic interpretation of physical objects under the impulse of feeling is an activity spontaneously performed, for good or for ill, by real people in their daily lives, under the impulse of emotion. It is not just an intellectual performance by the narrator of a novel who says, "This equals that," or, "These things are a parable." We all of us grave or light get our thoughts, our perceptions, and our feelings entangled in metaphors. We live our lives according to our abilities as readers of signs, but no readings are true in the sense of being objectively confirmed by the mute texts we read and make into emblems of our inner states. Another viewer might see the scene outside Dorothea's window as an inspiriting sign of his or her ownership of valuable property and as evidence of high social standing.

Money as Metaphor

For George Eliot there is always an incommensurability between what is there to be seen and the semiotic, or one might say "semioptic," function which is projected into it. To put this another way, what is there to be seen can never be seen neutrally as it is in itself. Seeing is always interested. To see with interest is to add the plus value that makes what is seen a sign, as an innocent piece of paper or metal becomes a bill or a coin when it is stamped. It is possible, in this perspective, to understand the significance of the monetary metaphor that insinuates itself into several passages already cited as examples of one or another of the non-monetary master figures of *Middlemarch*. The figure of money also figures in other passages not yet quoted. This trope presents itself so insistently in *Middlemarch* that any full account of the metaphorical texture of the novel would have to "take account" of it as one filament in the web. One would need to add it in, so to speak.

Money is a familiar example of the incommensurability between a sign and its meaning. A piece of money is nothing much in itself. It is nothing of great use. It is a mere bit of paper or metal. The value of a coin or a bill derives from the image that is stamped on it and from the collective faith a given community has in its value. Suppose I were to present a fifty dollar bill in payment for groceries and were to be told that I am just proffering a worthless piece of paper. That meaning printed on a coin or on a paper bill can multiply itself in a way outside the logic of material production. The addition of zeroes on a piece of money can turn a penny into a dime, a dollar into ten, a hundred, or a thousand dollars.

This property of money is emphasized in various passages in *Middlemarch*. In these passages the monetary metaphor adds itself as a metaphor of metaphor to some apparently substantiated metaphorical correspondence that has already been established. By "substantiated" I mean based on something having solid reality within the first level of representation in the novel. When the narrator, in a passage already cited, compares his investigation of Mrs. Cadwallader's match-making to the use of lenses of different powers in a microscope, the comparison is grounded in the substantial person of Mrs. Cadwallader. She is substantial, that is, as long as we take the novel as history. When the little creatures seen under the microscope are compared to "so many animated tax-pennies," a monetary metaphor adds itself to the first one in a metaphor of a metaphor no longer directly grounded in the first level of reality of the novel. The effect of this is odd. It cannot easily be evened out in a total accounting of the interplay of literal and figurative language in the novel. As Wallace Stevens says, "There is no such thing as a metaphor of a metaphor."[3] What was the vehicle of the first metaphor, the microscope, becomes the tenor of the second. This means that the reader tends to ascribe to the microscope a first-level status as a solid reality that the narrator is "describing" or "representing," carrying it from here to there in the vehicle of a metaphor in the same way as he describes or transfers Mrs. Cadwallader. The reader also knows, if she thinks of it, that there is no literal microscope at this point in the novel. The microscope oscillates back and forth before the reader's eyes between being really there and being only metaphorically there. This calls attention to the play of figuration. It moves the reader's attention back to the surface of the text and away from the supposed psychological and social realities it describes. It foregrounds the verbal activity of the novel and, for the moment, hollows out the "realities" it describes. It makes the reader see these realities as an effect of the text, rather than as something objective the text imitates. The final sentence in the passage about Mrs. Cadwallader's match-making affirms this overtly in the phrase "metaphorically speaking." This phrase makes a self-conscious allusion to the way the activity of interpreting one metaphor with another metaphor and that with yet another brings metaphor-making and metaphor-reading to the surface.

The metaphor of money, however, is more than just one example among others of "metaphorically speaking." The same piece of paper, as I have said, can be taken as a dollar, as ten dollars, or as a hundred dollars, depending on what is printed on it. This, as George Eliot sees, is a powerful image of the non-representational logic of representation. The failure of representational correspondence in monetary symbolism follows from the fact that all signs are originally metaphors. They take one thing, in this case a bit of paper or metal stamped with an image, as something else. All signs draw their meaning from some baseless projection into a material substratum of an arbitrary value that exceeds the value of the substratum as such. This value may proliferate to infinity in the compound interest of its crediting, or it may fall back to zero if its lack of base is exposed. This inflation and deflation arises not so much from the arbitrariness of the sign as from the fissure between the stamped image and what it is stamped on. There is no sign without its material base, but that material base is indifferent as long as it will hold the image. One could imagine dollar bills made of slices of bread or of oak leaves, though they would not last so well as paper. What is money, according to one now outmoded idiom, but "bread"?

A sequence of passages using the metaphor of money threads its way through *Middlemarch*. The sequence functions as an implicit commentary on the operation of those other three families of metaphors I have been identifying. To put this another way, the figure of money puts in question both the family resemblances within each group and the distinctions between groups that have allowed me, like Mr. Casaubon or Mr. Brooke, to pigeon-hole the different examples of each "family" in three convenient compartments: objective spatial design; the act of seeing; the act of interpreting a text.[4] If the figure of money can be added as a figure of figure to any member of all three families of metaphors, then the distinctions among the families are broken down in a kind of promiscuity or intermarriage, a miscegenation making the family lines impure. Each metaphor, that of the web, that of seeing, that of reading, is contaminated by its demonstrable similarity to the metaphor of money. At this point the genealogical lines break down into a confused tangle like the unsorted contents of Mr. Brooke's mind or of his unarranged papers, not to speak of Casaubon's disordered notes. Everything leads to everything else, or bears a family resemblance to it. On the other hand, the monetary metaphor, as George Eliot presents it, disconnects genealogical or causal relations. It indicates for signs a power of autogenesis that exceeds anything that has fathered or mothered the signs. Signs, George Eliot's analysis of the monetary figure implies, are a kind of immaculate conception bringing into existence something outside the sequence of causality in legitimate marriage and family lines where the effect is seen as commensurate with its cause.

In putting in question explanation by paternal or maternal causality, the monetary metaphor reinforces the implications of the strange tangle of secret family connections, absent parents, and quasi-incestuous marriages across generations that characterize "actual" family relations in Middlemarch. Claude Lévi-Strauss might have had a field day identifying the skewed kinship system at work in the novel.[5] "You are not angry with me for thinking Mistress Second-Cousin the most perfect young

Madonna I ever saw?" asks Naumann of Will Ladislaw in their discussion of Dorothea. "[As] a painter," he continues, "I have a conception which is altogether *genialisch*, of your great-aunt or second grandmother as a subject for a picture ... This is serious, my friend! Your great-aunt! 'Der Neffe als Onkel' in a tragic sense—*ungeheuer*!" (19: 211, 212, 213). Second cousin, great-aunt, second grandmother—which is she? Is Will a nephew or an uncle?

"'Der Neffe als Onkel' ['The Nephew as Uncle'] in a tragic sense"— that is an exceedingly odd phrase. What did Marian Evans mean by it? Can there be an oblique reference to Marx's *The Eighteenth Brumaire of Louis Bonaparte*, a reference, that is, to Marx's interpretation of the relation of Napoleon III to Napoleon Bonaparte? This would also be a reference to the way, for Marx, all the tragic shows of history repeat themselves as farce. In the economy of repetition in *Middlemarch*, which is the tragedy, which is the farce? Should not the label "farce" be given to Dorothea's disastrous but to some degree comic marriage to Casaubon, repetition of Milton's disastrous marriages, or of Ariadne's marriage to that self-righteous and forgetful prig Theseus? Does not Naumann mean to say that Will's infatuation with his great-aunt or second grandmother has tragic possibilities, reversing the usual Marxist sequence from tragedy to farce? Alas, no evidence that I know of exists that George Eliot ever read Marx. This makes their burial a few yards from one another in Highgate Cemetery outside London somewhat ironic. Critics have plausibly claimed that the phrase in quotation marks is a reference to the name of a play by Friedrich Schiller: *Der Neffe als Onkel*. Marx also refers to this play, but apparently the echo is coincidental.[6]

Money is like kinship terms, genealogical tables, and marriage relations in several ways at least. In both marriage and money, arbitrary labels and arbitrary values are given to individual entities, paper or metal in one case, persons in the other. In both cases the labels and values derive from differential relations within a system. In both cases, the system has the same structure as language, though which is prior, sexual relations, economic relations, or linguistic relations, can never be told, since each system always already presupposes the others. In all three cases, the system, to those living within its hegemony, seems part of the given natural world, not something arbitrary or conventional that could be otherwise. Or rather, each system seems that way until something goes wrong with it, an incestuous marriage, a runaway inflation turning money back into mere paper and metal, a recession brought about by the limitless greed, folly, and chicanery of banks, financial institutions, and government officials such as we in the United States and in the whole world have experienced in the last three years (I write in

2011), or a deconstructive analysis of literature or of philosophy such as those performed by Marx, Paul de Man, or, in her own way, by George Eliot.

The monetary metaphor in *Middlemarch* appears at least six times at widely spaced intervals. It is part of that network of passages reticulating the text. This network repeatedly calls attention to the arbitrariness of naming. I have already cited passages about slang and about calling things by the old names. Another example is the narrator's remark about "that mysterious influence of Naming which determines so much of mortal choice" (23: 263). This mysterious influence persuades Fred that the sordid and boring business of following the horses with Messieurs Bambridge and Horrock and losing money at it is "pleasure" and "gay:"

> Under any other name than "pleasure" the society of Messieurs Bambridge and Horrock must certainly have been regarded as monotonous; and to arrive with them at Houndsley on a drizzling afternoon, to get down at the Red Lion in a street shaded with coal-dust, and dine in a room furnished with a dirt-enamelled map of the county, a bad portrait of an anonymous horse in a stable, His Majesty George the Fourth with legs and cravat, and various leaden spittoons, might have seemed a hard business, but for the sustaining power of nomenclature which determined that the pursuit of these things was "gay." (23: 263)

Among examples of this "sustaining power of nomenclature" none is more socially powerful than our confidence in money. All the places where George Eliot uses money as a figure produce an odd equation between one thing and another that calls attention to the baselessness of this confidence. Even so, confidence in the value of money and in the value of someone who has money is of the utmost importance in the society of Middlemarch. At the same time, the monetary metaphor works as a figure to undermine our confidence in some other activity. That activity is said to work, surprisingly, in a way analogous to the coining and circulation of money, that is by the ascription of value to a material base that does not in itself have enough substance to carry that value, so that the value must always be taken on credit.

I referred above to the passage comparing the difficulty in interpreting Mrs. Cadwallader's match-making to looking at animalcules through microscopes of different strengths. This optic figure is then further figured in a monetary image. The passage must be cited again so that the reader can look at it now with a stronger lens:

> Even with a microscope directed on a water-drop we find ourselves making interpretations which turn out to be rather coarse; for whereas under a weak

lens you may seem to see a creature exhibiting an active voracity into which other smaller creatures actively play as if they were so many animated tax-pennies, a stronger lens reveals to you certain tiniest hairlets which make vortices for these victims while the swallower waits passively at his receipt of custom. In this way, metaphorically speaking, a strong lens applied to Mrs Cadwallader's match-making will show a play of minute causes producing what may be called thought and speech vortices to bring her the sort of food she needed. (6: 65)

What, exactly, does this passage say? To look through any lens, weak or strong, it says, is to interpret. Seeing is reading, and reading, as the passage demonstrates, means seeing one thing as another thing. To see one thing as another thing is to name it, but to name it in metaphor. Seeing is interpreting, but interpreting is naming figuratively. All things are always already from the beginning seen as tropes. Each thing is a parable throwing one thing beside another thing. There is no language of realism, if that means naming things literally. All seeing is tropological, and all speaking is "metaphorically speaking." The narrator's activity of interpreting Mrs. Cadwallader's match-making is named in the metaphor of looking through a microscope. Apparently it cannot be named adequately or "interpreted" in literal language. Looking through a microscope is in its turn not a literal base. It must be named, or rather what is seen through microscopes of different strengths, little creatures eating voraciously, must be named in metaphor in its turn, this time in the monetary metaphor of gathering tax-pennies. The metaphor of eating, in another turn, is an implicit interpretation of what goes on in the circulation and accumulation of money in a society.

A movement in the other direction whereby the tenor becomes vehicle and interprets that which interprets it goes counter to this *mise en abyme* structure of the text, metaphor behind metaphor behind metaphor potentially *ad infinitum*. Tax gathering interprets eating but is also interpreted by it. The hierarchical sequence is also an oscillation. This reversal is a usual feature of such metaphorical chains. Match-making, looking through a microscope, reading or "interpretation," eating, tax gathering—a movement back and forth occurs among all these basic physiological, psychological, and social functions whereby each interprets all the others and is interpreted by them. All are versions of, or perhaps one should say "functions within," the valuation, circulation, distribution, production, consumption, and interpretation of "goods" in society—men, women, money, food. The society of *Middlemarch* is already an example of that modern capitalist society organized around conflicting use-value and exchange-value, along with commodity fetishism, that Marx so pitilessly analyzes in *Das Capital*.

No one function, of the four I just listed, is the ground of all the others, its literal base. Each is literal, something that "really" exists in society. At the same time, in its most literal existence, it is always already tropological or metaphorical, turned from itself, or carried over, transported. The "real" ground of the passage about Mrs. Cadwallader is the process of sign making and sign reading in society, the movement or circulation of signs that makes us human. The passage brilliantly exemplifies this as well as simply describing it. Insofar as the circulation of money in tax gathering is the "bottomless bottom," the deep beneath the lowest deep of the miniature *mise en abyme* in this passage, it gives the law to the others. It serves as the model for the other forms of the circulation of signs and values in a capitalist society. I note in passing that *Middlemarch* contains relatively little of *Adam Bede*'s constant comparison of human beings to animals and plants. The tropological repertoires of the two novels are quite different.

A tax-penny is not just an ordinary penny used to pay taxes, as one might assume. An archaic meaning of the word penny is "the part of an amount of money indicated by a specified ordinal," as when Adam Smith writes that "interest was reduced from the twentieth to the fiftieth penny or from five to two percent." This then led to the use of the word "penny" to indicate "the sum exacted by a specified tax or customary payment." The word existed in such compounds as "earnest penny," "ale-penny," or "fish-penny," as well as in "tax-penny."[7] The reader will now see the point of George Eliot's phrase, "as if they were so many animated tax-pennies." The ordinary monetary transactions of daily life, such as the buying of ale or fish, cause so many tax-pennies to be automatically paid out of the sums I spend for the ale or the fish. These "pennies" are a kind of plus value or minus value added to the transaction or subtracted from it without the volition of either buyer or seller. They are "animated" because they seem to have a life of their own. They add to the price but subtract from the amount of fish or ale I get, as a metaphorical term or an allegorical sign means more and at the same time less than its literal meaning. It means more because the literal things named, for example tax-pennies or the little creatures under a microscope, stand for something other than themselves and so have an added value. It means less because being made to stand for something other than themselves hollows out the literal meaning and negates it, just as the tax-penny part of my payment for fish or ale does not go to pay for fish or ale. The behavior of tax-pennies is a brilliant paradigm of the way signs work in human intercourse. This, as I have said, is the real subject of the passage. The "undecidable" in this model, as in the other figures it models and is modeled by, is the unanswerable question of whether the making and movement of signs is active or passive, controlled by human beings or controlling them. It is both and neither, since will and passion cannot by any means be detached from the movement of signs that incorporates them, generates them, and is generated by them, in a perpetual coming and going.

Mrs. Cadwallader, for example, in the paragraphs surrounding the texts I am discussing, is called "the diplomatist of Tipton and Freshitt," that is, someone to whom "for anything to happen in spite of her was an offensive irregularity" (6: 66). She is shown circulating from household to household in her pony-phaeton, a living emblem of the relation of tenor and vehicle in a metaphor. She accommodates herself promptly to her failure to marry Dorothea to Sir James Chettam and shifts instantly to more successful match-making between Sir James and Dorothea's sister Celia. In her movements from household to household she makes something happen. She brings people together. She acts as a catalyst to marriages that keep bloodlines pure. She insures the correct distribution of men, women, and property that keeps the community alive and consistent with itself. On the other hand, she is intensely conservative, programmed by prejudices about "birth and no-birth" (6: 65) that make her the passive instrument of an impersonal, self-perpetuating system of naming and valuing, for example in judgments about who ought to marry whom. She is no more than a function within that system. She is both causer and caused, both active and passive. Whatever she does as calculating master diplomatist she also does as unwitting victim of prejudices she cannot see from the outside. She embodies that feudal class structure still so active in England as capitalism took over, all the way down to World War II, and even to a considerable degree today. Like the voracious creatures under the microscope, she both waits passively to be fed and also makes the little whirlpools that sweep her food toward her. The "play of minute causes" which produce "what may be called thought and speech vortices to bring her the sort of food she need[s]" are both the deliberate actions she performs to make the "right" sorts of marriages occur and at the same time those more impersonal causes which act through her and make her believe and do in a certain way. The notion of "minute causes" in George Eliot's thought moves toward the idea of a complex self-sustaining and self-regulating system in which causer is also always caused. In such a system, the possibility of thinking in terms of uni-directional causality governed by origin and end, as in the complex Aristotelian analysis of cause, breaks down.

The model for this is the movement of money in society, as in tax paying and tax gathering. This movement is both deliberately controlled by man and at the same time self-governing, according to an intrinsic tendency in money to move around, to circulate. The tax-pennies seem uncannily "animated" by a will of their own, though the buyer, the seller, and the tax gatherer are also making them move, in another version of the uncertainty as to which is active, which passive, which causer, which caused.

The passage, like *Middlemarch* as a whole, depends on an opposition between, on the one hand, a traditional logocentric pattern involving beginning, ending, and underlying cause or ground, embodied in feudal society and in Christianity, and, on the other hand, the model of a self-sustaining system of circulating signs in which neither beginning, end, nor cause can be identified. Paul de Man, famously, called the latter system "allegorical," a sign-to-sign relation across a temporal gap rather than the spatial sign-to-thing relation of symbol. A formulation in Walter Benjamin's *Trauerspiel* book, a strong but relatively covert influence on de Man's definition of allegory, is even closer to what Eliot says about lords and loobies: "Any person, any thing, any relationship can mean any other thing you like." ("*Jede Person, jedwedes Ding, jedes Verhältnis kann ein beliebiges anderes bedeuten.*")[8] Money is one of George Eliot's prime examples of an allegorical sign system. The subversive implication of the passage I have been discussing, as of other examples of the monetary metaphor in *Middlemarch*, is that the distribution of men, women, property, food, and other things of value takes place in the same arbitrary, groundless, and yet necessary way as does the coining and circulation of money. All the examples of the money metaphor in *Middlemarch* contain the *mise en abyme* of metaphor behind metaphor that dismantles the logocentric hierarchical structure. This subversive alternative version of the serial pattern is further contaminated by the image of circulation, which does not even allow the implicit placement of priority still present in the *mise en abyme*. The ladder of image within image becomes a round of perpetual displacement in which no beginning, ending, or predominant function can be found.

Casaubon believes, for example, that miser-like he can hoard unused passion, "that his long studious bachelorhood had stored up for him a compound interest of enjoyment, and that large drafts on his affections would not fail to be honoured" (10: 93). In fact, what circulates in his veins is neither blood nor passion but marks of punctuation. As Mrs. Cadwallader says, "Somebody put a drop under a magnifying-glass, and it was all semicolons and parentheses" (8: 77). This passage once more adds language to the chain of figures circulating in constant replacement one for another. Not quite language, though, is in question, but two of those unvoiced marks that indicate pauses, rhythms, breaks, ligatures, turning a jumbled chain of signs into articulated sentences. Semicolons and parentheses are especially appropriate for Casaubon and perhaps secret figures for *Middlemarch* itself. Casaubon has not only sought origins, the key to all mythologies. He has also sought to write a great work that will correspond to the form he assumes cultural history has taken. It will have a beginning, middle, end, and a total grounded unity. Instead, Casaubon's efforts have produced an endless series of notes. These could be strung together at best by that most ambiguous mark of punctuation, the semicolon, neither quite a full stop nor quite a connection. The semicolon indicates analogy at a distance or apposition.

Do the multitudinous plots and figures of *Middlemarch* perhaps make no more than one long compound sentence held together by semicolons? The only published production of Casaubon's pen is several *parerga*, literally *hors d'oeuvres*, something beside or outside the main work, as the bits of food called *hors d'oeuvres* are eaten before the main meal. Casaubon's *parerga* are neither wholly part of the great systematic work he is trying to write nor wholly separate from it. They are parenthetical, or rather they are examples of that odd sort of parenthesis which is at the edge, marginal, like the provincial town of Middlemarch itself, at once in the middle and at the edge, a middle march. The word "march" designates a marginal territory. Casaubon's *parerga* are something put down like milestones or boundary markers in the middle of his march toward the completion of his work, the *ergon* proper: " . . . the difficulty of making his Key to all Mythologies unimpeachable weighed like lead upon his mind; and the pamphlets—or 'Parerga' as he called them—by which he tested his public and deposited small monumental records of his march, were far from having been seen in all their significance" (9: 311–12). The comic scatological nuances of these "deposits" will not escape the careful reader, nor the covert reference in "march" to "Middlemarch."

Versions of the image of matter stamped with signs surreptitiously circulate throughout *Middlemarch*, appearing here and there like a pulse-beat on a temple and insinuating the fact that all valuation is arbitrary. Of the young Lydgate, for example, before he gets his vocation for medicine, George Eliot says: "he had no more thought of representing to himself how his blood circulated than how paper served instead of gold" (15: 160–1). That the meaning of a sign arises from our trust in it, as paper serves in place of gold, makes Lydgate, in his turn, a blank cipher for other people to add zeroes to, rather than being, as he wants to be, a substantial number, at least a number one, "a unit who would make a certain amount of difference towards that spreading change which would one day tell appreciably upon the averages" (15: 163). Lydgate has been correct in believing "that a change in the units was the most direct way of changing the numbers" (ibid.), but a later passage indicates the kind of unit he is. The power over Rosamond of Lydgate's entering into the room, while she is still infatuated with him, is said to have "the effect of a numeral before ciphers" (63: 712). Rosamond projects into Lydgate a value that turns a row of nothings into a huge sum, thereby fulfilling the law stated earlier whereby in Middlemarch each person is "known merely as a cluster of signs for his neighbour's false suppositions" (15: 158). Rosamond prints Lydgate into money, so to speak, and prints herself into money too, turning her boredom into a full imaginative and emotive life by her response to a Lydgate she has created through a process of bad reading.

In another such passage Fred Vincy's imaginative propensity for gambling is figured as the power of multiplication latent in numbers, falsely thought of as having a genetic propensity for growth; "he had kept twenty pounds in his own pocket as a sort of seed-corn, which, planted with judgment and watered by luck, might yield more than threefold—a very poor rate of multiplication when the field is a young gentleman's infinite soul, with all the numerals at command" (23: 261).

The Boomerang Effect of the Monetary Metaphor

One final example of the monetary metaphor is the most important. The narrator uses those discussed so far as tools of interpretative mastery over the characters or over the society in which they live. In one use of the monetary metaphor, however, an intrinsic danger in all that family of metaphors involving the figure of interpreting signs comes to the surface. This is their propensity to turn back on the narrator's mastery and on that of the author. To put this in the most general terms: the metaphor of metaphor differs from the metaphor of the web or the metaphor of seeing in that it necessarily applies to its own activity. It deconstitutes itself as much as it deconstitutes what it is used to analyze.

The passage in question begins as an ironic comment on the "lowness" of the scene just concluded. That scene has described the reading of old Peter Featherstone's will. Like so many passages of the narrator's commentary this one expands to make wide generalizations on the basis of the particularity just presented. In this case the generalization has to do with the parabolic method of *Middlemarch*. Here, even more than in the "parable" of the pier-glass, the mode of representation in *Middlemarch* as a whole is figured and made salient by the text itself. The novel here exposes the strange connection between realism on the one hand, in the sense of straightforward reference to historical, social, psychological realities, naming things as they are, and, on the other hand, an emblematic, parabolic, pastoral, or allegorical technique. In the latter the realities named are never merely themselves. They always stand for something else that they are not really like or analogous to, but are only arbitrarily, at a distance, said to represent in parabolic figure. They function in the same way as a piece of paper that becomes a banknote when it is stamped with an appropriate design. The narrator (explicitly an "I" or "he") speaks here with characteristically delicious Eliotic irony. *Middlemarch* is, among other things, often a wonderfully comic book:

> And here I am naturally led to reflect on the means of elevating a low subject. Historical parallels are remarkably efficient in this way. The chief objection to them is, that the diligent narrator may lack space, or (what is often the same thing) may not be able to think of them with any degree of particularity, though he may have a philosophical confidence that if known they would be illustrative. It seems an easier and shorter way to dignity, to observe that—since there never was a true story which could not be told in parables where you might put a monkey for a margrave, and *vice versa*—whatever has been or is to be narrated by me about low people, may be ennobled by being considered a parable; so that if any bad habits and ugly consequences are brought into view, the reader may have the relief of regarding them as not more than figuratively ungenteel, and may feel himself virtually in company with persons of some style. Thus while I tell the truth about loobies, my reader's imagination need not be entirely excluded from an occupation with lords; and the petty sums which any bankrupt of high standing would be sorry to retire upon, may be lifted to the level of high commercial transactions by the inexpensive addition of proportional ciphers. (35: 379)

This passage speaks for itself, but it is perhaps even richer than may at first appear. It may even be interest-bearing. It may be able to sustain the capital gains of a commentary. Does my commentary, on the contrary, perhaps rather tax it, deplete its value, use it up? In any case, the passage is odd rather than even. It taxes itself, perhaps even to bankruptcy, not least in the uncertainty of its defensive irony and in the strangely multiplied negatives. Does George Eliot really mean to apologize for the "low mimetic," to use Northrop Frye's term, mode of his realism? Surely he does not mean the reader to take seriously the absurd invitation to think about lords while reading about these loobies? Is the reader then to take seriously the alternative theory of parable (George Eliot's name for something akin to de Manian allegory) the passage proposes, even though it seems also to be presented ironically? This alternative theory would undermine any referential function of the descriptions of loobies, making them merely the parabolic vehicle of a different "truth." Does the word "true" or "truth" mean the same thing both times it appears here ("true story"; "truth about loobies")? What is the exact functioning of those double negatives with their qualifying adverbs, "more," "entirely," "figuratively": "not more than figuratively ungenteel," "need not be entirely excluded from"? To say something "is not . . . not," "not . . . un-." or "is not . . . ex-" is not entirely the same thing, is it, as to say that it "is"? Or is it?

The passage opposes two modes of elevating a low subject. One is "objective" in the sense that it deals with external realities and external analogies. A "historical parallel" is presumably one that compares the low subject to some grander historical event on the basis of an analogy that is "really there," external and objective. Revolutionary France repeats classical Rome. Both the hypothetical historical event and the sociological facts imitated in the "low subject," for example Peter Featherstone's funeral, are taken as really there. The "philosophical confidence" of which the narrator speaks is belief in these objective realities and objective analogies. This is the mode of analogy between one event and another appropriate to realism as it is often understood. Why the lack of space and the failure to think of the historical parallels "with any degree of particularity" are "often the same thing" is a little puzzling. What mode of analogy makes them "often the same thing"? Is this analogy to be understood parabolically or historically, that is, "realistically"? The comic irony makes these questions impossible to answer. Their undecidability is just the point. Irony is the linguistic expression of undecidability. Does the diligent narrator say he lacks space (as George Eliot, in another important passage where *Middlemarch* exposes its own workings, has said he lacks space for the expansive meditations of Fielding), when he really means something different? Does he mean that there is a blank space in his mind where the analogous particularities of history ought to be? Or does George Eliot mean to call attention to a problem inherent in realism, namely the superabundance of historical particularities? These inexhaustible particularities might be placed in metonymic contiguity beside any low subject. This would make a potentially endless serial work in which this is like this is like this is like this is like this, and so on. It is a requirement of realism that all things be thought of with particularity. The double bind of this mode is that if low subjects are left unadorned in their lowness, not "illustrated," they are merely low, "bad habits and ugly consequences" surrounded by a blank. If the particularities of history are adduced to "elevate" them, there could never be enough space for the narration.

The untying of this knot is achieved by a shift to the alternative way of elevating a low subject, the "easier and shorter way to dignity." It is shorter because the mode of analogy is parabolic rather than historical, particular, and accumulative. In the parabolic or allegorical mode anything can stand for anything, since the kind of equivalence is arbitrary and linguistic rather than objective and realistic. The smallest, briefest, simplest thing can stand for the largest and most complex. This is a laconic pastoral mode where little stands for great and much is said in less. Two models or figures are given in the passage for this parabolic mode. These are parables for parable. One is the arbitrary character of linguistic signs. The other is the way money works.

The word "monkey" just happens to sound like the word "margrave." One word alliterates with the other, as "lord" sounds like "looby," though the things designated by these pairs have no (apparent) similarity. In historical reality a monkey is not like a margrave, nor a lord like a looby, but in parable they are, by the accidental similarity of the sounds. There are two meanings for the word "truth" in the passage, one historical or "realistic," the other parabolic. When the narrator says, "while I tell the truth about loobies," he means representational, mimetic truth, the truth of correspondence. When he says, "there never was a true story which could not be told in parables where you might put a monkey for a margrave, and *vice versa*," the truth is of a different sort. The mode of representation appropriate to parable is not that of one-to-one correspondence, but that of a figurative standing for, a sign-to-sign temporal relation like de Manian allegory. It is temporal because, as de Man implies, language is always a temporal sequence, one sign after another.[9] Eliot's parabolic mode is the substitution of one thing in emblematic shorthand for something that it "not more than figuratively" resembles.

To call parable figurative, however, is misleading, since the concept "figurative" derives from the concept "literal" and depends on it. In the case of parable, the relation is reversible. You can put a monkey for a margrave, and *vice versa*. The most literal representation, for example George Eliot's description of Peter Featherstone's funeral, is also emblematic, which is why it is "not more than figuratively ungenteel." This, paradoxically, is a way of saying that figuratively it is genteel. It is figurative through and through, and at the same time literal, which would also be the case of any conceivable description of a monkey, a looby, a margrave, or a lord. The distinction between literal and figurative breaks down in parabolic representation, or is scattered. It is replaced by a mode of truth generated by the relation between two interchangeable signs, for example monkey and margrave, or lord and looby, or Jupiter and Judy, each of which is both literal and figurative, each of which can stand for the other or be stood for by it. Each is figurative, a parable for the other as literal, but the other, when the reader turns to it, is figurative in its turn. The relation between these signs is not that of objective similarity but a relation as arbitrary and conventional as the contingent fact that they start with the same letter. The truth-generating relation here is like that between two negatives—"not . . . not," or "not . . . un-," or "not . . . ex-." In copulation these produce not a literal positive but a parabolic positive. It is a positive always ironically hollowed out by the negatives that have gone into its making.

The truth-value of parable is, moreover, like the value of money. It is like the ascription of an arbitrary exchange-value to bits of paper or metal that do not intrinsically have that worth. The same bit of paper or metal may, absurdly, be made more valuable by stamping more zeroes on it. The "transactions" among parabolic signs, like the "commercial transactions" carried on with money, are performed always with remnants left over from a prior bankruptcy or reducing to zero. The truth of a parabolic emblem is made of the ruin or emptying out of the referential truth-value of the elements that enter into it. This odd fact about money and about parables—that their value is always constructed over a zero, or with what is left after a reduction to zero—is indicated in the introduction of the notion of bankruptcy in the sentence which ends the paragraph: "the petty sums which any bankrupt of high standing would be sorry to retire upon, may be lifted to the level of high commercial transactions by the inexpensive addition of proportional ciphers."[10]

If the parable of money as a parable for parable is set against the parable of the pier-glass, a difference emerges. The difference is that the latter is presented as an emblem of the universal egotism of mankind and womankind, whereas the former is an emblem of the working of parable itself. Nevertheless, as I argued in my discussion of the pier-glass passage, an element of self-analysis is intrinsic to the parabolic method as George Eliot uses it. One passage in any case interprets the other. The parable of the banknote indicates that the parable of the pier-glass does not just have to do with "seeing," nor does it just argue that each man's or woman's egotistic perspective on the world distorts what is seen according to the needs and desires of the ego. Nor is its "literal" subject Rosamond's distorted vision. Both sides of the equation it makes are parables for the universal act of interpretation that encompasses them. Interpretation confronts things as signs to be read, not as objects to be seen correctly or incorrectly. To see something as sign is to see it as figure. To see it as figure is to see it as standing for something else with which it is not identical or which it does not literally picture. If the series of scenes of Dorothea looking out a window or looking at the colossal spectacle of Rome show her spontaneously reading the world parabolically, the parable of the pier-glass and the parable of the banknote show the narrator reading the world in the same way. This is true not only when he is most overtly emblematic but also when he seems most "real-

istic," most intent on "telling the truth about loobies" with full historical, sociological, and psychological particularity.

The narration as a whole is simultaneously realistic and parabolic or
allegorical throughout. It tells the truth about loobies. By means of that
as vehicle it tells at the same time that sort of allegorical truth that may
be told as well by means of a monkey as by a margrave. Or rather, such
truth is told by their substitution one for the other in a relation in which
each is a figure for the other, and neither has the priority of the literal.
The relation among the various plots in *Middlemarch* is an example of
this. Each repeats the others in a different mode, but none, not even the
story of Dorothea, is, in the completed text, the "original" of which
the others are repetitions with a difference. George Eliot indicates this
multi-centered nature of *Middlemarch* when, in a passage already cited,
he says, "But why always Dorothea? . . . Mr Casaubon [too] had an
intense consciousness within him" (29: 309, 310). This consciousness is
"an *equivalent* centre of self" (21: 235, my italics).

Money as Universal Measure

My discussion of money's properties as a figure of figure in *Middlemarch*
will help understand the role of money in the various plots. All the
stories Eliot tells involve money as an essential ingredient. A shorthand
formulation would assert that *Middlemarch* as a totality registers a
certain historical stage in England's transition from a feudal society
based on putative absolute or transcendent values to a capitalist society
in which money is the universal standard and the universal solvent.

On the one hand, remnants of the feudal class structure still have
great power in Middlemarch, as in the "nice distinctions of rank" (23:
258) that all to some degree accept and that Mrs. Cadwallader's ideology embodies. Rosamond marries Lydgate in part because she has a
fantasy that his aristocratic relatives will accept her and that she will
thereby leap much higher on the social ladder. Dorothea's marriage to
Casaubon rather than to the eminently eligible Sir James Chettam was
bad enough, but her ultimate marriage to Will Ladislaw, an outsider of
low birth, is even worse. It destroys her social standing in the eyes of her
Middlemarch neighbors.

On the other hand, money enters decisively into the lives of all the
characters. Lydgate's hopes of becoming a distinguished medical scientist
are dashed by Rosamond's profligate spending in order to keep up her
idea of her social rank and by his inability to make enough income from
his medical practice to support their household at the level Rosamond

quietly but inflexibly demands. In order to marry Ladislaw Dorothea must give up her inheritance from Casaubon, according to the cruel but prescient terms of Casaubon's will. She becomes a relatively poor woman, with an income of only 700 pounds a year from the bequest of another relative, but she lives happily ever after. Fred Vincy must learn from Caleb Garth to give up gambling as well as his vague hopes that Providence will be good to him. He must decide to work for a living as a farmer in order to deserve marriage to Mary Garth. Bulstrode's social standing is destroyed when his previous secret chicanery to disinherit Will Ladislaw and make himself rich is revealed. Specific details are given about the amounts of money Bulstrode gives to Raffles to bribe the latter to keep his secret. The Reverend Farebrother has to use his earnings from card-playing to make ends meet before Dorothea, as Casaubon's heiress, grants him a living as rector of Lowick.

The comedy of the way that clever old rogue Peter Featherstone fools all his relatives as well as Fred Vincy into thinking they are named in his will as rich legatees is a version of a common motif in Victorian fiction: the sinister power a rich man has by way of his ability to make wills and then cancel them in new wills. Featherstone "loved money," but "perhaps he loved it best of all as a means of making others feel his power more or less uncomfortably" (34: 359). Anthony Trollope's late novel, *Mr. Scarborough's Family* (1883), is a good example of the persistence of this narrative motif of the rich man's ever-renewed will-making. The motif often involves questions of legitimacy and illegitimacy, as well as extremely tangled and often secret family relationships, such as those that are conspicuously the case in *Middlemarch*. In that novel everyone seems to be related to everyone else, either by birth or by marriage. When Featherstone's will is read before all his assembled relatives, it turns out that he has left almost all his estate to an unpleasant frog-faced stranger, his illegitimate son Joshua Rigg.

Mrs. Cadwallader believes in "birth or no-birth" (6: 65) as an absolute standard. The novel shows that "money or no money" is instead rapidly becoming the sovereign standard in England around 1830, that is, at the historical moment just before the Reform Bill of 1832 that did much to weaken the feudal system in England. This acceptance of money as universal measure is hyperbolically the case, by the way, for that suicidal plutocracy, the United States, in 2011, though without a counterforce in any belief in a feudal class system. Just what is the difference between the two standards? The feudal class system assumed a ground in a transcendental source, support of transcendent values. In short, it was a version of "logocentrism." As I have shown, *Middlemarch* is a devastating critique of logocentrism. It shows the malign effect of various forms of fatuous belief in assumptions about teleological sequence held by the main characters. These beliefs are not only shown to be false. They are also shown to be the source of much suffering for those beguiled by them. As the analysis of money presupposed in the chain of money figures I have interpreted shows, money has no transcendent ground. It is an immanent system of valuation governed by fictitious exchanges subject to speculative inflation, as in the periodic bank and financial crises in Victorian England, not to speak of the recent twenty-first-century global financial "meltdown."

The hyperbolic mirror of the power of zero is the global Great Recession of 2008 and subsequent years. This was brought about by the unregulated ability by those running banks and financial institutions, in their limitless greed, to make money out of money through "derivatives" and other complex financial instruments, such as "credit default swaps." These unscrupulous villains learned how to add zeroes to digits and make 10 into 100, 1,000, 10,000, *ad infinitum*, until the Ponzi scheme bubbles burst. This financial collapse has caused great suffering to ordinary people in the form of high unemployment, foreclosed mortgages, loss of pensions, and so on. The financial crisis has caused great suffering, that is, to everyone but the bankers and financiers. They have, most of them, escaped scot free. They are already making huge profits once more. They are busy paying themselves big salaries and bonuses. They are setting things up for the next financial crisis. They are doing this with much help from politicians, especially but not only, in the United States, Republican politicians. The latter are already (February 2011) plotting how to weaken the Financial Reform Bill that the United States Congress passed when the Democrats still controlled both houses of Congress. Eliot shows in *Middlemarch*, in a quasi-Marxist way, the dangerous power of money as supreme fiction. She did not, apparently, know Marx's work, but she had read many of the political economists Marx read.

Eliot's novels can nevertheless have quasi-conventional happy endings, at least for Fred and Mary, Dorothea and Will. I shall later discuss what is problematic about the endings of *Middlemarch*. These endings are marriages that are based on affection and sympathy. Those emotions exceed the actual worth, both financial and personal, of the loved person. These happy marriages are seen as not dependent on the dying feudal class system, or on the capitalist money system. The ungrounded human power of love and sympathy is George Eliot's replacement for the vanished transcendent logos. Marian Evans's own domestic happiness came through a liaison with a married man, G. H. Lewes, in defiance of the sanctity of marriage.

The Uses of Art

In the context of the ironic passage about raising a low subject by making it stand for aristocrats (loobies for lords), it is possible to assess the complex irony of another place where the question of art surfaces. This is the sequence of two scenes in Rome in which Will Ladislaw and Dorothea discuss art in general and Will's grandiose paintings in particular. The overt purpose of the scenes seems to be to manifest again Dorothea's uneasiness about art. They also aim to debunk the Hegelian theory of art as it is represented by the work of Naumann, the "Nazarene,"[11] and, in self-conscious parody, by Will's paintings. "[I]n Rome," says Dorothea to Will Ladislaw, "it seems as if there were so many things, which are more wanted in the world than pictures" (21: 230). She continues in a later conversation with Will: "I should like to make life beautiful—I mean everybody's life. And then all this immense expanse of art, that seems somehow to lie outside life and make it no better for the world, pains one. It spoils my enjoyment of anything when I am made to think that most people are shut out from it" (22: 244). This sentiment finds its echo now (2011) in my anxiety about what good art and literature can be in these bad times of climate change and global recession. To Dorothea's "fanaticism of sympathy," as Will calls it, he opposes his own piety of enjoyment: "The best piety is to enjoy—when you can. You are doing the most then to save the earth's character as an agreeable planet. And enjoyment radiates. It is of no use to try and take care of all the world; that is being taken care of when you feel delight—in art or in anything else" (22: 244). Will's attitude corresponds, more or less, to my Kantian conviction, and, in a different way, to that of Harold Bloom, for example in his new book, *The Anatomy of Influence: Literature as a Way of Life*,[12] that enjoyment of literature and art is its own end. Art and literature are an inexhaustible enrichment of the lives of those who open themselves to such things. Such a conviction does not cut much ice with many people these days.

There is no doubt that matters of fundamental importance are at stake here. These include the historical, ethical, and ontological issues that are woven into the fabric of *Middlemarch* throughout. They include also questions about the function of the novel itself that keep appearing obliquely here and there. An example is that opening scene in which Dorothea, in spite of herself, takes pleasure in the beauty of her mother's gems. Should we take pleasure in the beauty of *Middlemarch*? In a not altogether obscure way *Middlemarch* raises the question of Marian Evans's vocation as an artist, the uneasy question of the utility of *Middlemarch* itself, and the even more uneasy question of the relative claims, in Marian Evans's ethical life, of renunciation, of a masochistic narrowing and giving up (which have their pleasures), as against open "enjoyment" of art or of even more forbidden sensuous pleasures. Reading novels was still considered immoral by many in the Victorian era because such reading was thought to give a pleasure obscurely, or not so obscurely, like sexual pleasure. No doubt activating the imaginary, whether in dreams, reveries, or reading literature, always has a sexual component. These large issues are not unrelated to the question of the relative values of the parabolic/allegorical and realistic modes in art. Both are part of Marian Evans's attempt to find meaning and value in a world lacking transcendent ground. In place of such a ground Eliot places what she calls, in a notable passage, "the roar on the other side of silence," that is, a formless, inarticulate chaos, something like the imaginary "in itself," as Iser defines it. I shall return later to that roar.

Dorothea's error is to try and take care of all the world. She thinks in terms of all-embracing totalities. She is unwilling to make one life beautiful if she cannot make them all beautiful, one by one. Her problem, as the reader learns in the early chapters of the novel, is that she wants each particular person to remain what he or she is, and at the same time she wants each person to play an effective role in the total march of history toward an ideal end. On one side, her attitude corresponds to a naive realism in art, with its respect for particulars; on the other side, to a naive idealism in real life, with its millennial hopes. This mixture indicates the secret relation of realism to teleological systems such as Hegel's.

Will Ladislaw, on the other hand, recommends a blind enjoyment in what is near at hand, without thought for ideal ends. These will take care of themselves, since "enjoyment radiates." Such enjoyment is both concretely itself and at the same time radiates out into the whole. As Will says, "all the world" is "being taken care of" when one person, Dorothea for example, "feel[s] delight—in art or in anything else." Such enjoyment corresponds to the parabolic or allegorical method in art. It stands for the whole while at the same time being different from it, in a form of particularity differing essentially from the concrete universal of Hegel or from the "idealistic in the real" (22: 239), in Naumann's phrase for Casaubon's physiognomy. Naumann sketches Casaubon as St. Thomas Aquinas. It is a comic allegorical representation, with the egregious Casaubon standing for Aquinas. The concept of the "all" in Will's pronouncements must be also different from the Hegelian one. It must be a non-synthesizable totality, a totality not oriented toward an absolute goal, and not open to dialectical "sublation" or *Aufhebung*. It is an assemblage of just those things and people that happen to be there. Into this assemblage a particular example of enjoyment "radiates," having such effect as it does have. This effect is unpredictable and immeasurable. It is "incalculably diffusive" (Finale: 924), like a good person, or like a work of art—like *Middlemarch* itself. This novel has had, over the years, incalculably diverse effects on its readers. The manifest reduction, these days, in the number of people capable of reading, or willing to read, *Middlemarch* is a significant loss for human life. You cannot read *Middlemarch* and play World of Warcraft, or "text," or "Tweet" at the same time, though some young people, adept at multitasking, might claim that you can.

The notions of enjoyment, of ethical quality, and of the function of art in *Middlemarch* define them all as, in different ways, performatives. Enjoyment, the state of being good, and a work of art are each of value because they make something happen. When Will says being a poet means having "a soul in which knowledge passes instantaneously into feeling and feeling flashes back as a new organ of knowledge," Dorothea answers: "But you leave out the poems ... I think they are wanted to complete the poet. I understand what you mean about knowledge passing into feeling, for that seems to be just what I experience. But I am sure I could never produce a poem." To which Will replies: "You are a poem" (22: 249). She *is* a poem because, like a poem, she "produces" by being what she is. She performs by being herself, as in its way does a great novel like *Middlemarch*. The exact form of these performatives remains to be identified.

Discussion of an earlier interchange between Will and Dorothea will explain this further. The passage passes judgment on the Hegelian theory of art in one direction and on Marian Evans's parabolic method in the other. The Hegelian system is present in the derived form of the Nazarene theory of art. Naumann is "one of the chief renovators of Christian art, one of those who had not only revived but expanded that grand conception of supreme events as mysteries at which the successive ages were spectators, and in relation to which the great souls of all periods became as it were contemporaries" (22: 237). Naumann's current painting is "the Saints drawing the Car of the Church" (ibid.). Will Ladislaw's painting is a parodic mockery of Naumann's. It is not simply negative, however, since it obliquely presents an example of George Eliot's parabolic method. It ironically mocks *Middlemarch* itself. At the same time it exposes the novel's mode of working for those who have eyes to see and read. Will's painting is a sketch of Marlowe's "Tamburlaine Driving the Conquered Kings in his Chariot" (22: 237). Will's interpretation of his painting and the shared irony of the interchange between Will and Dorothea about it, evidence of an intimacy growing in spite of their intent, must be cited in full:

"I take Tamburlaine in his chariot for the tremendous course of the world's physical history lashing on the harnessed dynasties. In my opinion, that is a good mythical interpretation . . ."

"The sketch must be very grand, if it conveys so much," said Dorothea. "I should need some explanation even of the meaning you give. Do you intend Tamburlaine to represent earthquakes and volcanoes?"

"Oh yes," said Will, laughing, "and migrations of races and clearings of forests—and America and the steam-engine. Everything you can imagine!"

"What a difficult kind of shorthand!" said Dorothea, smiling towards her husband. "It would require all your knowledge to be able to read it." (22: 237–8)

For Naumann and Will Ladislaw, as for Walter Benjamin's theory of allegory, anything can stand for anything you wish, though in different ways in each case. Naumann's Car of the Church and Will's chariot are both emblems of history's process. Naumann's history has origins, grand events, and goals. Will's history is physical nature as it affects human culture. It has no discernible goal. It is "just one damn thing after another." What Naumann paints and the meaning of his painting are related by an evident similarity, since the Car of the Church drawn by the Saints stands for the Church as the chief determiner of world history. Will's painting is parabolic in the sense that there is no evident similarity between the overt subject of the painting and what it stands for. One relatively insignificant particularity, Tamburlaine in his chariot, stands for "everything you can imagine." (Its covert significance may be the evidence it gives that George Eliot, like Shakespeare, Milton, and others, was influenced by Marlowe's stylistic grandeur, in this case in Marlowe's play, *Tamberlaine* [1587].) As in the case of George Eliot's parables in *Middlemarch*, interpretation is necessary to make such meanings clear. George Eliot gives such interpretations of her parable of the pier-glass and of what might be called her parable of the banknote. As a piece of paper or metal can be stamped or coined into money of any denomination, so Will makes Tamburlaine stand for anything whatsoever. It is "a difficult kind of shorthand" based on difference and on the arbitrary assignation of meaning or value.

Conclusions About Metaphor

I can now draw conclusions about the effect on the meaning and artistic procedure of *Middlemarch* of the third family of metaphors, the one involving signs and the reading of signs. The working of such metaphors is essentially different from that of the web family or the optic family.

In several ways this working subverts both the apparent meaning of the novel and the procedure I have ostensibly employed to read it. It breaks down the distinction between the blind infatuation of the characters and the sovereign insight of the narrator. Both the narrator's rhetoric and my reading have tended to accept this distinction. It breaks down the distinctions among the families of metaphors on which my interpretation has depended. It breaks down the distinction between objective reality and figural description of that reality on which both the novel and my interpretation of it have seemed to depend, in spite of my caveat about "metaphor of metaphor." If the working of a figure for sign making and sign reading puts in question the narrator's enterprise of total insight into the characters and into the society in which they live, it also puts in question the power of the reader or critic to make total sense of the novel. The reader is caught in the same predicament as the narrator's, just as the narrator is caught in the same predicament as the characters'. The narrator's "unweaving" of the characters' subjective webs turns back to unravel the web of interpretation woven by the narrator and by the reader. What is true of the characters must be true of the narrator and true also of you and me.

What is true of the characters, the reader knows. They get their thoughts entangled in metaphors and act fatally on the strength of them. They take figurative similarities as identities and assume that those identities are governed by some absolute origin or end. The implication of the narrator's analysis of the characters may seem at first to be that they could see clearly and live happily if they would only disentangle their thoughts from metaphors and live in terms of lucid perception and literal naming of things as they are. Such seeing and naming would make no false assumptions that things as they are make up a grand totality coming from one source and bound for an ideal end. The narrator's analysis indicates that this is impossible. The only alternative to one metaphor is another metaphor. Metaphors may be fatal, but there is no thinking or doing without them. This fact may be hidden in the analysis of a fictive person, Dorothea or Casaubon, Lydgate or Fred Vincy, characters each of whom is beguiled primarily by only one network of related figures. It would appear that the single person could be cured of his single error. One might even be tempted to believe Eliot is saying that the fatal danger in living in terms of a private metaphorical system is not that it is a fiction but that it is an unshared fiction. A viable society is a community living together in terms of a single metaphorical system, such as Christianity.

The trouble with this argument is that Eliot shows how any metaphorical system, even a collective one, leads to fatal errors of judgment and action. It does this apparently because it collides with "reality," things as they are. The fatal results of our politicians' ideological mistakes today are an example or this, for example the false assumption that tax cuts for the rich will "trickle down," or the denial of climate change. Dorothea comes up against what the narrator calls the damp emotional coldness of Casaubon and his almost irremediable egoism. These make him entirely different from Dorothea's mistaken reading of him. But "damp" and "cold" are metaphors too. The narrator's interpretation of Casaubon is as metaphorical as Dorothea's, as when he says; "There is a sort of jealousy which needs very little fire: it is hardly a passion, but a blight bred in the cloudy, damp despondency of uneasy egoism" (21: 234–5). Egoism is here expressed in the powerfully suggestive figure of a blight-breeding swamp. Though passions such as jealousy have literal names, their force can best be expressed in tropes. The narrator dismantles Dorothea's metaphorical reading of Casaubon not by presenting the unadorned "truth" about him, but by presenting an alternative metaphorical picture. This remains the case even if we think of Casaubon as an "objective reality" existing outside George Eliot's language, which of course he is not.

O Aristotle!

Something of Marian Evans's understanding of what it means to say that the only alternative to a metaphor is another metaphor, the only tool to deconstruct figure is figure itself, is indicated in a sad and yet comic passage written over a decade before the time of *Middlemarch*'s writing. The passage appears in *The Mill on the Floss* (1860). Here the narrator already formulates his recognition of an alarming power inherent in figurative language. This is its power to undo any attempt to make a completely coherent picture of human life. If we can seldom say what a thing is without saying it is something else, without speaking parabolically, then there is no way to avoid the possibility of altering the meaning by altering the metaphor. No one metaphor or even group of metaphors can give a total picture. The possibility of adding yet another trope, and then another, always exists, as, in *Middlemarch*, the metaphor of eating is added to the metaphor of the microscope, and the metaphor of tax gathering added to the metaphor of eating. Each of these metaphors works differently. Each makes something happen, but each is curiously ineffective in dealing with things as they are. The method of description by metaphor is intrinsically non-totalizable. The passage has to do with poor Tom Tulliver's sufferings at school at the hands of his teacher, Mr. Stelling. It might have as title "The Beaver, the Camel, and the Shrewmouse":

> Mr Broderip's amiable beaver, as that charming naturalist tells us, busied himself earnestly constructing a dam, in a room up three pairs of stairs in London, as if he had been laying his foundation in a stream or lake in Upper Canada ... With the same unerring instinct Mr Stelling set to work at his natural method of instilling the Eton Grammar and Euclid into the mind of Tom Tulliver ...
> [Mr Stelling] very soon set down poor Tom as a thoroughly stupid lad; for though by hard labour he could get particular declensions into his brain, anything so abstract as the relation between cases and terminations could by no means get such a lodgment there as to enable him to recognize a chance genitive or dative ... Mr Stelling concluded that Tom's brain being peculiarly impervious to etymology and demonstrations, was peculiarly in need of being ploughed and harrowed by these patent implements: it was his favourite metaphor, that the classics and geometry constituted that culture of the mind which prepared it for the reception of any subsequent crop. I say nothing against Mr Stelling's theory: if we are to have one regimen for all minds, his seems to me as good as any other. I only know it turned out as uncomfortably for Tom Tulliver as if he had been plied with cheese in order to remedy a gastric weakness which prevented him from digesting it. It is astonishing what a different result one gets by changing the metaphor! Once call the brain an intellectual stomach, and one's ingenious conception of the classics and geometry as ploughs and harrows seems to settle nothing. But then it is open to some one else to follow great authorities, and call the mind a sheet of white paper or a mirror, in which case one's knowledge of the digestive process becomes quite irrelevant. It was doubtless an ingenious idea to call the camel the ship of the desert, but it would hardly lead one far in training that useful beast. O Aristotle! if you had had the advantage of being "the freshest modern" instead of the greatest ancient, would you not have mingled your praise of metaphorical speech, as a sign of high intelligence, with a lamentation that intelligence so rarely shows itself in speech without metaphor,—that we can so seldom declare what a thing is, except by saying it is something else?[13]

This admirable passage rises from height to height to a high summit, or falls from depth to depth of bathos, by a continual process of capping itself or going itself one better. It might be said that it constantly deconstructs itself. The passage speaks of the activity of reading, proffers a model of that activity, and invites us to read it according to the method it employs. Though good reading perhaps does not occur as often as one might expect or hope, it is by no means confined to one historical period. It may appear at any time, perhaps most often in those who, like George Eliot, are also good writers. The deconstructive movement of this passage, if I may dare to call it that, is made up of the proffering and withdrawal of one metaphorical formulation after another. Each metaphor is dismantled as soon as it is proposed, though the sad necessity of using metaphors is at the same time affirmed. No doubt most teachers of English grammar and composition, like teachers of Latin, such as remain, have experienced Mr. Stelling's exasperation at the obduracy and denseness of their students' inability to remember the rules of grammar or to grasp syntactical concepts. Nevertheless, such students speak with fluency and force, just as Tom Tulliver "was in a state bordering on idiocy with regard to the demonstration that two given triangles must be equal—though he could discern with great promptitude and certainty the fact that they *were* equal" (ibid., 208). Though Tom cannot learn Latin grammar, he uses English with devastating cruelty toward his sister.

It might seem that Eliot is opposing the use of literal language to the abuse of metaphorical language. She may be counseling the former in a way that recalls the late-seventeenth- and eighteenth-century tradition alluded to in her Lockean figure of the mind as a white sheet of paper. On the contrary, the passage demonstrates that "rarely" or "seldom" seems to be "never." The only weapon against a metaphor is another metaphor, along with an awareness of our linguistic predicament in not being able—or in being so seldom able that "rarely" is "almost never"—to declare what a thing is, except by saying that it is something else. Mr. Stelling's problem is not that he uses the metaphors of plowing and harrowing for his teaching of Euclid and the Eton grammar, but that he takes his metaphors literally. He has no awareness of their limitation. He uses them as the excuse for a brutally inappropriate mode of instruction for Tom. The pedagogy of English composition these days for the most part eschews rote learning. I was as a child, however, still taught to diagram sentences and to distinguish a gerund from a gerundive. The double (and highly problematic) assumption was that grammatical terms derived from Latin grammar apply without problems to English grammar, and that knowing a gerund from a gerundive makes you a better writer. Mr. Stelling teaches "with the uniformity of method and independence of circumstances, which distinguishes the actions of animals understood to be under the immediate teaching of nature," such as that beaver who builds a dam "up three pairs of stairs in London," in sublime indifference to the absence of water (ibid., 206). The beaver, like Mr. Stelling, is a literalist of the imagination. To take a metaphor literally is the aboriginal, universal, linguistic error, something we may even share with animals. We all get our thoughts entangled in metaphors and act fatally on the strength of them.

The escape from this entanglement in the net of metaphor (another metaphor!) is not a substitution of literal language for misleading figures. It is rather the replacement of one metaphor by another. The second metaphor may neutralize the first or cancel out its distortions. This is a cure of metaphor by metaphor, a version of homeopathy. So Eliot replaces the metaphor of plowing and harrowing, which has already replaced the more covert metaphor in "instilling," with the metaphor of eating. Forcing geometry and Latin grammar on Tom is like curing an inability to digest cheese with doses of cheese, or, the reader might reflect, replacing one kind of cheese with another kind of cheese. It is at this point that the narrator draws himself up and makes the exclamation about how astonishing it is what different result one gets by changing the metaphor.

To the other figures here must be added irony and prosopopoeia, irony as the pervasive tone of the narration and personification as the trope whereby the ironic discrepancy between narrator and character is given a name and a personality in the putative storyteller, "George Eliot." That narrator pretends to have made Mr. Stelling's mistake, or the beaver's mistake—namely, to have used metaphor without reflection—and then to have been surprised by the results into having a metalinguistic insight into the role of metaphor in social life, for example in pedagogical theory. But of course the narrator has been aware of this all along, He (she? it?) is manipulating the metaphors in full deliberate awareness. He only pretends to be astonished. The sentence is ironic in the strict sense that it says the opposite of what it means, or rather it says both things at once, indiscernibly or undecidably, as is the way with irony. It is astonishing and not astonishing. The reader is challenged to ally herself with one side or the other, though at the same time she is put in a double bind. If she is not astonished, she may be putting herself unwittingly in the same camp as the beaver and Mr. Stelling. Another way to define a literalist is to say that she is incapable of being astonished by the workings of language. If the reader is astonished, then she is admitting that, until a moment ago at least, she was a linguistic innocent, lagging behind the all-knowing narrator, who only ironically pretends to be astonished by something that he has known all along.

The digestive metaphor is then followed by two traditional metaphors for the mind—the Lockean one of the blank sheet of paper and the figure of the mirror, which, as my discussion of chapter 17 of *Adam Bede* has shown, has had a long history in descriptions of realism in the novel, all the way down to sophisticated twentieth-century theorists like Georg Lukács, and including of course George Eliot along the way.

The next metaphor, that of the camel as the ship of the desert, seems to be irrelevant or non-functional, not part of the chain, no more than a textbook example of metaphor.[14] It allows, however, the bringing in of

Aristotle and the opposition between the ancients who naively praised metaphor, on the one hand, and the moderns, such as Locke, who lament its presence in language and try (unsuccessfully) to expunge it, on the other. Aristotle did not, strictly speaking, "praise . . . metaphorical speech as a sign of high intelligence," as Eliot says. Aristotle affirmed, rather, that "a command of metaphor" is the "mark of genius," "the greatest thing by far," in a poet, the one thing that "cannot be imparted by another."[15] A command of metaphor is for Aristotle not so much a sign of intelligence as an intuitive gift, "an eye for resemblances" (ibid.). The poet does not rationally think out metaphors. They just come to him or her in a flash, or they just fall under the poet's eye. The passage from *The Mill on the Floss*, however, shows that "*command* of metaphor" is impossible, however fecund a good poet may be in inventing or discovering good ones.

The figure of the camel as a ship makes three simultaneous moves in the intricate sequence of Eliot's thought in the passage as a whole.

First move: the image of the camel more or less (though not quite, as I shall show) completes the repertoire of exemplary metaphors that makes the passage not only a miniature treatise on metaphor, but also, unostentatiously, an anthology, bouquet, herbarium, or bestiary of the basic metaphors in the Western tradition—that is, coming down from the Bible and the Greeks. No choice of examples is innocent. It is no accident that metaphors of farming and sowing (for example, in Plato's *Phaedrus* or in Christ's parable of the sower [Matt. 13: 3–23], with the sun lurking somewhere as the source of germination); metaphors of specular reflection, the play of light, of images, of mirroring, and of seeing; metaphors of eating, or of writing on that white sheet of paper, or of journeying from here to there (that is, of transport, whether by camel or on shipboard)—all tend to reappear, whenever someone from Aristotle down to the freshest modern teacher of composition pulls an example of metaphor out of his or her pedagogical hat. These remain the basic metaphors still today. Though a good reader will not necessarily have the poet's instinctive "command" of them, she can thread her way adeptly from one to another in their interchangeability and at least confront the problems they raise. If the ship plowing the waves (an example from Aristotle) mixes the agricultural with the nautical regions of figure, the sowing of seed, for both Plato and Jesus, is a form of writing, a dissemination of the word. And does not the assimilation of learning to eating appear in that extraordinary image of Ezekiel eating the magically proffered scroll (Ezek. 2: 9–10; 3: 1–3), as well as in Hegel's interpretation of the Last Supper in "The Spirit of Christianity and Its Fate" (written 1799, published posthumously), or in the Communion

Service itself, in which the communicants eat the *Logos,* or in that strange passage in *Middlemarch,* already discussed, about the voracious little creatures seen under a microscope that figure Mrs. Cadwallader's circulation in the community to learn things, that is, to pick up gossip, which is "the sort of food she needed," so she can make new things happen (6: 65)?

Second move: the camel as ship of the desert is not just a random example of a metaphor. It is a metaphor of metaphor. It figures transfer or transport from one place to another. That is not only what "metaphor" means etymologically, but also what metaphor does. It effects a transfer. If George Puttenham's far-fetched Renaissance name for metalepsis is the "Far-fetcher," he elsewhere calls metaphor the "Figure of Transport."[16] Metaphor gets the writer, reader, speaker, or listener from here to there in her argument, whether by that "smooth gradation or gentle transition, to some other kindred quality," of which Wordsworth speaks in the "Essay upon Epitaphs,"[17] following Socrates in the *Phaedrus* on "shifting your ground little by little,"[18] or by the sudden leap over a vacant place in the argument, of which George Meredith writes: "It is the excelling merit of similes and metaphors to spring us to vault over gaps and thickets and dreary places."[19] Pedagogy is metaphor. It takes the mind of the student and transforms it, transfers it, translates it, ferries it from here to there. A teaching method, such as Mr. Stelling's, is as much a means of transportation as is a camel or a ship. My own "passage" from Eliot is a synecdoche, a part taken from a larger whole and used as a figurative means of passage from one place to another in my readings of *Adam Bede* and *Middlemarch.*

Third move: the sentence about the camel brings into the open the asymmetrical relation between the opposition between theory and figurative language, on the one hand, and the opposition between theory and practice, on the other. The reader may be inclined to think that these are parallel, but this probably depends on a confusion of mind. One thinks of literal language as the clear, non-figurative expression of ideas or concepts: for example the abstract concepts of grammar, such as the relations between cases and endings in the genitive and the dative. Tom Tulliver has as much trouble learning these as a modern student of English composition has learning the rules of English grammar. Knowing those rules is, however, evidently not required in order to be able to write clearly and correctly. Tom Tulliver can see clearly that the two equal triangles are equal, though he cannot prove it, just as he speaks forceful and correct English. Those old Romans, educated and uneducated, presumably spoke good Latin without necessarily knowing anything about the abstract rules of conjugation, declension, and case

endings. One thinks of literal language as the act of non-figurative nomination, calling a spade a spade and a camel a camel, not a ship of the
desert. We tend to think of figure as applied at either end of the scale
from abstract to concrete. Figure is an additional ornament making
the literal expression "clearer," more "vivid," more "forceful," more
"concrete." As Eliot's passage makes clear, however, the trouble with
theory is not that it is abstract or conceptual, but that is always based on
metaphor—that is, it commits what Alfred North Whitehead in *Science
and the Modern World* calls "the fallacy of misplaced concreteness."[20]

Original thinking is most often started by a metaphor, as Whitehead
and such literary theorists as William Empson and Kenneth Burke affirm
in different ways. An example would be the assumption in old-fashioned
behaviorism that human beings are like rats in a maze. Therefore study-
ing rats tells you something about human beings. Each metaphorically
based theory, however, such as the various alternative pedagogical
theories that Eliot sketches out, has its own built-in fallacious bias and
leads to its own special form of catastrophe in the classroom. John B.
Watson's behaviorist theories of child-rearing led to cruel neglect of
babies when they were put into practice. If a camel is not a ship, the
brain is neither a field to plow, nor a stomach, nor a sheet of paper,
nor a mirror, though each of these metaphors could, and has, generated ponderous, solemn, and intellectually cogent theories of teaching.
Neither theory nor literal meaning, if there were such a thing (which
there is not), will help you with that camel. As soon as you try to tell
someone how to manage a camel, Eliot seems to think, you fall into
theory, that is, into some metaphorical scheme or other. The opposition
between theory and practice is not like that between metaphorical and
literal language, but is an opposition between language, which is always
figurative through and through, and no language—silent doing. If the
praxis in question is the act of writing, the habit of writing well, it can
be seen that problems will arise in teaching it, more problems even than
in teaching someone to drive a camel, or to butcher a carcass, cutting
it at the joints (one of Plato's examples), or to make a chair. That the
terms for the parts of a chair are examples of those basic personifying
catachreses, whereby we humanize the world and project arms and legs
where there are none, may cause little trouble as the apprentice learns
from watching a master cabinetmaker at work, but it might cause considerable trouble to someone who is writing as literally as possible about
chairs and how to make them.

After what has been said so far, the function of one more animal in
George Eliot's bestiary, the shrewmouse—the vehicle for the last metaphor in the sequence that I have lifted from her narrative—appears clear

enough. Having seemingly aligned herself with those fresh moderns who would opt for an antiseptic "speech without metaphor," Eliot, far from speaking without metaphor, goes on to present the most ostentatious and elaborate of all the metaphors in this sequence. It is ostentatious in the sense that the literal elaboration of the vehicle of the metaphor, a bit of Midlands agricultural folklore, seems far to exceed its parabolic application to Tom's suffering. The narrator, after putting metaphors in question, is almost immediately driven to use an ostentatious and force-ful figure. It is as if the narrator, in spite of himself, were compelled to provide another demonstration of the fact that we can seldom say what a thing is except by saying it is something else. Rather than burying this dependence on metaphor, the narrator somewhat shamefacedly brings it out in the open. The metaphor he uses is not at all inappropriate, but it is grotesque and wildly imaginative. It calls attention to itself, in part by the elaborate specificity with which it is worked out. This specificity exceeds its application to Tom. The metaphor proves that George Eliot has that gift for coining original figures that Aristotle said was the mark of genius in a poet. I cite it once more: "Tom was in a state of as blank unimaginativeness concerning the cause and tendency of his sufferings, as if he had been an innocent shrewmouse imprisoned in the split trunk of an ash-tree in order to cure lameness in cattle." The reference is to a folk belief that Eliot implicitly sees as a foolish superstition, as well as a cruel treatment of innocent shrewmice. The shrewmouse figure not only shows that "we can . . . seldom declare what a thing is, except by saying that it is something else." It also shows that the only cure for metaphor is not literal language, but another metaphor that so calls attention to itself that no one could miss that it is a metaphor. We cannot take the shrewmouse trope as innocently "dead," as one might with the term "instill" used for Mr. Stelling's goal of importing Latin grammar and Euclidean geometry into Tom Tulliver's mind. If literal language is pos-sible, it is likely, paradoxically, to occur in the elaboration of the vehicle of a figure, as in this case or as in the parables of Jesus in the Gospels. It is possible to speak literally about shrewmice in the Midlands or about the details of farming, fishing, and household care in Jesus's lifetime in Judaea, Samaria, and Galilee, but this literal speech often turns out, by a fatality intrinsic to language, to be the means of speaking parabolically about something else. The most figurative language, it would follow, is the language that appears to be the most literal, like the phrase "impris-oned in the split trunk of an ash-tree," or like Jesus' "Some fell upon stony places, where they had not much earth" in the parable of the sower. The good reader or writer is one who, like George Eliot, brings this distressing fact into the open, as secret writing in sympathetic ink beneath the writing on the surface is brought out by the application of heat or the right chemicals.

What is the source of my metaphor of "cure"? Is it my own licit or illicit addition, my reader's or interpreter's license? No, it is of course already there in my citation from Eliot. I have said that the shrewmouse is the last animal in George Eliot's bestiary and that the literal details of the shrewmouse's suffering exceed its figurative application. Obviously, neither of these is the case. The last animals are those lame cattle. They function to make the figure of the shrewmouse, at a second remove, a figure for the failure of teaching to cure lameness in the sense of linguistic incapacity—for example, an inability to learn the rules of Latin grammar. Mr. Stelling's pedagogy, based as it is on the magic literalizing of several metaphors, is as much a piece of superstition as is the countryman's belief about shrewmice and lame cattle. Which of us twenty-first-century teachers can be sure that our method is not another such blind belief in an unread metaphor?

The reader at the end of my sequence from *The Mill on the Floss* remains as trapped as ever within the linguistic double bind of not being able to say what a thing is, except by saying it is something else. Tom is imprisoned within the obstinate rigors of Mr. Stelling's pedagogy, rigors that result from the literal application of metaphors. His situation makes him like a poor innocent imprisoned shrewmouse. The melancholy, but also comic, wisdom of this passage affirms that the reader or writer of any sort—you or I—is imprisoned as much as Tom, Mr. Stelling, the shrewmouse, or George Eliot within the linguistic predicament that the passage both analyzes and exemplifies. The most that one can hope for is some clarification of the predicament, not escape from it into the light of day.

Both ordinary readers and professional literary critics should aim to become as good readers as Plato, George Eliot, or, in our day, Paul de Man or Jacques Derrida,[21] as wise in the ways of tropes, or else they will be even more likely to be bamboozled by ideological aberrations in what they read or in what they see in the media. If the medieval trivium of grammar, logic, and rhetoric is a place where these three disciplines come together at a crossroads, as the etymology of *trivium* suggests (*triviae*, "three roads"), it may be that rhetoric is not so much the climax of a progressive mastery of language both for reading and for writing as it is the place where the impossibility of mastery is decisively encountered. The road called "rhetoric" is always marked "impassable," or "under construction; pass at your own risk," or, as it is, or was, succinctly put on road signs in England: "Road Up!"

Paul de Man certainly thought this was the case with rhetoric as wrestling with tropes. In an interview with Robert Moynihan near the end of his life, de Man, in answer to a question about irony, asserted that "the claim of control, yes, when it is made, can always be shown to be unwarranted—one can show that the claim of control is a mistake, that there are elements in the text that are not controlled, that it is always possible to read the text against the overt claim of control."[22] In another essay, "Semiology and Rhetoric," discussing Archie Bunker's question about lacing one's shoes over or under, "What's the difference?" de Man asserts: "The grammatical model of the question becomes rhetorical not when we have, on the one hand, a literal meaning and on the other hand a figural meaning, but when it is impossible to decide by grammatical or other linguistic devices which of the two meanings (that can be entirely incompatible) prevails. Rhetoric radically suspends logic and opens up vertiginous possibilities of referential aberration . . . I would not hesitate to equate the rhetorical, figural potentiality of language with literature itself."[23]

At the end of *The Mill on the Floss* the grown-up Tom Tulliver is still "imprisoned within the limits of his own nature." "His education," says the narrator, "had simply glided over him, leaving a slight deposit of polish" (bk 7, ch. 3: 630). "Polish": that is a traditional metaphor for what education accomplishes. Such "polish" is like a commentary added to an unchangeable underlying text. In the passage I have discussed, Tom is already implicitly presented by the narrator as a text that cannot be read without the superimposition of a commentary in the form of one trope or another. As *Middlemarch* was over a decade later to demonstrate, Tom's kind of "blank unimaginativeness" about origin and end, "cause and tendency," could only be filled up by some archeological or eschatological metaphorical system like those that beguile Dorothea, Lydgate, or Bulstrode. Metaphors tend to proliferate, as the passage in *The Mill on the Floss* shows. One metaphor breeds another, as in my figure here of "breed." The attempt to demystify metaphor or to do without it only leads, by a kind of fatality, to more metaphors. Eliot's reference to Aristotle in *The Mill on the Floss*, as well as much else in her work, shows that she had extensive knowledge of Western theories of tropes from Aristotle on up to the nineteenth-century German rhetorical and hermeneutical tradition.[24]

The Roar on the Other Side of Silence

Why one metaphor "breeds" another, as if they were multiplying rabbits, is suggested by a disquieting implication of passages about figures cited earlier, for example: "Probabilities are as various as the faces to be seen at will in fretwork or paper-hangings," since "every form is there, from Jupiter to Judy, if you only look with creative inclination" (32: 337). The creative interpretation which sees one thing as something else, that is, as metaphor, is performed on a ground which already has a humanized form, the regular repeating patterns of manmade fretwork or paper-hangings. What is there before this first act of order-giving? About this nothing can be affirmed directly. There is no direct experience of it. Of the lines on the pier-glass it can be said: "It is demonstrable that the scratches are going everywhere impartially" (27: 294). "It is demonstrable"—the impersonality of this "it" and the impersonality of the passive construction remove the random disorder of the scratches from direct experience by any willing and seeing "I." But there is no experience except through a willing and seeing ego. The random scratches are removed from literal naming too, if literal naming depends, as it has since Aristotle, on having the object named under one's eyes. There can be no proper name, says Aristotle, for the sun when it is beneath the horizon, since it can never then be seen. It must always be named in figure. The "it" is at once an object, a state of affairs, and the effaced remnant of an absent active agent turned into a passive construction, as in *es gibt* in German, or *il y a* in French. "It" can be demonstrated. By whom? By someone, though not by the "I" who speaks. "It" can be proved by the scientist, perhaps, who figures in the pier-glass passage: "a learned man of my acquaintance." "It" can be proved by the scientists, with their impersonal and indirect modes of demonstration. They show that what the eye shows by *Augenschein* is not the case. "It" can never be seen and named directly, by ocular proof, since the looking ego instantly sees the random scratches in metaphor, as concentric circles, just as we see faces in wallpaper. We see in metaphor, never what is really there. What is "really there" is therefore not susceptible to literal naming. The metaphorically transformed world, on the other hand, may paradoxically be named with minute particularity, as, for example, George Eliot spells out in detail his folkloristic metaphor of the shrewmouse imprisoned in the ash-tree or as the base of any parable, Featherstone's funeral for example, may be described exactly. This is "realism," the scrupulous fidelity to detail in the description of what is originally and irreducibly a tissue of metaphors. These metaphors are better called catachreses. They do not substitute for any literal terms, and they are not literal themselves. Since no literal seeing exists, but only seeing this as that, the one true thing that may be said literally is that no literally true statements exist, only metaphors and metaphors of metaphors. What is "really there" is imperceptible and unnamable except in figure. "It" is "chaos" or "ruins," but to call it these is already to speak in figure, as a ruin is not something original but the reduction to formless fragments of something once shaped and orderly, with a human meaning and value, and as "chaos" is a concept with a long religious, philosophical, and scientific genealogy. "Chaos" is a good name for the roar on the other side of silence. That roar is a disorderly and meaningless multitudinousness, a loud but inaudible susurrus. It is a "chaos," in the literal sense of a formless, uncreated confusion.[25] This chaos is not unlike the diffuse and unformed imaginary, in Wolfgang Iser's definition, before that imaginary is "pragmatized," given shape and form, in a literary work.[26]

This underlying disorder, without origin, goal, tendency, or ground, is figured parabolically in a number of ways throughout *Middlemarch*. It is the shapelessness of the random scratches on the pier-glass. It is the ruins of Rome, layer on layer, that Dorothea confronts on her honeymoon as the reflex of her internal disorder, the ruin of her illusions. It is the labyrinthine disorder of Casaubon's notes for the "Key to all Mythologies." These notes are always proliferating in excess of the pigeon-holes he devises to keep them in order. It is the "ruins" Rosamond briefly confronts when her illusory inner world of mistaken interpretation is momentarily demolished by Will Ladislaw's declaration of his love for Dorothea. When the interpreting, ordering candle goes out, Rosamond is left face to face with fragments. She confronts an inner chaos that is to be defined, within the logic of the pier-glass parable, not so much as a glimpse of the random scratches (these are on principle invisible) but rather as a confrontation of bits of disconnected arcs, once making neat circles around a single center: "The poor thing had no force to fling out any passion in return; the terrible collapse of the illusion towards which all her hope had been strained was a stroke which had too thoroughly shaken her: her little world was in ruins, and she felt herself tottering in the midst of a lonely bewildered consciousness" (78: 864). Rosamond usually has a strong ego. Here she momentarily becomes depersonalized, a "poor thing," like the dead Lucy in Wordsworth's "A Slumber Did My Spirit Seal": "She seemed a thing that could not feel / The touch of earthly years." Rosamond's "I" depends on her "force," her power to sustain a metaphorical system. That system and the energy behind it hold her ego together. The "I" is a fragile product of the will to power, always poised to become ruins.

Can I dare to generalize this in a way analogous to George Eliot's own generalizations? Such a formulation would assert that the self for George Eliot is the "force" to make a coherent system of metaphors and stick to them. When the system collapses into ruins, the self vanishes too. It becomes a "lonely bewildered consciousness," no longer a force-ful, ordering ego. If the self is a force, the force that creates coherent fictional metaphorical systems, that force also seems to have a fatal ten-dency, sooner or later, to deconstruct the airy aberrant structures it has built, if I may dare to use the word "deconstruct." It thereby also dis-mantles the self that is a fragile correlate of the structure. The structure as a whole self-destructs. It reduces itself to ruins. It seems as if it must have secretly incorporated the "underlying" chaos into itself. Perhaps the "force" which sustains the self and its fictions is another name for the roar on the other side of silence.

The roar on the other side of silence is named in a striking passage that few readers of *Middlemarch* have failed to notice.[27] The passage comes as part of the magisterial description of Dorothea's association of the ruins of Rome with her inner "confusion" during the first months of her marriage. This confusion is "heightened" by "the very force of her nature." The force must go somewhere. If it can no longer be used to maintain the systematic structure of her illusions, it functions to exacer-bate the confusion. This is a revolt of Dorothea's personal force against its normal function, even though "permanent rebellion, the disorder of a life without some loving reverent resolve, was not possible to her" (20: 217). At the moment, however, her inner world is in disorder. This is so usual an event for a girl in the first weeks of marriage, says Eliot, that he does not expect his readers to view it as tragic or to be deeply moved by it. Then comes one of those shifts to a universal generalization that is so important a part of the rhetoric of *Middlemarch*:

> That element of tragedy which lies in the very fact of frequency, has not yet wrought itself into the coarse emotion of mankind; and perhaps our frames could hardly bear much of it. If we had a keen vision and feeling of all ordi-nary human life, it would be like hearing the grass grow and the squirrel's heart beat, and we should die of that roar which lies on the other side of silence. As it is, the quickest of us walk about well wadded with stupidity. (20: 216–17)

"Human kind / Cannot bear very much reality."[28] The overt referent of the "roar" is "all ordinary human life." The reader will remember that the protagonist of George Eliot's *The Lifted Veil* is destroyed by his telepathic ability to have a keen vision and feeling of all ordinary human life. That hidden reality, however, is figured as something more occult: the roar on the other side of silence. In question for George Eliot is not that terrifying transcendent religious ground of which his twentieth-century namesake speaks. It is something rather closer to the "X which remains inaccessible and indefinable for us" of Nietzsche's early essay,

"On Truth and Lies in a Nonmoral Sense."[29] It is the invisible, inaudible, imperceptible "roar" that can only be given in figures and that has always already been turned into figures whenever it is encountered or named.

Two sorts of figures are in question here. The images of the sounds made by growing grass and by the squirrel's heartbeat are of actual noises too soft to be heard. They function as figures for the inaccessible X, the roar on the other side of silence. Even the word "roar" is itself a figure, since sound here is of course a parabolic metaphor for all that obscure human pain which seems less than tragic because it is so common. The other figure is the cushioning of stupidity that luckily lies between humankind and the roar. That protective wadding is the barrier of coarse emotions and flawed vision that incarnates itself in the system of illusory metaphors according to which each man or woman lives. It is like that shield Freud speaks of which protects us from the barrage of sense impressions.[30] This wall of error, for George Eliot, as for Freud or Nietzsche, in their different ways, is necessary to continued human life. Not only does it give order, purpose, and resolve, so that constructive existence can continue. It also hides from us the annihilating roar, the chaos that is "really" there, happily imperceptible to our coarse feeling and to our coarse vision and weak hearing.

Chaos cannot be described literally. Genuine disorder cannot be imagined. As Conrad's Marlow says in *Heart of Darkness*, "The inner truth is hidden—luckily."[31] True formlessness is unthinkable, unnamable, except in negatives. As soon as it is thought or named it becomes some form or other, a labyrinth, a network, a stream, a face, concentric circles, or it becomes the negation of some such form. The sensed data are taken as signs standing for something other than what they are. They are read as emblem, as parable, as allegory. The word "chaos" does not have meaning in the same way as the word "web" has meaning. It is possible to have a mental image or a direct perception of a web, never of chaos as such. Chaos is like those black holes astronomers hypothesize without ever being able to see them, in order to account for phenomena they *can* see. The multitudinous scratches are initially seen as concentric circles. Their "actual" lack of order can only be named in terms of the way they are not this particular order or that. They seem to be concentric circles, but they are not. Rosamond's momentary glimpse beyond her illusions can only be defined as the ruin of those illusions.

Eliot's insight here again closely matches Nietzsche's. (Ironically so, since the misogynistic Nietzsche mistakenly disdained Eliot as no more than a "little moralistic female.")[32] Nietzsche's postulation in *The Gay Science* of a labyrinthine chaos in its relation to a prior image of circular regularity is like the shift from order to disorder in Eliot's parable of the pier-glass or in her passage about the roar on the other side of silence:

> *Parable [Gleichniss]*—Those thinkers in whom all stars move in cyclic orbits are not the most profound [*die tiefsten*]. Whoever looks into himself as into vast space [*in einem ungeheuren Weltraum hineinsieht*] and carries Milky Ways [*Milchstrassen*] in himself, also knows how irregular [*unregelmässig*] all Milky Ways are; they lead into the chaos and labyrinth of existence.[33]

Nietzsche's parabolic method of expression here is like Eliot's. Human beings' interiorities are like cosmic space. For both writers, the origin is not literal, representational, or "realistic," but always from the beginning metaphorical. It is a taking of what is seen as a sign, and then it is the figurative interpretation of that sign. If signs are small measurable things, interpretations are illimitable. This is to say that all signs are open to a limitless multitude of incompatible readings. Every sort of face, from Jupiter to Judy, may be seen in fretwork or paper-hangings if one looks with creative inclination. To look at all is to look creatively. There is no looking which does not take what is seen as something else. No sign or configuration of signs exists that is not open to a plurality of interpretations. Rather than saying the origin is the act of seeing and naming what is seen as something else, one should say that the origin, for Eliot, is the possibility of multiple simultaneous incompatible interpretations, each a figure. For this reason, each passage, of all those cited here to exemplify this or that metaphor, turns out, when it is examined closely, not to be based on a single metaphorical model. Each is the superimposition of a multitude of conflicting metaphors, any one of which contradicts the others and gives "a different result." No one has priority over the others. It has only been for the convenience of my interpretation that I have singled out one metaphor as dominant in a given passage I have cited. The fact that we can seldom say what something is without saying it is something else means the possibility of saying it is more than one thing, perhaps even the necessity of doing so. The theoretical statement of this in *The Mill on the Floss* is confirmed by Eliot's habitual practice in *Middlemarch*.

It is, as Eliot says, lucky that we are well wadded with stupidity because we should otherwise die of the roar that lies on the other side of silence. To hear that roar would be lethal. Another name for that roar is not chaos, but death. As in Benjamin's theory of allegory the mask of death, the *facies hippocratica*, underlies all the play of allegorical signs,[34] so for George Eliot the lethal roar on the other side of silence is her name for death as an ubiquitous but invisible and inaudible other, that is, for what stupidity, another name for those illusions Eliot denounces in *Middlemarch*, must protect us from if we are to go on living. *Middlemarch* is punctuated by deaths, the death of Casaubon, the death by miscarriage of Rosamond's baby, the death of old Featherstone. Set against that inaccessible roar on the other side of silence, all our actions and valuations are nullified, including the discourse of the narrator, just as actions, valuation, and discourse are nullified by death. All our "chat" (Eliot's word) becomes, in the narrator's grotesquely resonant phrase, "thin and eager, as if delivered from a camp-stool in a parrot-house" (15: 158). That has always seemed to me a truly weird phrase. Just what is a camp-stool doing in a parrot-house? And why would one want to chat from such a location? Why is such chat "thin and eager"? Perhaps because whatever is said in a parrot-house turns into the mocking echoes of parrot-talk and is echoed mockingly by the parrots.

The Ruin of Totalization in a Cascade of Misreadings: A Summary Description of the Ground Gained So Far

The ruination of George Eliot's project of totalization in *Middlemarch* occurs in a number of interconnected ways. By "totalization," the reader will remember, I mean the attempt to give a complete and completely objective view of Middlemarch society. I have shown already how the narrator's dismantling of the way the characters think according to archeological or teleological historical models turns back to undermine the narrator's own attempt to justify his, her, or its enterprise by an analogy with the writing of history or with history itself. The same thing may be said of that other form of totalization discussed in this book: the use of metaphors, each providing a model by means of which the reader can think both of the details of Middlemarch life and of the whole in its complex interconnections. If the narrator demystifies each character's belief in some history with a beginning, a middle, an end, and a transcendent ground, he also shows the dependency of that erroneous belief on getting one's thinking entangled in metaphors. What is true for the characters must be true also for the narrator. His thinking according to metaphors must also be guilty of the error of taking similarities as identities and of drawing false universal conclusions from that error. He too must be guilty of that power of generalizing which gives man so much the superiority in mistake over the dumb animals.

Moreover, if the reader looks at the narrator's actual practice in the use of totalizing metaphors, as I have attempted to do here, it can be seen that the narrator uses not one metaphor or family of metaphors but several. Each asks to be taken as an adequate model of the whole.

It has an inherent tendency toward totalization. This is indicated by the many places where the narrator, on the basis of one or another of the metaphors, makes a judgment claimed to apply absolutely to all humankind at any time or place. Each figure, however, gives a different picture of the whole. This picture is incompatible with the pictures given by the others. Nor do they add up to a single complete picture if they are set side by side in an effort to defeat perspectivism by multiplying perspectives. It is not possible to add them up to create a kind of three-dimensional stereoscopic vision. If one is true, the others must be false, and yet no one of them seems to be complete in itself. Each seems to leave some residue of interpretation not fully worked out. Another metaphor has to be added to the first one as a "reading" of it, another one yet to that, and so on, without ever reaching an exhaustive interpretation of the signs being read.

The models for human life in *Middlemarch* are multiple and incompatible not in the sense that one is more naive and gives way to a more sophisticated paradigm, but in the sense that any passage, when looked at closely, reveals itself to be a battleground of conflicting metaphors. This heterogeneous or "unreadable" aspect of the text of *Middlemarch* jeopardizes the narrator's effort of totalizing. It suggests that one gets a different kind of totality depending on what metaphorical model is used. The presence of several incompatible models brings into the open the arbitrary and partial character of each. It thereby undoes the claim of the narrator to have a total, unified, and impartial vision. Like the characters, the narrator gets entangled in metaphors. The web of interpretative figures cast by the narrator over the characters becomes a net in which he himself is trapped, his sovereign vision blinded, his claim to be a good reader of signs nullified.

The incoherence of the text of *Middlemarch* lies not only in the presence of several incompatible families of metaphors. It lies also in the impurity of the genealogical line of each family. This is a little like the tangled genealogical lines in the stories told in *Middlemarch*. Each metaphorical model already implicitly contains the others. Each has a disquieting tendency to call forth the others to complete itself. At the same time it contaminates itself, as if, to mix George Eliot's own metaphors, there were some inevitable tendency in that roar on the other side of silence to produce ruins, to turn concentric circles back into scratches going impartially everywhere. The optical model is already implicit in the web figure, insofar as the latter implies a patterned field on which the narrator's "light" of understanding must be "concentrated." The optical metaphor already contains the metaphor of text and reader by implying that all seeing involves taking something as a sign standing for something other than itself, the multitudinous scratches as concentric circles, wallpaper as faces. The metaphor of the web implicitly contains the metaphor of the text, *textus*, something woven. The web of Middlemarch life is a text to be read. The monetary metaphor, finally, acts as a commentary on the parabolic quality of all these metaphors. The metaphor of text and interpretation has a different status from the other metaphors not in the sense that it is more "correct" than they are, but in the sense that it reveals what goes on in any thinking according to metaphors, including thinking according to itself as model. All metaphors are readings, not acts of vision. All reading is false reading, the grouping of unique entities under a common erring figure apparently governed by a beginning, end, and ground.

The peculiarity of the metaphor of metaphor is the following: the functioning of metaphorical models, like the definition of metaphor, depends on the distinction between figurative and literal uses of language. The model is a figure by means of which the reader can think about what is "literally" there, Rosamond's egotism, the interwoven minutiae of Middlemarch society, or whatever. The metaphor of metaphor undermines this bifurcation. It sets up a confusion in which the definer enters into the defined, the defined into the definer. It is like a Möbius strip, which clearly has two sides and yet can be shown to have only one side. In the metaphor of metaphor both tenor and vehicle are figures. A making problematic of figure short-circuits the use of a metaphor as a way to think of something non-figurative. The metaphor of metaphor calls attention to the words there on the pages of *Middlemarch* and to their role as performative creators of meaning. The words, the reader is led to see, make an alternative imaginary "world." This virtual reality exists nowhere but as brought into putative existence for the reader through those words. In addition, the figure of figure in *Middlemarch* insinuates that what is literally and originally there is a text to be read, signs to interpret, not an extra-linguistic reality. It thereby breaks down the distinction between tenor and vehicle, literal and figurative, on which the notion of metaphorical models depends.

What both the characters and the narrator of *Middlemarch* see is signs that veil an unknown X, the inaudible roar on the other side of silence. The metaphors in *Middlemarch* have a propensity to turn into one another because all are catachreses. They are arbitrary names given to an unknown X for which there is no literal name. No control on their adequacy exists such as might be presumed to operate in realistic narrative as it is usually understood. Such understanding would think of realism as the representation in words of a physical, social, and psychological world that is really there, outside language. For George Eliot, what is "really there" is the roar, the random scratches. Out of this chaos, in real life as in the writing of a novel, we make signs and coherent networks of signs, and then read them, in a doubly aberrant veiling of the hidden "truth."

The metaphor of the web is therefore the covert image in *Middlemarch* of the textuality of the text. There is no fabric which has not been woven, fabricated, and on which more weaving may not be added as embellishment. The pilulous web of pre-matrimonial romantic dreaming spun between Rosamond and Lydgate is a text, a set of signs. It is, in addition, the interpretation of a previous set of signs. Lydgate, the reader will remember, is described, when Rosamond and the others first encounter him, as "a cluster of signs for his neighbours' false suppositions" (15: 158). Rosamond makes another text out of the text she reads, as if she were a literary critic or the commentator on a text. On this web woven on a web the narrator in his turn stitches another needlepoint of interpretation. Like any reader, he follows one line or another in the web, giving a weight and value to this node or that in relation to the others. The web is not there as an object to have light cast on it by the narrator. The narrator weaves the web himself in his activity of interpretation. He sees things as signs and then reads those signs. His work, moreover, is as much a covering over as it is a revelation. The web he weaves is a falsifying veil cast over dispersed data to make them a pattern, the scratches into circles, the fretwork into faces.

You and I in our turn, as readers of *Middlemarch*, are the next in the series. The reader fashions another web superimposed on the narrator's web, which is superimposed on the web spun between Rosamond and Lydgate, itself already an interpretation of those signs Lydgate offers to his neighbors' misreadings. What is true for the characters, for the narrator, and for the author, must be true also for the reader who writes a silent commentary as she or he reads, and for the critic who puts his or her commentary down on paper, as I am doing now. A final effect of the metaphor of interpretation in *Middlemarch* is to remind the reader that his or her own activity is also represented parabolically in the novel. She or he too is a reader of signs. What undermines the narrator's enterprise of totalization must undermine also any idea the reader might have of providing a correct and complete interpretation of *Middlemarch*. The meaning of *Middlemarch* is indeterminate not in the sense that useful commentary may not be written on it, or that one can say anything about it one likes, but in the sense that no commentary can be exhaustive or wholly coherent. It will be the less coherent insofar as it yields to the richness of the text.

"Undecidability" in reading does not arise from the reader, from the possibility of seeing the text from many angles or perspectives. It arises from the text itself. It arises from a propensity toward heterogeneity in language, manifest, for example, in puns, homonyms, and word play. This means that no storyteller can master language and make it say unequivocally one thing without at the same time saying something else. So-called "undecidability" arises from the power a text has over the reader or critic, not from a power the reader or critic has over the text. An irresistible coercion in the words of the story forces the critic, sometimes in spite of herself, to repeat in her commentary the heterogeneity of the text, betraying what she would repress, the evidence that undoes any unified reading, in the act of repressing it. This happens, for example, by the procedure of citation, which always exceeds the commentary that would fit it into a single reading. The difference between one reading and another is the varying degrees of awareness of this universal predicament of criticism.

The predicament manifests itself in a certain feeling of dissatisfaction in the critic. This small book on *Adam Bede* and *Middlemarch*, for example, necessarily mimes in one way, or another, whether I have wished to do so or not, this discomfort of reading. This happens both in the detail of comment on particular passages and in the overall order of my sections. If criticism is a parable of the act of reading, the displeasure of the text is a multiple dissatisfaction. It is the sense of having said too much and too little at the same time. The critic feels that there would always be something important more to say, even about a brief citation that has been discussed at length. I never quite get my formulations just right. I can never quite say everything that needs to be said, say it correctly, and have done with *Adam Bede* and *Middlemarch*. The prolonged process of palimpsestic revision my manuscript has undergone, so easy now on the computer, is evidence of that endless dissatisfaction.

Form as Repetition in Unlikeness

In spite of its insight into the necessary failure of any effort of comprehensive vision—by imaginary person, by storyteller, by reader, or by critic—*Middlemarch* is essentially affirmative. No reader can doubt that. Its affirmations depend on a notion of repetition different from Dorothea's wish to marry another Milton, different from any theory of storytelling as exact mimesis of an extra-verbal reality, and different from any notion of criticism as the identification of a single determinate meaning. To this alternative theory of repetition I now turn in conclusion. In this alternative mode, metaphysical notions of history, of storytelling, of individual human lives, and of criticism are demystified and rejected, though of course never banished with entire success. At the same time they are countered by different concepts. The images of origin, of end, and of continuity are opposed by categories of repetition, of difference, of discontinuity, of openness. Life is seen positively as the free and contradictory struggle of individual human energies, each a center interpreting the whole. Interpretation, it will be remembered, is always misinterpretation. It never sees things as they are. It is affirmation without solid determinable ground in truth or reality.

History, for George Eliot, is not chaos, but it is governed by no ordering principle or aim. It is a set of acts, not a passive, inevitable process. It is the result of the unordered energies of those who have made it, as well as of the interpretations these energies have imposed on history after the fact. History, for Eliot, is stratified, always in movement, always in the middle of a march, always open to the reordering of those who come later. Rome, for example, in the great chapter describing Dorothea's reaction to it, is a "spiritual centre" not because it is an occult origin but because it is "the interpreter of the world." Rome is the place where over the centuries has congregated the most intense activity of interpretation. For Eliot, "souls live on in perpetual echoes, and to all fine expression there goes somewhere an originating activity, if it be only that of an interpreter" (16: 179). The most likely origin is an act of interpretation, that is, an act of the will to power imposed on a prior "text." That text may be the world itself seen as signs to be read.

Such signs are not inert. They are nothing but matter, like the "stupendous fragmentariness" of Rome. At the same time, they are always already heavy with a weight of previous interpretations. They embody those interpretations in material form. Dorothea's response to Rome adds itself to the layer upon layer of interpretations of it that have been made before. In a similar way, the great passage on the ruins of Rome near the beginning of Freud's *Civilization and Its Discontents*, if you happen to know it, retrospectively alters the reader's response to the passage in *Middlemarch*. It adds one more stratum to the sedimentation.[35] As Harold Bloom might say, it seems as if Eliot must have read Freud. "The gigantic broken revelations of that Imperial and Papal city," says George Eliot, in a passage I have already cited, "thrust abruptly on the notions of a girl who had been brought up in English and Swiss Puritanism" form "one more historical contrast" and take a new meaning in her response to it (20: 215). Though Dorothea's life does not have intrinsically a given aim any more than it has an other than accidental origin, nevertheless she may give it an aim, as she ultimately does in her decision to marry Will Ladislaw. In the same way, though the past does not have a fixed meaning I may give it meaning, as Walter Benjamin affirms, in the way I appropriate it for the present, just as the narrator gives the imaginary Dorothea's life a meaning by telling it as a story, and just as the reader in her turn adds herself to the chain when she interprets the novel.

Against the notion that a good work of art must be an organic unity and against the notion that a human life gradually reveals its destined meaning and wholeness, George Eliot proposes the notion that a literary text is made of differences and the concomitant notion that human lives have no unitary meaning. For all men and women "every limit is a beginning as well as an ending" (Finale: 917). Their lives have meaning not in themselves but in terms of their influence on other people, that is to say, in the affective interpretation that other people make of them. I shall return to these presuppositions. In place of the erroneous assumptions about origin, end, and wholeness that cause the characters in *Middlemarch* so much suffering, Eliot presents each fictive life in the novel as justifiable by no ideal origin or end. Each has such effect as it does have on those around it. This is an influence not capable of being generalized or predicted.

Moreover, in place of the concept of elaborate organic form in art, George Eliot presents a view of artistic form as inorganic, a-centered, and discontinuous. Such a view sees form as based on unlikeness and difference. This view is expressed in her extraordinary little essay, "Notes on Form in Art" (1868).[36] It is manifested in the actual narrative structure of *Middlemarch* (not least in its metaphorical texture), as well as in explicit statements in the novel. "Fundamentally," says George Eliot in "Notes on Form in Art," "form is unlikeness, . . . and . . . every difference is form."[37]

What does this mean? In several passages in *Middlemarch* the narrator argues that all generalizations are falsifications because they derive from the illicit amalgamation of specific instances that are all different. As a result, the narrator must say categorically: "I protest against any absolute conclusion" (10: 92). "But this," he says of the stimulation of imagination by emotion, "which happens to us all, happens to some with a wide difference" (47: 520–1). In another place the narrator says, "all conceit is not the same conceit, but varies in correspondence with the minutiae of mental make in which one of us differs from another" (15: 167). A final example is the observation that "there are many wonderful mixtures in the world which are all alike called love, and claim the privileges of a sublime rage which is an apology for everything (in literature and the drama)" (31: 333–4). In such passages the narrator is not a seer but an expert reader of signs. He is one who knows that no two cases are identical. He understands that no interpretation is absolutely correct, since an interpretation always depends on the assertion of similarities over differences. Interpretation puts two and two together. George Eliot, in the essay on form in art, asserts that form emerges from the juxtaposition of differences rather than from a wide view that sees things whole, as a pattern of similarities making an organically unified tissue.

Middlemarch itself is an example of form arising from unlikeness and difference. Its form too is governed by no absolute center, *arche*, or *telos*. *Middlemarch*'s meaning is generated by the juxtaposition of its several plots. The three love stories, for example, are as much different from one another as they are similar. Even the styles in which they are written differ. The story of Dorothea, Casaubon, and Will employs an abstract vocabulary, as in the early descriptions of Dorothea as "ardent" and "theoretic," in search of the way to an "ideal end." A covertly manipulated parallel with the myth of Ariadne and Dionysus supports this elevated style and implicitly justifies it, as I shall show. The rationale for this repetition of an ancient myth in modern England is doubtless George Eliot's version of the theory of myth she had learned from David Friedrich Strauss, Ludwig Feuerbach, and others, in her omnivorous reading. This theory anticipates similar conceptions of myth latent in the "imaginary portraits" of Walter Pater, for example "Denys L'Auxerrois" and "Apollo in Picardy." The story of Rosamond and Lydgate, on the other hand, is told in a middle style, the basic style of nineteenth-century realistic fiction, for example as that style is used in Anthony Trollope's novels or, in a different way, in Flaubert's *Madame Bovary*. A lower, pastoral, comic, or ironic style is used for the courtship of Fred Vincy and Mary Garth, as it is in Hardy's *Under the Greenwood Tree*. The story of Bulstrode and his wife Harriet echoes the "well-made play" conventions of Eugène Scribe, as well as the "vaudevilles" of Danish playwright and poet Johan Ludvig Heiberg, and anticipates Henrik Ibsen's plays. As Leonardo Francisco Lisi has brilliantly shown in *Aesthetics of Dependency: Early Modernism and the Struggle against Idealism in Kierkegaard, Ibsen, and Henry James*,[38] these conventions characteristically involve the collision of religious values with commercial values and the revelation of some hidden secret about a financial crime usually involving inheritance. Bulstrode's story can be seen as an exemplification of Tawney's famous thesis about the role of religion in the rise of capitalism.[39] Bulstrode justifies his criminal act of cheating Will Ladislaw's mother and Will himself out of their birthright by telling himself it is for the greater glory of God and for his own salvation. His becoming rich shows that he is specially chosen. It allows him to do God's work in the world.

Critics have erred in expecting *Middlemarch* to be in one homogeneous "realistic" style throughout. They have misunderstood and misjudged it as a consequence, for example in what they have sometimes said about Will Ladislaw's implausibility as a character. Each of the styles I have mentioned goes along with certain conventional plot assumptions common in popular novels, dramas, and operas at the time, though every great novel, *Middlemarch* included, plays against those reader or spectator expectations in one way or another and puts the conventions in question. Eliot would have known some of these conventions in part through the many operas she witnessed in Germany as well as in England. These operas were the equivalent in George Eliot's day of popular films and television dramas in our own day.

Middlemarch is also an example of form as difference in its effect on its readers. The novel, like Dorothea, has such effect on its readers as it does have, as they thread their ways through its labyrinth of words. Each reader makes such an interpretation of it as she can. None is absolute. Each is a misreading in the sense that the text is expanded for what the reader can put into it. The reader of the novel, like Dorothea, Lydgate, or Casaubon, links similar elements and makes patterns out of diversity. This activity is shown within the narrative to be both entirely human and also inevitably in error, an error perhaps for good, perhaps for ill. In either case, it is the imposition of an unjustified will to mastery over the text.

It is no accident that *Middlemarch* has been so consistently misread as affirming the metaphysical system of history it so elaborately deconstructs. That system is there, along with its subversion. It is there in the apparent parallelism of the various plots. It is there in the penchant for absolute generalization of the narrator. It is there in the apparent organization of the whole text according to the totalizing metaphors I have already discussed—the metaphor of the web or that of flowing water or that of a text. *Middlemarch* is an example of the inevitable reweaving of the spider-web of metaphysics even in a text explicitly devoted to contracting it to its "pilulous smallness" and so showing it as what it is.

Nevertheless, for those who have eyes to see it, *Middlemarch* not only dismantles the metaphysical system of history, and not only affirms it again, but also proposes, beyond that contradictory doubleness, an alternative that is consonant with the propositions of Friedrich Nietzsche and Walter Benjamin in the citations with which I began the *Middlemarch* part of this book. Like Benjamin, Eliot as narrator rejects historicism with its ideas of progress and of a homogeneous time within which that progress unfolds. Like Benjamin, he proposes a view of history writing as an act of repetition. In that repetition the present takes possession of the past and liberates it for a present purpose, thereby exploding the continuum of history.

A passage in Benjamin's "Theses on the Philosophy of History," just prior to my initial epigraph from him, presents a model of a relation to history that would be consonant with Dorothea's relation to the history she confronts in Rome, George Eliot's relation to the story he tells, and the reader's relation to the text of *Middlemarch* as she seizes it out of the past in order to understand one aspect of the connection between history and narrative. The difficulty of Benjamin's formulation lies in the way it may be read, and sometimes has been read, like *Middlemarch* itself, as reaffirming the metaphysical system it seems to subvert. The Hegelian terminology and the language of Jewish Messianism Benjamin uses cannot be easily twisted away from their usual implications, that is, from the large contexts into which they are folded.[40] The passage contains both metaphysics and its deconstruction, like all such attempts to win freedom from what is inescapably inscribed in the words we must use to speak at all. I cite the last sentence in German once more, so the reader can savor again its special flavor:

> Thinking involves not only the flow [*Bewegung*] of thoughts, but their arrest [*Stillstellung*] as well. Where thinking suddenly stops in a configuration [*Konstellation*] pregnant with tensions [*von Spannungen gesättigten*], it gives that configuration a shock, by which it crystallizes into a monad. A historical materialist approaches a historical subject [*Gegenstand*] only where he encounters it as a monad. In this structure he recognizes the sign of a Messianic cessation of happening, or, put differently, a revolutionary chance in the fight for the oppressed past. He takes cognizance of it in order to blast [*herauszusprengen*] a specific era [*Epoche*] out of the homogeneous course of history—blasting a specific life out of the era or a specific work out of the lifework. As a result of this method the lifework is preserved in this work and at the same time canceled [*aufbewahrt ist und aufgehoben*]; in the lifework, the era; and in the era, the entire course of history. The nourishing fruit of the historically understood contains time as a precious but tasteless seed [*Die nahrhafte Frucht des historisch Begriffenen hat die Zeit als den Kostbaren, aber des Geschmacks entratenen Samen in ihrem Innern*].[41]

This is by no means an easy passage to understand. It turns on the opposition between time as a flowing liquid, a current, and time as analogous to the way a supersaturated liquid can suddenly crystallize into a solid that remains fixed but that contains within it the tensions that created it. The Messianic cessation of happening, as one can tell from others of the "Theses on the Philosophy of History," is not a "now" in the sense of the German word *Gegenwart*. It is not the presence of the present, and not, as the note to the English translation claims, "the mystical *nunc stans*."[42] It is the *Jetztzeit* of time as repetition. Such a time is the freezing or crystallizing of the present by way of its eternal reiteration of a past in which the Messiah had not yet come but was coming. In such a now once more the Messiah has not yet come but is coming, according to the aphorism from Karl Kraus that Benjamin quotes: "*Ursprung ist das Ziel*" ("Origin is the goal").[43] Benjamin's Messianism is, like Kafka's, the eternal waiting for a Messiah who never comes until it is too late. As Kafka puts this, "The Messiah will first come [*erst kommen*] only when he is no longer necessary; he will come only on the day after his arrival; he will come, not on the last day, but on the very last [*allerletzten*]."[44] The *Jetztzeit* is a now that is the monadic and crystallized repetition of a past which never was a presence. The reference to Leibniz's windowless monads indicates how cut off the *Jetseit* is once it crystallizes out of the flow of history, just as de Man's allegorical signs are cut off from the signs they echo. At the same time this monad is a prolepsis of the future as "something evermore about to be." "Thus," says Benjamin, in echo of Marx's *Eighteenth Brumaire*, "to Robespierre ancient Rome was a past charged with the time of the now [*Jetztzeit*] which he blasted [*heraussprengte*] out of the continuum of history. The French Revolution viewed itself as Rome incarnate [*wiedergekehrtes*]. It evoked ancient Rome the way fashion evokes the costumes of the past."[45]

The tasteless seed of time released by the fruit of history understood as repetition is not time as homogeneous continuity. It is time as the eternal absence of any *locus standi*. This tasteless seed of time is one name for that "nowhere" of fiction Henry James so fears to confront. Like any seed, however, it is capable of generating a future. The discontinuity of a repetition blasts a detached monad, crystallized into immobility, out of the homogeneous course of history, in order to take possession of it in a present that is not present. It is the cessation of happening in a metaleptic assumption of the past, making the past depend on the present, preserving and annulling that past in the movement of a Hegelian *aufhebung* (a word that means both "cancel" and "preserve"). Such a repetition disarticulates the backbone of logic and frees both history and fiction, for the moment, before the spider-web of logocentrism is rewoven, from the illusory continuities of origin leading to aim leading to end. Monad, crystal, seed, *Jetztzeit*—none of these figures is more literal than any of the others. All are catachreses for something that has no literal name. All are needed, in their incoherence, to give some idea of what Benjamin is talking about. The crystallized time of the *Jetztzeit* is a tasteless seed, but also an explosive monad that brings about an unpredictable future.

Middlemarch, I claim, is in anticipatory resonance with the passage from Benjamin I have just discussed. Benjamin, one might say, without meaning to do so, blasted *Middlemarch* out of the course of history and gave us the means to understand it retrospectively and to reappropriate it for present uses. Our *Jetztzeit*, alas, is a time when, in W. B. Yeats's formulation, "the best lack all conviction, while the worst / Are full of passionate intensity."[46] It is a time when we need all the help we can get from what the old books say.

A Finale in Which Nothing is Final

Where should I end this long discussion of *Middlemarch* but with a consideration of its end, the celebrated Finale? The Finale, in its grave, compassionate, and somewhat melancholy affirmations, lacks the explosive assertions of Benjamin's "Theses." The two texts nevertheless belong to a chain of repetitive reversals of Hegel that includes Feuerbach, Marx, Nietzsche, and many twentieth-century writers. This is an uneasy fraternity by no means simply in brotherly consonance, as Marx's splendidly ironic putdown of Feuerbach in *The German Ideology* sufficiently indicates. Nor does one escape from Hegel by simply "reversing" him, as *Middlemarch* abundantly shows. That is why it must be done again and again. We are all Hegelians, that is, logocentrists, often without knowing it.

The Finale, it would seem likely, is the place to look for an "ending" to *Middlemarch*, drawing all its threads tight. The Finale, however, it turns out, ends the novel only by presenting generalizations about openness. The first sentence of the Finale, already cited, says this clearly enough: "Every limit is a beginning as well as an ending" (Finale: 917). The novel's eighth book, of which the Finale is a part, is entitled "Sunset and Sunrise." What this might mean is indicated by what is said by anticipation in the Finale about the future lives of Dorothea and the other characters. The narrator clearly tells his story from a point long after the marriages that end the novel, since he knows the outcomes of those marriages. The marriages of Dorothea and Will, Fred Vincy and Mary Garth, end the narrative conventionally enough. The narrator reminds the reader, however, that marriage too is a beginning as well as an ending, in real life and in realist fiction, as well as in epics and in the Bible: "Marriage, which has been the bourne of so many narratives, is still a great beginning, as it was to Adam and Eve, who kept their honeymoon in Eden but had their first little one among the thorns and thistles of the wilderness. It is still the beginning of the home epic—the gradual conquest or irremediable loss of that complete union which makes the advancing years a climax, and age the harvest of sweet memories in common" (Finale: 917). Note that Eliot allows for "irremediable loss" as well as for "conquest" of "complete union." The conventional "happily ever after" is by no means certain for her. (It is hard not to think of the Finale as spoken by George Eliot herself.)

George Eliot here calls attention to a relation of similarity and difference between epics and realist fiction. She invites the reader to think of *Paradise Lost* as though it were a bourgeois novel, and of *Middlemarch* as if it were an epic. All marriages are "home epics." We all in our marriages repeat Adam and Eve. This both domesticates the epic and raises "low mimetic" realism to epic status, universalizing it. *Paradise Lost* already does this by inviting all Protestant readers to think that each moment of their lives repeats the momentous alternatives open in the instant before Eve ate the apple. No final end comes to human history, until the last end. The meaning of each human life, moreover, remains open as long as the person is alive. That meaning remains open even after the person's death, insofar as the meaning of each life is his or her effect on others, down through the generations.

The openness of *Middlemarch* is also demonstrated in the way the Finale modulates for the last time, though not in any definitive way, the key metaphors of the novel: the tropes of history, of the web, of flowing water, of seeing, and of interpretation. These figures appear for the last time in a dissonant mode, not as a harmonious assemblage in a grand concluding chord. One by one, the power of each figure adequately to image human life is dismantled. Speaking of the newlyweds' futures, for example, the narrator says there is no way to be sure that their after-lives will be continuous with the fabric which has been woven up to the fictive "now" that ends the novel: "Who can quit young lives after being long in company with them, and not desire to know what befell them in their after-years? For the fragment of a life, however typical, is not the sample of an even web: promises may not be kept, and an ardent outset may be followed by declension; latent powers may find their long-waited opportunity; a past error may urge a grand retrieval" (Finale: 917). If what Nietzsche called "*monumentalische* (monumental)" history, that is, the history of great men,[47] is, for Eliot, not a straightforward sequence governed by cause and effect, neither is a given human life. A speech act such as a promise does not guarantee the future. The promise may not be kept. Emotion as motive does not necessarily continue through time with the same force. It may "decline." An error, such as Dorothea's or Bulstrode's, does not necessarily lead to permanent disaster. It may, paradoxically, be the cause of a turn for the better, as in the touching solidarity in catastrophe of Bulstrode and his wife at the end of his story.

Eliot's figure of the uneven web rejects both the method of synecdoche so basic to narration in *Middlemarch* and the assumption that the totality of *Middlemarch* society, or of human life generally, may be thought of as a web of regular pattern permitting universal judgments. The validity of synecdoche has been presupposed in all those places in which the narrator moves from particular examples to absolute generalizations, for example when, apropos of "poor Mr Casaubon," the narrator says, in a passage cited more than once here, that "we all of us, grave or light, get our thoughts entangled in metaphors, and act fatally on the strength of them" (10: 93). The fragment of a particular life, the Finale now says, cannot be counted on to stand for the whole of social existence. If human life, in its minute particulars and in its total configuration, is like a web, it is like that particular form of web that is uneven. It does not form a unified design that can be seen at a glance. It may shift unpredictably from one pattern to another, for example when a promise made in good faith is not kept. As a result, no safe generalizations about the texture of human life may be made, though the narrator makes yet another in saying that the fragment of a life is not the sample of an even web.

A similar doubt is cast on the figures of vision and of interpretation. As the narrator says:

> Certainly those determining acts of [Dorothea's] life were not ideally beautiful. They were the mixed result of young and noble impulse struggling amidst the conditions of an imperfect social state, in which great feelings will often take the aspect of error, and great faith the aspect of illusion. For there is no creature whose inward being is so strong that it is not greatly determined by what lies outside it. A new Theresa will hardly have the opportunity of reforming a conventual life, any more than a new Antigone will spend her heroic piety in daring all for the sake of a brother's burial: the medium in which their ardent deeds took shape is for ever gone. (Finale: 924)

The word "error" used here is part of the vocabulary in *Middlemarch* that describes the act of reading. Interpretation is often, George Eliot asserts, a misreading of signs motivated by "great feelings" that are in themselves good, like Dorothea's infatuation with Casaubon. Her "great faith" in him produces a mistake in seeing, an optical illusion. She sees concentric circles where there are only random scratches, to borrow a celebrated trope from the novel (27: 294), discussed earlier in this book. Dorothea's "affectionate ardor" and her "Quixotic enthusiasm" (43: 468), to use Casaubon's words for her most salient qualities, are the motivating energy that drives her to read badly and to see wrongly.

Eliot places the blame partly on outward conditions, for example the genteel sexism that contributes to Dorothea's misery. When she returns from her wedding journey she finds that no one, especially her husband, expects her to do anything in particular. "What shall I do?" she asks

Casaubon, and is answered, "Whatever you please, my dear" (28: 305). Dorothea's ardor and her theoretical bent need some male partner who can match her idealism and who can tell her what she should do. In her society no such men exist (did they ever?), and so she misreads Casaubon as like Pascal or Milton or John Frédérick Oberlin (3: 31, 35; 7: 69). Even these patriarchal worthies, seen in close domestic surroundings, the final twist of George Eliot's irony implies, might not have matched Dorothea's ideal image of the man she would like to marry. In any case, Saint Theresa and Antigone were lucky enough to have a surrounding social "medium" equal to their heroic ardor, and lucky enough never to marry, while poor Dorothea has no such medium and no luck in her first marriage choice. I have shown earlier how important the concept of a social medium is in the novel. The reference to Saint Theresa in the Finale echoes of course the description in the "Prelude" of Dorothea as a "Saint Theresa, foundress of nothing" (Prelude: 4) and as one of those "later-born Theresas" who "were helped by no coherent social faith and order which could perform the function of knowledge for the ardently willing soul" (Prelude: 3–4).

The reference to Antigone in the Finale is not fortuitous, since she has been mentioned once before in the novel. Antigone as the heroine of Sophocles's tragedy was a key figure in German romantic speculation about the conflict between individual ethics and the state, for example in work by Hölderlin, Hegel, and August Böckh. George Eliot herself published in 1856, long before she wrote *Middlemarch*, a little essay on Antigone that mentions Böckh. Böckh was perhaps one source of George Eliot's rhetorical and tropological sophistication in *Middlemarch*, for example in her recognition of the disquieting effects of figurative language.[48]

The last paragraph of *Middlemarch* ends the novel on a note of eloquent openness to an unpredictable future. It also gathers up one last time the image of human life as flowing water. That image has been present in the novel since the "Prelude." In the "Prelude," Dorothea is a cygnet reared among ducklings in a brown pond and deprived of fellowship with its own kind in "the living stream" (Prelude: 4). That stream in the Finale is modulated into a river that disperses itself in the sand. The last paragraph also makes one last reference to the stream of history that has provided a (false) model throughout for the writing of narrative. If the reference to Cyrus, taken from Herodotus, draws a last parallel between *Middlemarch* characters and grand personages on the stage of world history, the passage goes on to say that Dorothea's life was "unhistoric." Her effect on those around her exceeded the public power of naming that makes the writing of monumental histories possible. The result is that her influence cannot be measured except hypothetically. What cannot be named exactly cannot enter into that precise calculation of cause and effect that historians pretend to make. It is impossible to understand Dorothea's life according to the gross model of visible historical causality. The parallel between writing history and writing fiction about ordinary middle-class people, important earlier in the novel, here breaks down. People like Dorothea are not historic:

> Her finely-touched spirit had still its fine issues, though they were not widely visible. Her full nature, like that river of which Cyrus broke the strength, spent itself in channels which had no great name on the earth. But the effect of her being on those around her was incalculably diffusive: for the growing good of the world is partly dependent on unhistoric acts; and that things are not so ill with you and me as they might have been, is half owing to the number who lived faithfully a hidden life, and rest in unvisited tombs. (Finale: 924)

The somber echoes of Gray's "Elegy Written in a Country Churchyard" at the end of this passage may remind the reader that George Eliot's tomb in Highgate Cemetery outside London is apparently not visited all that often and was in a rather shabby state when I last saw it, a good many years ago. Karl Marx's tall and elaborate marble gravestone with an elegant bust, however, just a few feet away, was, when I saw it on the same pious visit, in highly polished splendor. It was adorned with fresh flowers just being put there by a Soviet delegation wearing the shapeless black suits Soviet officials affected in those bygone days. This was before the disintegration of the Soviet Union, the putative vanishing of communism, and Francis Fukuyama's exuberantly mistaken pronouncement of an end to history in the worldwide triumph of capitalism or "liberal democracy."[49] I wonder how Marx's grave is managing today, in 2011.

Middlemarch, in deconstructing the characters' possibilities of verifiable knowledge, implicitly deconstructs also both its own power to make an orderly narrative and the reader's power to comprehend the novel integrally. *Middlemarch* may therefore be called a "parable of unreadability." The word "parable" is taken here in George Eliot's own sense, as she uses it in chapter 27 (27: 194), already discussed above. The characters' stories parabolically dramatize the narrator's problems and those of the reader. If that is the case, the novel is, paradoxically, readable. It invites the reader to master it as the story of challenges to cognitive mastery, though the invitation takes away with one hand what it offers with the other. Insofar as the reader understands what the text is saying, masters it, he or she understands any reader's powerlessness to understand verifiably either this particular text or his or her own actions on the stage of history. The reader is overmastered or deprived of mastery.

Dorothea's Limitless "Yes"

A stage beyond this cognitive impasse is, however, dramatized in the novel. This stage is expressed in parable too, though in a different mode of saying one thing and meaning another. The performance of this further stage is Dorothea's commitment to Will, her marriage to him, and her after-life "only known in a certain circle as a wife and mother" (Finale: 922). The ending presents in Dorothea's marriage an exemplary expression of what might be called an ethical or ethico-performative evaluation of human life. Such an evaluation involves a return to the "real world" of the reader, as when the narrator says, in a direct appeal to you or me: "that things are not so ill with you and me as they might have been . . ." (Finale: 924). The ending therefore involves a form of reference, though not a straightforwardly mimetic one. The reference takes place rather by way of a performative appeal to the reader to recognize and accept a debt. Beyond the dismantling of the characters' efforts to comprehend totally, beyond the turning back of that on similar efforts by narrator and reader, beyond the ruination of any cognitive enterprise of totalization, the novel proposes the positive affirmation of a performative power, possibly for good, possibly for evil, in actions and in words. These words and actions are necessarily blind to their full meaning and effect. They are, in George Eliot's precise formulation, "incalculably diffusive" (Finale: 924). They have power to make something happen, but exactly what that is, to what degree it will be for good or for ill, may not be calculated or known, neither before nor after the fact.

The move from cognitive to performative language occurs when Dorothea, in a scene shortly before the "Finale," throws herself into Will's arms in a "flood" of "passion" that matches the storm outside the window before which she and Will stand, just as, much earlier in the novel, Dorothea's honeymoon forlornness is matched by the ruins of Rome and by the crimson banners, "like a disease of the retina," in St. Peters: "Oh, I cannot bear it—my heart will break, . . . I don't mind about poverty—I hate my wealth" (83: 898). This episode is parabolic in the sense that Christ's inscrutable stories in the Gospels are exhortations to certain kinds of ethical action that are enjoined by what he says, though the cognitive justification for those actions can never be clearly given. You must believe, not know, that right action is a way to earn entrance into the Kingdom of Heaven. Even exactly what kind of action should be performed in a given situation remains not wholly clear. How would I ever know that I was correctly imitating Dorothea? Just what sort of action does Jesus's parable of the sower enjoin (Matt. 13: 4–23)? Such a performative parable as Dorothea's commitment of herself to Will lacks the more or less unambiguous cognitive meaning of George Eliot's parable of the pier-glass, enunciated in a celebrated passage earlier in the novel (27: 294) and discussed already in this book.

Dorothea's spontaneous and unpremeditated commitment of herself to Will is the last of the important decisions she makes in the novel. Each is ratified in one way or another by an explicit speech act or writing act. Each in one way or another has to do with a commitment to marriage. In Dorothea's social milieu, the acceptance or refusal of a marriage proposal was the chief place where a gentlewoman had the opportunity to make a free decision. Dorothea refuses Sir James Chettam's marriage proposal. She accepts Casaubon's marriage proposal. In various scenes of solitary meditation after her marriage, scenes that apparently influenced Henry James's *The Portrait of a Lady*, Dorothea recognizes that she has misinterpreted Casaubon. She has misread him. She resolves nevertheless to do the best she can with the marriage state she has erroneously chosen. Ultimately, after Casaubon's lucky death, lucky for Dorothea that is, since it occurs just before she might have committed herself to life-long futility by promising to finish Casaubon's "Key to all Mythologies," Dorothea entrusts herself to Will Ladislaw by throwing herself into his arms and uttering the words I have cited above. Her decision is a felicitous speech act even in the legal sense. It activates the clause in Causabon's will disinheriting her if she marries Ladislaw after Casaubon's death. Dorothea says: "We could live quite well on my own fortune—it is too much—seven hundred a year—I want so little—no new clothes—and I will learn what everything costs" (83: 898).

Though Dorothea's decision to marry Will may be unpremeditated, she ratifies that decision in a later deliberate speech act uttered to her sister Celia. Celia asks her why in the world she has given up all that money to marry Will Ladislaw. "I have promised to marry Mr Ladislaw; and I am going to marry him" (84: 908), says Dorothea. She will marry Will even though it activates a will that disinherits her. The implicit play on the word "will" indicates that Ladislaw's given name is not unmotivated. Will Ladislaw is willful, impulsive, motivated by emotion. That is part of his attraction for Dorothea. That Dorothea's commitment to Will is a true decision and not the preprogrammed following of a moral rule is indicated by what Dorothea says to her sister Celia when the latter asks the former just how it came about that she decided to marry Will Ladislaw. Dorothea says this is something that is impossible for Celia to "know." "Can't you tell me?" asks Celia. "No, dear," answers Dorothea, "you would have to feel with me, else you would never know" (84: 908).

A true decision is a matter of feeling, of unpredictable and inexplicable "ardor." It is never a matter of rational choice based on balancing pros and cons, or on coldly following a moral law, or on obedience to what family and friends tell you you should do. Dorothea defies her whole community in choosing to marry Ladislaw. Because it is based on ardor, not prudence, her decision constitutes a true historical event. It is a break in the predetermined sequence of happenings, in a way recalling Benjamin's analysis of monadic, crystalline, tasteless seeds of time. Isabel Archer, in James's *The Portrait of a Lady*, says much the same thing as Dorothea says to Celia. When Isabel's rejected lover, Caspar Goodwood, her aunt, Mrs. Touchett, and her cousin, Ralph Touchett, in succession, ask her to explain why she has decided (disastrously) to marry Gilbert Osmond, she answers each in the same evasive way. To Caspar: "Do you think I could explain if I would?"[50] To Mrs Touchett: "I don't think it's my duty to explain to you. Even if it were I shouldn't be able. So please don't remonstrate; in talking about it you have me at a disadvantage. I can't talk about it" (4: 55). To Ralph: "I can't explain to you what I feel, what I believe, and I wouldn't if I could" (4: 72).

The commitment to family life and political action by Will and Dorothea after their marriage confirms the rechanneling of Dorothea's ardor when she throws herself into Will's arms. Dorothea, the novel makes clear, does not move from blindness to full insight, from illusory misinterpretation to clear seeing of the way things are. She comes, it is true, according to the narrator, to see that Casaubon has his own center of perception, from which "the lights and shadows must always fall with a certain difference" from those which fall from her own center, or from anyone else's (21: 235). Dorothea is never, however, shown as able to articulate her understanding as clearly as the narrator does. The narrator must speak for her more or less inarticulate intuitions and feelings.

In another celebrated scene, Dorothea looks from her window in the early morning, after her night of sorrow over Will's supposed betrayal of her with Rosamond. She sees a man and a woman moving across the landscape. The woman is carrying a baby. This scene repeats in the modern world that moment when Adam and Eve, who celebrated their honeymoon in paradise, had to nurture their first child in the thorny wilderness outside Eden. Seeing this emblem of our fallen state leads Dorothea to feel her kinship with "the manifold wakings of men to labour and endurance" (80: 873). In this moment her insight more or less coincides with that of the narrator. The narrator must still, however, give words to what Dorothea sees and feels. Her spirit from the beginning has been both ardent and "theoretic" (1: 8), but her hunger for theoretical certainty, if one may use that phrase, can never be satisfied, anymore than can ours. Dorothea's falling in love with Will and her decision to give her life to him are based on ardor, feeling, and "will" (in the sense of spontaneous life force), rather than on clear-seeing theory.

The final determining act of Dorothea's life is, like her other decisions, performative rather than cognitive. Her love for Will is as much an "error," in the sense of overvaluing and in the sense of blind submission to the guidance of another, as is her love for Casaubon. It just happens to be a good love rather than a disastrous one. Dorothea is never shown as making out her own way clearly. The lesson her life teaches is that such clear seeing is impossible: "She had now a life filled also with a beneficent activity which she had not the doubtful pains of discovering and marking out for herself" (Finale: 921). Such irresponsibility was just what she wanted to get by marrying Casaubon. The difference is that she actually gets what she wants by marrying Will Ladislaw.

The difference, the reader may protest, is that Dorothea's choice of Will is good. It has good effects, both for her and for others, whereas her choice of Casaubon was mistaken and had bad effects. Is that so certain? By what right, on what grounds, does Dorothea, or the narrator, or the reader, make this judgment? The last paragraph of the novel forbids the possibility of making a final evaluation, in spite of the apparent confidence expressed in a beneficent teleological orientation of history in the phrase, "the growing good of the world" (Finale: 924). The world's good will grow only if we are lucky enough to have a sufficient number of Dorotheas. I have stressed that Dorothea's life is said to be "incalculably diffusive" (Finale: 924). The world "incalculably," as I have said, forbids definitive cognitive judgment. It deprives the narrator of his authority of understanding. It deprives the reader too of the power to make an authoritative judgment, to render full justice to Dorothea's choice. Another way to put this is to say that any judgment the narrator or the reader makes is itself performative rather than cognitive. It is another act of will following Dorothea's impulsive choice and repeating it.

Dorothea as Ariadne

Middlemarch puts all these ardent acts under the aegis of Ariadne.[51] Dorothea's decision to marry Will may be called Ariadne's choice. Many hints scattered here and there throughout the novel invite the reader to think of Dorothea's story as a repetition with difference of the myth of Ariadne. The difference lies not only in the change from archaic Greek times to nineteenth-century England, but also in the way Dorothea is Antigone and the Virgin as well as Ariadne. The narrator presents her as an uneasy incarnation of several conflicting mythological archetypes. Within the re-enactment of the myth of Ariadne, Casaubon is both a grotesque parody of Theseus and at the same time the devouring Minotaur at the center of the labyrinth. It might be better to say that Dorothea's masochistic notions of self-sacrifice in the name of an imaginary grand goal make Casaubon into her Theseus and also into her Minotaur. Dorothea's misreadings of Casaubon transform him, but the danger is real enough. "You have been brought up," says Will impetuously to her, "in some of those horrible notions that choose the sweetest women to devour—like Minotaurs. And now you will go and be shut up in that stone prison at Lowick: you will be buried alive. It makes me savage to think of it!" (22: 245). If Casaubon is Dorothea's Minotaur, he is also, in a conflation of two myths characteristic of George Eliot's use of mythology, the Creon who buries her alive as another Antigone. Like Theseus, Casaubon is self-righteous and cold, a prig. Like Theseus, he marries his Ariadne and then abandons her, though, unlike Theseus, he has not even accepted her proffered help in escaping that self-made labyrinth of moldy notes and outmoded theories in which he dwells.

Dorothea is made into a Christian and modern repetition of Ariadne in the scene in which Will Ladislaw and his German painter friend Naumann find her in the Vatican beside the statue of "the Reclining Ariadne, then called the Cleopatra" (19: 210). Naumann calls her the "antithesis" of Ariadne, as well as her modern replica. The parallel with Ariadne, moreover, is complicated by accompanying references to Cleopatra, to Antigone, and, a little later, to Santa Clara. In the "Prelude" she is likened to Saint Theresa, and late in the novel to the Madonna. "This young creature has a heart large enough for the Virgin Mary" (76: 852), says Lydgate, in grateful praise of her decisive intervention in his life. What a bewildering set of comparisons! If Dorothea is Saint Theresa, Cleopatra, Antigone, Santa Clara, and Mary, as well as Ariadne, there is much doubt implicitly cast on solemn Hegelian theories of repetition to which the novel makes oblique reference. Both Will Ladislaw and the narrator make fun of such theories. Casaubon's futile search for a key to all mythologies hardly inspires confidence in the reader that he or she might find some key to the mythological references in *Middlemarch*.

Nevertheless, the reader is invited, with whatever ironic qualifications, to think of Dorothea as in some way like Ariadne. "What do you think of that as a fine bit of antithesis?" asks Naumann, as he and Will watch Dorothea beside the statue of Ariadne/Cleopatra in the Vatican. "There lies antique beauty, not corpse-like even in death, but arrested in the complete contentment of its sensuous perfection: and there stands beauty in its breathing life, with the consciousness of Christian centuries in its bosom" (19: 211). Naumann apparently thinks it is a statue of Cleopatra, as many mistakenly did at that time, though both identifications had been proposed. A moment later Naumann describes Dorothea as "antique form animated by Christian sentiment—a sort of Christian Antigone—sensuous force controlled by spiritual passion" (19: 212). If Dorothea reincarnates Cleopatra and Antigone, she does so with the crucial difference that she also embodies centuries of Christian ascetic renunciation that says, "If you enjoy it, it must be sinful." Dorothea is shown inhabited by such a fear of pleasure at the beginning of the novel when she catches herself enjoying the gems in her dead mother's jewelry for their beauty (1: 14–15). Will, to be sure, pours scorn on Naumann's reading of Dorothea and on his corresponding aesthetico-Hegelian notion of "the divinity passing into higher completeness and all but exhausted in the act of covering your bit of canvas" (19: 212). If metaphysical notions of repetition are firmly rejected in *Middlemarch*, it may be that the reader is left to devise, on the basis of the text, an alternative notion of repetition, one not controlled by any divinity or by any fixed mythological archetypes. The final paragraph of the novel gives the rationale for such an alternative notion.

Felicia Bonaparte, to my knowledge, was the first critic to argue cogently that the mode of George Eliot's novels is not straightforward realism but what I have been calling allegory. George Eliot, Bonaparte argues, habitually manipulates parallels between her mimetic narratives of everyday life and various mythological prototypes.[52] The realistic story re-enacts these in complex interfering patterns and with various degrees of ironic dissonance. My reading of Eliot differs from Bonaparte's, at least in what I find in *Middlemarch*, in seeing more irony and more dissonance than she does. Her reading of *Romola* sees a dialectic movement in the title character from Ariadne to Antigone to the Madonna. This, Bonaparte argues, involves a rejection of the pagan affirmation of selfish sensuous feeling and a replacement of this with the Christian values of sorrow, renunciation, and service. Bonaparte's interpretation of the ethical meaning of George Eliot's novels reaffirms what has often been said of them. I find, on the contrary, in *Middlemarch* at least, that Ariadne wins out over Antigone and over the Virgin, or that the three remain in uneasy and unreconciled tension as models for the understanding of Dorothea's marriage to Will. The marriage of Dionysus and Ariadne remains the dominant prototype, even though Dorothea may be an Ariadne with centuries of Christian understanding of sorrow to modify her apotheosis.

It might be possible to argue that Dorothea's repetition of Ariadne in her marriage to Will indicates her inferiority to Romola, the modern Mary. The tonality of *Middlemarch*, however, invites the reader to see Dorothea positively. We are asked to see her as having, somewhat blindly, made the right choice at last. She has done the best that can be done with her life within the lamentable circumstances of nineteenth-century England. The novel powerfully dramatizes a rejection of any large destiny that would make Dorothea a repetition of Saint Theresa or of the Virgin, a savior of her people, someone able to perform epic actions on the broad stage of history. In place of those impossibilities for the modern world are put the obscure affirmations of a Christian Ariadne. Those affirmations have a power to do a hidden incalculable good in a narrow circle. Dorothea, the reader is encouraged to believe, made the only possible good choice, given her historical predicament.

If Dorothea is a modern Ariadne, Will is her Dionysus. He is Dionysus-like in his association with art and light, in his irresponsibility, in his willingness to be guided by impulse and strong emotion. He is also Dionysus-like in having an obscure association with animals. That association is affirmed by the connection between the miniature of Will's grandmother and the tapestry of a stag. Both hang on the walls of Dorothea's boudoir at Lowick. Will is like Dionysus in his slight effeminacy, troubling to some critics. Like Dionysus, Will is given to metamorphosis. In the admirably somber chapter describing the newly married Dorothea at Lowick, the portrait miniature of Will's grandmother, "who had made the unfortunate marriage," turns into Will himself as Dorothea looks at it: "Nay, the colours deepened, the lips and chin seemed to get larger, the hair and eyes seemed to be sending out light, the face was masculine and beamed on her with that full gaze which tells her on whom it falls that she is too interesting for the slightest movement of her eyelid to pass unnoticed and uninterpreted. The vivid presentation came like a pleasant glow to Dorothea" (28: 306–7).

Various anomalies stand out in the presentation of Will throughout the novel. These are odd features that seem in excess of the requirements of realistic portraiture. They even seem in excess of the need to present Will as sexually attractive to Dorothea, as Rosamond is attractive to Lydgate, or as Fred Vincy is attractive to Mary Garth. The somewhat covert mythological parallel with Dionysus best explains these oddnesses. This hidden connection surfaces perhaps most openly in a passage in chapter 21, though still without explicit reference to Dionysus. Without the support of all the references to the myth of Ariadne to characterize Dorothea, one might have thought Will is as much Apollo as Dionysus, though the emphasis throughout on Will's strong emotions and on his power of shape-changing make him more Dionysian than Apollonian. As Felicia Bonaparte has seen, however, for George Eliot, as for Friedrich Nietzsche, there is a secret kinship as well as an antithesis between Apollo and Dionysus:[53]

> The first impression on seeing Will was one of sunny brightness, which added to the uncertainty of his changing expression. Surely, his very features changed their form; his jaw looked sometimes large and sometimes small; and the little ripple in his nose was a preparation for metamorphosis. When he turned his head quickly his hair seemed to shake out light, and some persons thought they saw decided genius in this coruscation. (21: 233)

Dorothea's marriage to Will, I claim, repeats that marriage on the Island of Naxos of Ariadne to Dionysus that changed Ariadne's situation from that of forlorn betrayal to semi-divine status. In her researches for *Romola*, as Bonaparte shows, Eliot had encountered many versions of the myths of Bacchus and Ariadne. She knew Ovid well. She knew many of the antique Greek statues of Bacchus, as well as that Ariadne in the Vatican mentioned in the novel. She knew the painting by Piero di Cosimo in the Vespucci Palace in Florence, *The Discovery of Honey*. This includes the figures of Bacchus and Ariadne in triumph. This was a favorite subject in Renaissance Florence, both for literary and for pictorial representation. The marriage of Bacchus and Ariadne in the moment when Bacchus puts a ring on Ariadne's finger was also an important Renaissance and post-Renaissance theme. Eliot may have known, for example, two admirable paintings of the marriage of Bacchus and Ariadne, one by Titian, one by Tintoretto. The marriage of Bacchus and Ariadne was often the subject of operas by composers from Monteverdi on through Jiri Benda in the eighteenth century (who composed a monodrama, *Ariadne auf Naxos*, in 1774), and of course down to Richard Strauss's glorious *Ariadne auf Naxos* in the twentieth century.[54] Alongside these many presentations of Ariadne's story, *Middlemarch* may claim an honorable place.

Dorothea's choice of Will is her spontaneous affirmation of the life force's unpredictable and contradictory energy. Almost against her will, she has embodied this force from the beginning, in her beauty and in her "ardor." This life energy is dangerous, disruptive. Just as Clara Middleton in George Meredith's *The Egoist* causes much trouble to all those around her, so Dorothea in *Middlemarch* in both her marriages upsets the conventional economy of marriage and the distribution of property in Middlemarch. Mrs. Cadwallader speaks for those conventions and proprieties. Dorothea's energy is the order-destroying, order-creating vitality of her emotions. This vitality is the fuel that feeds her illusions. It also, however, gives her such power to do good as she has. Her marriage is her choice for the expression of her ardor over her need for theoretic justification. If Dorothea is both ardent and theoretic, the lesson of *Middlemarch* is that the two needs cannot both be satisfied, or rather that her theoretical need cannot be satisfied, even if she were willing to abandon her ardor. Dorothea's failure implies that the narrator's wished-for theoretical clear-seeing is also impossible, as is the reader's. Dorothea's marriage is a spontaneous saying yes, like Ariadne's acceptance of Dionysus when he appears to her in her state of forlorn betrayal. Jacques Derrida calls such an acceptance, "*l'ouverture affirmative pour la venue de l'autre* [the affirmative openness for the coming of the other]."[55] Dorothea's "Oh, I cannot bear it—my heart will break" (898), the opening of the floodgates of her tears, is the moment, in Nietzsche's phrase, of her "*ungeheure unbegrenzte Ja*,"[56] her "immense limitless yes." This "yes" breaks the bind in which Casaubon's will has placed her.

Middlemarch ends with the narrator's analysis of the meaning of Dorothea's life. No evidence is given that Dorothea herself understands her life even so well as the narrator does. Her consciousness disappears from direct representation in the "Finale." The "openness" of the ending of *Middlemarch* lies partly in the still remaining gap between what the narrator and reader know and what Dorothea is shown as knowing. Neither narrator nor reader can calculate precisely the meaning of Dorothea's life. Nevertheless, they have more insight than she is shown as having. Dorothea's choice of Will imposes a pattern on that roar on the other side of silence that the narrator names in another celebrated passage earlier in the novel, already discussed (20: 216–17). The freely imposed pattern, like the parables in the narrator's discourse, is not an accurate picture of the roar, nor is it justified by or grounded in the roar. No literal representation of the roar is possible. Any coherent pattern given a life by ethical choices lacks depth in that it is without solid ground in any archetype that it repeats. Nor is it founded on any metaphysical *logos*, not even one apprehended as a "roar" to which it can be shown to correspond.

Dorothea's commitment of herself to Will is a performative cata-chresis. It is a figure projected on the unknown and unknowable X. This figure covers the unknown X over rather than bringing it into the open. The X or roar cannot be brought into the open. Dorothea's choice repeats Ariadne's choice not in the sense of being grounded in it as avatar is grounded in archetype but in the sense of performing once more the blind affirmation figured in Ariadne's acceptance of Dionysus. The marriage of Ariadne and Dionysus, moreover, like the marriage of Dorothea and Will, exists in the artistic representations of it, not as some celestial archetype. It too is a human creation, a pragmatization of, or giving shape to, the shapeless imaginary. Each marriage helps to understand the other, but neither is the ground of the other, nor are they both versions of some more ancient model, some key to all mythologies. Dorothea's marriage to Will in *Middlemarch* is George Eliot's interpre-tation of the myth of Ariadne and Bacchus. The novel functions as a commentary on the myth that changes it, as all interpretation does. Each marriage, whether we think of it as an imagined actual event or as an artistic representation, is no more than what is made of it by those who come after. It is something incalculably diffusive, to be measured by the effects it has.

George Eliot's Life and Work as an Uneven Tissue of Ungrounded Repetitions

This alternative Benjaminian or Nietzschean mode of repetition, in its opposition to the traditional metaphysical one, is repeated in five dif-ferent ways in George Eliot's life and in her work. No one of these has priority over the others, as its "source" or "key." All five are related as Dorothea's marriage is related to Ariadne's. Each is a different manifes-tation of the same inaugural performative. One way is Marian Evans's own life in her relations with her father and with the various men with whom she was associated. Another way is in her writing of her novels. Another way is in the interpretation of the characters' lives by her novels' narrators and in the tropological modes of narration used. The latter might be called George Eliot's rhetoric of narration. Another is in the lives of the characters themselves. The fifth is in the interpretation of all these proposed by readers and critics.

In her own life Marian Evans repeatedly enacted an odd female version of the Oedipal triangle. This version has father, mother, daughter, rather than father, mother, son. Freud called this the Electra Complex. The reference is to the Greek myth, as dramatized in

Sophocles's *Electra*, of Electra's plotting with her brother Orestes the murder of her mother Clytemnestra in revenge for the latter's murder of Electra's father, Agamemnon. The myths of Ariadne, of Antigone, and even of the Virgin Mary, each in its own way, are different modes of this. In this story the daughter seeks to replace the mother in the father's affections. That would make possible a position of willing submission to the father's authority. The daughter hopes thereby to give her life an absolute justification. The father, in Eliot's versions of the story, is then recognized to have no valid authority. The daughter, discovering this, replaces the father in one way or another as the authority figure. Even the Virgin, in her submission to the divine mandate, takes on within the Catholic tradition a more or less independent power as mediator. The authority of these various figures has what might be called a peculiarly feminine nuance. In one way or another it challenges or displaces the divine fathering energy. This pattern was repeated at least five times, with variations, in Marian Evans's own life: with her father, with Dr. Brabant, with John Chapman, with G. H. Lewes, and a final time with J. W. Cross, whom she married a few months before her death.[57]

One salient way in which Marian Evans became an authority figure was in the assumption of a masculine persona as the narrator of her novels. Within the novels she plays the role of an omniscient paternal deity, all-knowing, all-wise, all-powerful. In *Adam Bede*, for example, she changes her real father into the fictive Adam and becomes, so to speak, the father of her father. In speaking as a putatively masculine narrator this "she" becomes a fictive "he." This imaginary "he" makes universal generalizations on the basis of the particular persons and events Marian Evans has invented. The narrator is like a God in judgment dividing the sheep from the goats (Matt. 26: 32). Marian Evans's decision to become George Eliot was an imperious assertion of masculine authority and power, even if that assertion remained in the mode of a fictive "as if." This was especially the case when, after everyone came to know the actual identity of "George Eliot," Marian Evans or Marian Lewes chose not to drop the pseudonym. She never published fiction in her own name. The presumed masculinity of the implied author and narrator of "George Eliot's" novels remains to the end a fundamental part of their mode of existence.

The narrators of Eliot's novels, however, deconstruct masculine authority, even though they employ it. Those narrators show that the conventions of realist fiction, in which a fictively "omniscient" narrator plays God, producing and judging an authoritative replica of things and people as they are, only exists in the mode of "as if." Moreover, that kind of authority is systematically dismantled in the discourse of the narrator himself. A feminine narrative authority that has no transcendent base replaces it. This authority takes responsibility for its own creative power. "George Eliot" becomes once again "feminine," within the pattern of sex differentiation the novel has set up, for example in the opposition between the deluded search for an originating "Key" by Casaubon or for a "primitive tissue" by Lydgate, on the one hand, and, on the other hand, Dorothea's abandonment of that kind of search. An expression of that "feminine" insight is Mary Garth's somewhat detached, thoroughly demystified, ironic wisdom. Mary is perhaps of all the characters in *Middlemarch* closest to Marian Evans herself. In the shift in the narrator back from masculine arrogation of justified cognitive power to a putatively feminine performative power, realism as referential mimesis becomes realism as a function of language's autonomous authority. It is narration under the aegis of Ariadne.

Some of the claims made for George Eliot as a feminist writer seem to me unpersuasive. She remained, in her novels at least, conservative on the issue of a woman's place. Dorothea fulfills herself by becoming a wife and mother. This destiny is hardly an argument for women's liberation. Nevertheless, in the subtle and pervasive dismantling of male claims to a divinely grounded authority in storytelling as well as in the conduct of life, and in the replacement of this by what might be called a feminine mode of narration, George Eliot, in spite of her masculine pseudonym, or rather because of what she does with it, is one of the most powerful of feminist writers. The ironical attack on traditional "male" forms of narration lies in part in the way Marian Evans goes on ironically calling herself "George Eliot," even when the secret of her gender is out, as if to indicate that what happens to her masculine claims to authority must happen to any male author too, as indeed it does.

If a female version of the Oedipal drama is enacted and re-enacted in Marian Evans's own life, and in what happens to the narrator's claims to authority, the same drama is in another way the figure in the uneven carpet in the stories told in the novels. As could be shown through detailed readings, this story is repeated in permutations and combinations in, for instance, *Adam Bede*, in *Silas Marner*, in *The Mill on the Floss*, and in *Daniel Deronda*. An example would be Adam's submission to Dinah's power in *Adam Bede*. Dorothea's story in *Middlemarch*, however, is perhaps the most powerful example. All George Eliot's stories dramatize in one way or another the failure of the search for a legitimate masculine authority to whom to submit. Such authority is in each case ultimately replaced in one way or another by what might be called Ariadne's authority. Ariadne's authority has the power of performative ethics. The latter generates its own authority by way of ungrounded speech acts, such as Dorothea's "Oh, I cannot bear it—my heart will break." Such authority is woman's work. It weaves a web-like pattern and casts it over random scratches, giving them apparent order. This is an authority without sovereignty, center, or *logos*.

The reader in his or her turn repeats the story once more by experiencing the bafflement of his or her search for a definitive interpretation of *Middlemarch*. The concept of organic form inviting cognitive mastery, often invoked in praise of *Middlemarch*, is deconstituted. It is replaced by the experience of a failure to make a definitive reading and in a recognition of the heterogeneity of this text. This failure may be defined by saying that the reader cannot know whether or not a definitive reading is possible. It may be possible, and the reader may have it in hand, but he or she can never know for sure. All reading and all criticism, this uncertainty would imply, are performative, productive. They are not a form of certain knowledge, but a form of construction. The constructive net of the critic's work of interpretation, concentric circles cast over random scratches, is subject to all the interpretative acts performed by narrator and characters within the novel, but it adds it own interpretation to those already made. A rhetorical reading, such as the one you are now reading, must, like the novel itself, or like the determining acts of Dorothea's life, or like Ariadne's marriage to Dionysus, take responsibility for effects that are unpredictable and "incalculably diffusive," whenever the reading happens to be read.

Dorothea repeats Ariadne. This repetition gives meaning to what it repeats rather than being grounded in it as an origin. Dorothea's life is a parable, in the strict sense in which George Eliot uses the word to define acts of narration, of reading, and of writing about what is read. The alternative form of repetition her life exemplifies may be detected in chain-linked fashion in all the regions of the novel. Dorothea's marriage is like the writing of the novel, or like the narrator's telling of it, or like our reading it or writing about it. All make something happen, but what exactly each makes happen is unpredictable. It cannot be exactly measured or valued. The reader or critic is no more able to get outside the human situation than is the narrator, the author, or the characters. All are inside the system of signs the novel proffers as an imaginary replica of ordinary human life. Like Dorothea, the reader, the narrator, and the author are "part of that involuntary, palpitating life, and [can] neither look out on it from [their] luxurious shelter as . . . mere spectator[s], nor hide [their] eyes in selfish complaining" (80: 873). Like Dorothea, the reader must act, but he or she must always act blindly. He or she must act from within the involuntary palpitating life, not on the basis of a clear vision of it. He or she can never see it whole as a spectator from outside might do. If Dorothea is blinded in her actions, so also are narrator and reader, in spite of their apparently superior breadth of vision and capacity for analysis. All three can know what they say and do, but none can know what effect these may have. Like Dorothea and like the narrator, the critic cannot know how what he docs will insert itself in an ongoing process of teaching, reading, and appropriation. The ending of *Middlemarch*, in what it says of the effects of Dorothea's life, provides an emblem of the novel's uncertainty of meaning and effect. If her effect is incalculably diffusive, so also is the effect of the novel on its readers. One effect of *Middlemarch* is the critical essays it generates. These tend to cover it over, to repress and limit its power in one way or another, but they also receive that power and pass it on. Dorothea's "Oh I cannot bear it—my heart will break," the breaking of the floodgates of her tears, is the moment of her *"ungeheure unbegrentzte Ja,"* her immense limitless yes. This "yes," her act of will accepting Will, breaks the double bind in which Casaubon's will has placed her. It also reaffirms the double bind in the uncertainty of its incalculable diffusion.

Dorothea's life cannot be justified by any ideal end. It produces such dispersed effects on other people as it does produce. In the same way, the novel, something Marian Evans has made out of words, is not the reflection or discovery of some pre-existing non-verbal truth, neither the truth about human nature in general nor a historical truth about England at a certain time and place within a certain social class. The novel is rather a web woven of language that produced then, and produces now, unpredictable effects on its readers. It cannot be justified by an idealist theory of art, nor by the symmetrical converse of that theory, the notion of an objective mirroring realism. The novel imitates neither things as they are, nor the "being" at the origin, end, or base of those things. *Middlemarch*, like Dorothea herself, is unpredictably diffusive. Though the text when read works as a performative or imperative imposing of meaning on its readers, this meaning can never be calculated in advance. It depends on an activity of interpretation that is always to some degree spontaneous, revealing some things in the text, occluding others by silence or evasion. The reading of any sign, in spite of the power of the sign over its reader, is always to some degree fortuitous.

This does not mean that the reader can make *Middlemarch* mean whatever he or she wants it to mean. The openness of *Middlemarch* is an intrinsic feature of the novel, part of its nature as a complex system of signs. The novel itself programs all the diversity of its interpretations. Any interpretation in one way or another repeats the indeterminacies of a text. This is true even of those readings which most try to reduce a given text to a single determinate meaning. The novel is not really like the random scratches on the pier-glass. It is, rather, like those scratches already organized into signs. Like the ruins of Rome with the living city atop, in another celebrated passage in *Middlemarch* (20: 215–16) that I have already discussed, these signs have a layered incoherence that forbids exhaustive coherent interpretation. The reader is not a sovereign power of seeing, motivated by feeling. Her or his interpretation of the novel is not a free perspective on it. A sign can only be interpreted by another sign. The reader too is inhabited by a system of signs. This gives him or her a certain power of interpreting other signs. He or she is open to certain possibilities of meaning in *Middlemarch*, blind to others, though what the reader is blind to will also reappear, in spite of that blindness, in the reading. The reader's own sign system too has its incompleteness, its too little or too much. Readers of *Middlemarch* are bound by possibilities of meaning inscribed there, but any reading will repeat in one way or another the openness of the text. The ruins of Rome exert power over Dorothea, but she can nevertheless appropriate them as an emblem of her own life. She can read the ruins as a parable of her state.

Middlemarch, like the ruins of Rome for Dorothea, is of no use now unless we take possession of it for some present purpose, repeat its performatives with a performative of our own. That taking possession, however, is always a dispossession, a being possessed by the power of the text. The language of the novel takes possession of the reader and speaks again through him or her, as those people Dorothea influences, Lydgate and Rosamond, for example, act in ways they would not have acted but for her. The reader of *Middlemarch* too is in the situation of Ariadne confronted by Dionysus and must make, in one way or another, Ariadne's choice, with its resonances all down through history.

The ultimate paradox or contradiction in the Finale is the double meaning it gives to the word and concept of "history." On the one hand, Dorothea's life is not historic. It could not find a place in any old-fashioned "monumental" history, with its tales of world leaders, kings, emperors, popes, battles, and wars. Herodotus can write about Cyrus, but not about ordinary women of his time. On the other hand, real history is made by innumerable almost invisible acts such as Dorothea's saying yes to Will. Such events are truly inaugural speech acts. They interrupt the course of history, as Antigone's defiance did. The effects of such events are unpredictably diffusive in the sense that they deflect the course of human history, in however minuscule a way.

People like Dorothea make things better for all of us, but they do this often against the understanding of the communities in which they live. One recurrent theme of the Finale is the pervasive misinterpretation of the characters by collective community judgment. People erroneously think that Mary Vincy must have written Fred Vincy's agricultural work on "Cultivation of Green Crops and the Economy of Cattle-Feeding," while, equally erroneously, they think Fred must have written the children's book Mary has written. "In this way," says the narrator somewhat acidly, "it was made clear that Middlemarch had never been deceived, and that there was no need to praise anybody for writing a book, since it was always done by somebody else" (Finale: 918). The reader may see this as a cryptic reference to the way a certain male impostor, Joseph Liggins, came forward and claimed to have written *Adam Bede*, to Marian Evans's amused chagrin. The Middlemarch community is wrong about Dorothea too. According to Middlemarch tradition, both her marriages were big mistakes: "Those who had not seen anything of Dorothea usually observed that she could not have been 'a nice woman,' else she would not have married either the one or the other" (Finale: 924). Even local history gets Dorothea wrong and does not recognize the incalculably diffusive good effects of her goodness. George Eliot's writing of *Middlemarch* is another on the whole beneficent historical event, like Dorothea's second marriage, as is, perhaps, in its more infinitesimal way, each reading of the novel, such as this one, however good or bad. That is still the case even if the reading never gets spoken publicly or written down. From this it may be concluded that the (im)possibility of reading should not be taken too lightly.[58]

Coda

This book is a palimpsest. It is the result of many revisions and additions to the original drafts, many changes of arrangement, emphasis, orientation, and nomenclature over the years, many interpolations, as layers were added to layers. I leave it to the astute reader to guess what came first and what layers have been superimposed on the ur-text. The difficulty is compounded by the way a computer-generated text (as though the computer did the writing!) exists in a perpetual present. The temporal layers of revision and addition vanish. The finished text seems to be there all at once floating in a single a-temporal cyberspace. One way to think of these alterations and additions is as changes in scale over the years of my context for the readings. Timothy Clark has recently written with persuasive eloquence of the need to perform the difficult task of viewing literary studies today at the wide and frightening scale of global climate change and the threat of species extinction, including the human species, in a looming imminent end to the anthropocene era.[1]

I began the "Prelude" to this book by raising the question of what value rhetorical readings of *Adam Bede* and *Middlemarch* might have in these days of climate change, global financial meltdown, the universal diffusion of computer technology, the rapid transformation of "developed countries" like the United States into third world countries, with a few super-rich and the rest living in misery and poverty, and, finally, collective "auto-co-immune" (as Jacques Derrida calls it) self-destruction of the human species through fossil-fuel use, environment destruction, and CO_2 emissions. Timothy Clark and Tom Cohen[2] reproach Jacques Derrida for ignoring, even in his latest work, catastrophic climate change and for remaining at the level of personal liberal politics within a horizon of the democratic nation state. I agree that Derrida is open to that reproach, and that though he died only a decade ago, worldwide change, what he called "*mondification*," particularly global climate change, the worldwide diffusion of the Internet, and global financial catastrophe, has happened so rapidly that the political side of Derrida's work, even his late work, may already seem outdated, as he feared would happen. "I have the feeling that two weeks or a month after my death, *there will be nothing left* [*quinze jours ou un mois après ma mort*, il ne restera plus rien],"[3] he said in his last interview. Derrida's phrasing is odd. I suppose he means nothing will be left of his work and its influence, since that is the context in the interview, but the phrase says "nothing will be left," as if everything, not just Derrida's work, will magically vanish with his death. I suppose we all secretly feel that way, though we know better. How can the world dare survive my death? The French title of Derrida's collection of memorial essays for dead friends and colleagues is *Chaque fois unique, la fin du monde* (*Each Time Unique: The End of the World*).[4] Derrida's work has certainly not been forgotten, far from it, but some readings of his work have seen it plausibly as recuperative of traditional values and outlooks. Nevertheless, I have not seen any better "explanation" of how and why we are collectively throwing ourselves off the cliff and into the rising waters than Derrida's theory of "auto-co-immunity." Derrida hypothesizes a built-in, undeliberate, and inescapable tendency in human beings living together in social orders of any sort to destroy themselves and their collectivity in a way that is analogous to mechanically acting autoimmune disease in the human body.[5]

I give a tentative answer to the question of the use of "Reading for Our Time" in my "Prelude," but I return to it now in my "Coda" in terms of the superimposed layers of my palimpsest. Clark distinguishes three "scales" in literary interpretation, that of the personal, that of the national, and that of the impersonally global or, as I would call it, the "ecotechnical." At the global scale, for example, my use of an automobile or of central heating contributes to the coming inundation of the Bangladesh floodplains by an inhuman, technical, machinal sequence that has little to do with my goodness or badness as a person or with my deliberate intent. It just happens, as increasingly violent hurricanes, tornadoes, wildfires, floods, and droughts worldwide are "just happening."

My readings of *Adam Bede* and *Middlemarch* started, innocently enough, with a formal literary-critical goal, that is, as attempts to show the function of repetition in the stories these novels tell and in the novels as texts. My acts of close reading, however, that is, my attempts to see how the texts really work, shifted my attention, willy-nilly, to the role of figurative language in these two novels. That then led, as layer was imposed on layer in successive revisions, to a study of speech acts in the novels, and then to a confrontation with the extreme oddness of the telepathic narrators Eliot used. I have also quite recently appropriated, with changes, Wolfgang Iser's distinction between the fictive and the imaginary. For me, as for him, the fictive is pseudo-reference to things that are like items in the real world, whereas "the imaginary" names the heterocosm that the ordering of fictive transpositions creates and that, pace Iser, can only be entered by reading the words on the page. Iser wants to give the non-linguistic imaginary an autonomous grounding power, whereas I give that power to language.

I by no means repudiate the bottom layers of my palimpsest, but I endorse the later developments too. A fascination with the complexities and strangenesses of George Eliot's language and a wish to explain those as best I can has persisted throughout all the writing. *Reading for Our Time* remains pretty much what it was from the beginning: primarily a study of figurative language's nature and function in the narrator's discourse in *Adam Bede* and *Middlemarch*. That is what I mean by "rhetorical readings."

In final revisions over the last year, I have asked myself, again and again, what use such readings are in the era of catastrophic climate change. That is the most recently added *couche*, layer, or stratum in my composite text. I claim that close rhetorical readings of these two novels at least can teach us to understand, insofar as it is at all open to cognition, as the waters rise up to our noses, how human beings can be led by ideological presuppositions to act self-destructively. I assert that there is some value in understanding as much as we can what is happening, how, and why, even though understanding will not keep it from happening. Learning to read the signs in the ways George Eliot teaches us to do it will perhaps (to make a final reference to my frontispiece) make some of us at least Ariadnes awakening, though not, alas, opening our eyes to confront a savior Dionysus.

My readings of *Adam Bede* and *Middlemarch* have revealed that these novels operate (in self-contradicting ways) on all three of Clark's "scales." The different layers of my palimpsest correspond, more or less, to these three scales. On the personal scale, *Adam Bede* and *Middlemarch* present four domestic stories of courtship and marriage, three of which have apparently unequivocal and reassuring "happy endings." On the national scale, these two novels are in manifold ways embedded in fictive representations of English Victorian history and culture. Much of the multitudinous secondary literature on these novels has been devoted to demonstrating just how that is the case. After all, *Adam Bede* is based on a real event of infanticide, and *Middlemarch* begins by asserting that Dorothea is a Saint Theresa born out of her time, that is, born into the Victorian era in England when the chances for leading a heroic life, such as Saint Theresa or Antigone lived, are nil. Reading at this scale is considerably less reassuring than reading at the personal scale. At the third scale, as my close readings of what these two texts actually say has gradually revealed, both *Adam Bede* and *Middlemarch*, in different ways, make generalizations about the universal penchant of human beings to make mistakes in interpretation and to act fatally on the strength of them. Those generalizations are asserted as valid everywhere at all times, in any conceivable human society.

Such insight into the way auto-co-immunity works "mechanically" for the whole human species corresponds to Clark's third and largest scale. Such insight can help us today, has helped me at least, to glimpse some explanation for why we (I mean the global "we," all 6.946 billions of us and counting) have done practically nothing globally, too little and too late, to confront the reality of climate change (human use of fossil fuels) or the causes of the global financial meltdown (unregulated greed of bankers and financiers) and to do anything about them. I doubt if understanding will lead to action in time, but quasi-understanding would nevertheless be of benefit as the ocean waters rise. At least we will know better what is happening to us globally, though to a considerable degree what is happening confounds comprehension. Clear seeing is often considered a basic human value. Rhetorical readings of *Adam Bede* and *Middlemarch*, I claim, will help achieve such understanding as is possible, if the reader practices the sort of lateral transfer that Eliot calls "parabolic." Such transfers would see, for example, our citizens' and political leaders' ideological delusions as something like Dorothea's misreading of Casaubon or like Fred Vincy's belief that Providence will be good to him because he is such a nice young man. Many people throughout the world today believe that surely Mother Nature would not let the human species die out. The evidence, however, indicates that global warming is an inhuman, mechanical process, a process that is falsified when it is personified. Put too much carbon dioxide into the atmosphere and the whole earth will warm up. It's as simple as that, and as mechanistic, just as Fred Vincy cannot help thinking Providence will be good to him. This failure in being able to understand ideological aberrations is one of the most terrifying things about them. Politicians go on believing in the "trickle-down" theory of economics, though it has been disproved by the hard facts again and again.

I suppose we should act on the basis of the irrefutable evidence of global climate change and, if we happen to read *Adam Bede* and *Middlemarch* and read them at all as I read them, also act on the basis of George Eliot's dark wisdom. "Should"? To whom or to what do we have that obligation? "Act"? Just how should we act? It is not easy to answer those questions. George Eliot's answer to them is dramatized in Dorothea's saying yes to Will Ladislaw. In my account of that "limitless yes," however, I have stressed what is enigmatic and uncertain about that saying yes.

Notes

Prelude

1. Paul de Man, "The Resistance to Theory," in *The Resistance to Theory* (Minneapolis: University of Minnesota Press, 1986), 11.
2. George Eliot, *Middlemarch*, with an introduction by A. S. Byatt, Oxford World Classics (Oxford: Oxford University Press, 1999), ch. 17, p. 193. All quotations from *Middlemarch* will be cited from this edition and will be identified by chapter numbers before page numbers, for the convenience of readers using other editions.
3. Paul de Man, *Allegories of Reading* (New Haven: Yale University Press, 1979), 245.
4. Nicholas Royle, *Veering: A Theory of Literature* (Edinburgh: Edinburgh University Press, 2011).

1: Realism Affirmed and Dismantled in *Adam Bede*

1. Friedrich Nietzsche, *The Will to Power*, trans. Walter Kaufmann and R. J. Hollingdale (New York: Vintage, 1968), 327; Nietzsche, *Nachgelassene Fragmente 1885–1887*, in *Sämtliche Werke*, ed. Giorgio Colli and Mazzino Montinari, Kritische Studienausgabe, 15 vols. (Berlin: Walter de Gruyter, 1988), 12: 154.
2. A list would include Mikhail Bakhtin, Viktor Shklovsky, Vladimir Propp, Roman Jakobson, Wolfgang Iser, Hans-Robert Jauss, Stanley Fish, Roland Barthes, Gerard Genette, Seymor Chatman, Paul de Man, Jacques Derrida, Wayne Booth, James Phelan, Jakob Lothe, Shen Dan, Arjun Appadurai, Kay Young, and many others, and even some of my own work. An immense number of books and essays in cultural studies and material culture have been published in recent years.
3. Gerard Genette, *Narrative Discourse: An Essay in Method*, trans. Jane E. Lewin (Ithaca: Cornell University Press, 1980); Genette, in French as "Discours du récit," in *Figures III* (Paris: Seuil, 1972), 67–273.
4. See Haight's introduction to the Rinehart edition of *Adam Bede* (New York and Toronto: Rinehart, 1948), p. xiii, and the chapter on *Adam Bede* in U. C. Knoepflmacher, *George Eliot's Early Novels* (Berkeley and Los Angeles: University of California Press, 1968), pp. 89–127. For Wordsworth's formulation, see "Preface to the Second Edition . . . of

'Lyrical Ballads,'" in William Wordsworth, *The Poetical Works*, ed. E. de Selincourt, II (Oxford: Clarendon Press, 1944), 384.

5. William Empson, *Some Versions of Pastoral* (New York: New Directions, 1974).

6. Gordon S. Haight, *George Eliot: A Biography* (New York and Oxford: Oxford University Press, 1968), 220. Haight has also ferreted out several people called "George Eliot," whose names George Eliot might have encountered (ibid.).

7. For a full account of the seriocomic Liggins episode, see Haight, *George Eliot: A Biography*, 280–92.

8. Nicholas Royle, "On Second Sight," in *Telepathy and Literature: Essays on the Reading Mind* (London: Blackwell, 1991), 89.

9. The French is in *L'Entretien infini* (Paris: Gallimard, 1969), 556–67; the English is in *The Infinite Conversation*, trans. Susan Hanson (Minneapolis: University of Minnesota Press, 1993), 379–87.

10. William Wordsworth, *The Excursion*, VI, 651–8, in *The Poetical Works*, ed. E. de Selincourt and Helen Darbishire, V (Oxford: Clarendon Press, 1949), 206–7. George Eliot has changed "shall" in line one to "may," and Wordsworth has in the fifth line "my flock," not "the flock," since the lines are spoken by the Pastor.

11. See Geoffrey Hartman, *Beyond Formalism* (New Haven and London: Yale University Press, 1970); Harold Bloom, *The Ringers in the Tower* (Chicago: University of Chicago Press, 1971); Paul de Man, "The Rhetoric of Temporality," in *The Rhetoric of Temporality: Essays in the Rhetoric of Contemporary Criticism*, 2nd edn (Minneapolis: University of Minnesota Press, 1983), 187–228.

12. William Wordsworth, *The Prelude*, VII, 650–2, 1850 text, ed. K. E. Selincourt, revised by Helen Darbishire, 2nd edn (Oxford: Clarendon Press 1959), 257.

13. Walter Benjamin, *Understanding Brecht*, trans. Anna Bostock (London: NLB, 1977), 11; Benjamin, *Versuche über Brecht* (Frankfurt: Suhrkamp, 1955, 1966, 1978), 27. Brecht wrote: "Oberste Aufgabe einer epischen Regie ist, das Verhältnis der aufgeführten Handlung zu derjenigen, die im Aufführen überhaupt gegeben ist, zum Ausdruck zu bringen." ("The supreme task of an epic production is to give expression to the relationship between the action being staged and everything that is involved in the act of staging *per se*.")

14. Citations from *Adam Bede* are taken from the Oxford World Classics Edition paperback, ed. Carol A. Martin (Oxford: Oxford University Press, 2008). Citations are identified by chapter numbers as well as page numbers for the convenience of readers using other editions.

15. George Eliot, *Essays*, ed. Thomas Pinney (New York: Columbia University Press, 1963), 266–99.

16. A paradox exists, it may be noted, in justifying a claim to realism in the novel by appeal to the conventions of another art medium. The paradox concentrates in itself the tension between mimetic and "allegorical" dimensions of *Adam Bede*, as I shall try to show.

17. Nicholas Royle, "The 'Telepathy Effect': Notes Toward a Reconsideration of Narrative Fiction," in *The Uncanny* (Manchester: Manchester University Press, 2003), 256–76.

18. See Edmund Husserl, "Fifth Meditation: Uncovering the Sphere of Transcendental Being as Monadological Intersubjectivity," in *Cartesian Meditations: An Introduction to Phenomenology*, trans. Dorion Cairns (The Hague: Martinus Nijhoff, 1960), 89–151. See esp. paragraph 50, "The mediate intentionality of experiencing someone else, as 'appresentation' (analogical apperception)" (108–11).

19. See ch. 2, n. 19.

20. Eliot, *Essays*, 266–7. Riehl's word *Volk* has a sinister sound to a post-Holocaust ear. Avrom Fleishman, in *George Eliot's Intellectual Life* (Cambridge: Cambridge University Press, 2010), 91, in his judicious account of Riehl's writings and of Eliot's essay, observes that Riehl was a proto-Fascist whose *Völkisch* ideology foreshadowed and was appropriated by the Third Reich. Right-wing politicians in the United States today routinely use our equivalent of the German word *Volk*, "the American people," for example when they claim "the American people want Obama's Health Care Law repealed." This is doubly a lie. Polls show that a majority of American citizens, diverse as they are, like the provisions of the Health Care Law. Moreover, no such thing as a monolithic "American people" exists. It is a dangerous linguistic fiction.

21. In *The Rise of the Novel* (Berkeley and Los Angeles: University of California Press, 1956).

22. For discussions of this vogue, see Simon During, *Modern Enchantments: The Cultural Power of Secular Magic* (Cambridge, MA: Harvard University Press, 2002), and J. Hillis Miller, *The Medium is the Maker: Browning, Freud, Derrida and the New Telepathic Ecotechnologies* (Brighton: Sussex Academic Press, 2009). See also Carol A. Martin's note on the Egyptian sorcerer in *Adam Bede*, 498. She shows that the most likely source is Edward William Lane's *Modern Egyptians*. Avrom Fleishman lists Lane's book as read by Eliot in 1867, that is, well after the publication of *Adam Bede*. See his *George Eliot's Reading: A Chronological List*, Supplement to No. 54–5, *George Eliot-George Henry Lewes Studies* (September 2008), 51.

23. I repeat here details about the edition of *Middlemarch* I have used: George Eliot, *Middlemarch*, with an introduction by A. S. Byatt, Oxford World Classics (Oxford: Oxford University Press, 1999), ch. 17, p. 193. All quotations from *Middlemarch* will be cited from this edition and will be identified by chapter numbers before page numbers, for the convenience of readers using other editions.

24. John Blackwood, when he read the first part of *Adam Bede* in manuscript, was disturbed by this equation: "It strikes me," he wrote, "that the passage page 53 about the identity of love, religious feeling, and Love of Art would be better modified a little" (*The George Eliot Letters*, ed. Gordon Haight, II [New Haven: Yale University Press, 1954], 445). Blackwood put his finger on something essential in the conceptual presuppositions of *Adam Bede*. The equations Eliot makes might, Blackwood apparently recognized, seem shocking or even blasphemous to a Victorian sensibility. George Eliot did not change the text of her novel. For a discussion of the correspondence between George Eliot and John Blackwood about *Adam Bede* see Roland Anderson, "George Eliot Provoked: John Blackwood and Chapter

Seventeen of *Adam Bede*," *Modern Philology*, LXXI (1973), 39–47. The passage from chapter 7 already cited describing Hetty's beauty anticipates my four passages in comparing that beauty to "the mounting lark," or to "still lanes when the fresh-opened blossoms fill them with a sacred, silent beauty like that of fretted aisles" (7: 77), that is, aisles of Gothic churches with complexly carved stone ceilings.

25. See ch. 2, n. 19.

26. Rachel Bowlby has written brilliantly on this passage, as well as on another passage in *Adam Bede* that I do not cite about Hetty as "a woman spinning in young ignorance a light web of folly and vain hopes which may one day close round her and press upon her, a rancorous poisoned garment, changing all at once her fluttering butterfly sensations into a life of deep human anguish" (22: 227). Bowlby productively and provocatively follows up these passages to their sources in the stories of Medea in Euripides's *The Medea* and of Deianira in Sophocles's *The Women of Trachis*. Bowlby teaches us to read Hetty's story as in complex and ironic resonance with these Greek myths. See Rachel Bowlby, "Introduction: Two Interventions on Realism," *Textual Practice*, 25:3 (2011), 432–3.

27. For a discussion of Derrida's theory of auto-co-immunity, see my "Derrida's Politics of Autoimmunity," in J. Hillis Miller, *For Derrida* (New York: Fordham University Press, 2009), 222–44.

28. *The Essence of Christianity*, trans. Marian Evans (George Eliot), Harper Torchbooks (New York: Harper, 1957; originally published 1854), xix, xvi.

29. "Adagia," *Opus Posthumous* (New York: Alfred A. Knopf, 1957), 167, 172.

30. On Eliot's reading of Böckh see Fleishman, *George Eliot's Intellectual Life*, 82.

31. See Gilles Deleuze, *Logique du sens* (Paris: Éditions du Minuit, 1969), 295.

32. Phillipe Sollers, *Logiques* (Paris: Éditions du Seuil, 1968), 253.

33. Friedrich Nietzsche, *The Will to Power*, paragraph 822, 435; Nietzsche, *Nachgelassene Fragmente 1887–1889*, in *Sämtliche Werke*, 13: 500: "Wir haben die *Kunst*, damit wir *nicht an der Wahrheit zu Grunde gehn*."

2: Reading *Middlemarch* Right for Today

1. This mixing has been argued for the case of Anthony Trollope. See James R. Kincaid, *The Novels of Anthony Trollope* (Oxford: Clarendon Press, 1977), especially 3–65. Avrom Fleishman, in *George Eliot's Intellectual Life* (Cambridge: Cambridge University Press, 2010), proposes various incompatible generic models for *Middlemarch*, including calling it in his chapter on the novel an encyclopedia ("The Encyclopedist: Transcending the Past in *Middlemarch*," 161–89).

2. I repeat here details about the edition of *Middlemarch* I have used: George Eliot, *Middlemarch*, with an introduction by A. S. Byatt, Oxford World Classics (Oxford: Oxford University Press, 1999), ch. 17, p. 193. All quotations from *Middlemarch* will be cited from this edition and will be identified by chapter numbers before page numbers, for the convenience of readers using other editions.

3. George Meredith, *Works*, Memorial Edition, 27 vols. (London: Constable, 1909–11), 13: 2.

4. George Eliot, *Essays*, ed. Thomas Pinney (New York: Columbia University Press, 1963), 271. Fleishman (*George Eliot's Intellectual Life*, 83–7) has shown how problematic Riehl's writing is, how dangerously close to later Fascist ideas about the German *Volk*. Riehl's work, as I have said, actually influenced Nazi ideology. Fleishman has also brilliantly discussed the complexities of Eliot's thinking about rural life in England in relation to Riehl's account of German peasant life.

5. Friedrich Nietzsche, *Unpublished Writings from the Period of Unfashionable Observations*, trans. Richard T. Gray, in *Complete Works*, ed. Ernst Behler, 20 vols. (Stanford: Stanford University Press, 1995), 11: 225–6. For the German original see Nietzsche, in *Sämtliche Werke*, ed. Giorgio Colli and Mazzino Montinari, Kritische Studienausgabe, 15 vols. (Berlin: Walter de Gruyter, 1988), 7: 660–1. The quotations from Hegel are from "*Die Weltgeschichte*," *Enzyklopädie der philosophischen Wissenschaften im Grundrisse* (1830), para. 549, *Zusatz*, ed. F. Nicolin and D. Poggeler (Hamburg: F. Meinr, 1969), 426, 428.

6. Walter Benjamin, *Illuminations*, trans. H. Zohn (New York: Schocken, 1969), 263; in German: *Illuminationen* (Frankfurt: Suhrkamp, 1961), 278.

7. Odd because rather than speaking directly as the character, as Edgar Bergen speaks as Charlie McCarthy, or as Joyce speaks as Molly Bloom in the interior monologue of her soliloquy, the author in indirect discourse pretends to be a narrator who speaks in third person, past tense for character's first person, present tense discourse, lending her or him words in a form of language that always involves some degree of ironical distance or difference. The displacement involved is present in the linguistic strategy employed.

8. Anthony Trollope, *The Warden*, World Classics (London: Oxford University Press. 1963), 163.

9. J. Hillis Miller, *Reading Narrative* (Norman: University of Oklahoma Press, 1998), 108–9.

10. Henry James, "Anthony Trollope," in *Literary Criticism: Essays on Literature; American Writers; English Writers* (New York: Library of America, 1984), 1342–3. The same polemic appears in "The Art of Fiction" (1884), in ibid., 46–7: "Such a betrayal of a sacred office seems to me, I confess, a terrible crime; it is what I mean by the attitude of apology, and it shocks me every whit as much in Trollope as it would have shocked me in Gibbon or Macaulay. It implies that the novelist is less occupied in looking for the truth (the truth, of course I mean, that he assumes, the premises that we must grant him, whatever they may be), than the historian, and in doing so it deprives him at a stroke of all his standing-room. To represent and illustrate the past, the actions of men, is the task of either writer, and the only difference that I can see is, in proportion as he succeeds, to the honor of the novelist, consisting as it does in his having more difficulty in collecting his evidence."

11. James applied this phrase to Thackeray's *The Newcomes*, to Dumas's *The Three Musketeers*, and to Tolstoi's *War and Peace*. See the Preface to the New York Edition of James's *The Tragic Muse*, in Henry James, *Literary*

Criticism: French Writers; Other European Writers; The Prefaces to the New York Edition (New York: Library of America, 1984), 1107.

12. For analyses of James's use of an extravagant narrative style see my *Literature as Conduct: Speech Acts in Henry James* (New York: Fordham University Press, 2005).

13. For an essay on this topic by Barthes, see "Le discours de l'histoire," in *Information sur les sciences sociales* (1967), trans. in *Introduction to Structuralism*, ed. M. Lane (New York: Basic Books, 1970), 145–55. A powerful passage in Jacques Derrida's celebrated early essay, "Structure, Sign and Play in the Discourse of the Human Sciences," states his position on totalization: "If totalization no longer has any meaning [*sens*], it is not because the infiniteness of a field cannot be covered by a finite glance or a finite discourse, but because the nature of the field—that is, language and a finite language—excludes totalization. This field is in effect that of *play* [*un jeu*], that is to say, of infinite substitutions within the enclosure of a finite gathering [*dans la clôture d'un ensemble fini*]. This field only allows these substitutions because it is finite , that is to say, because instead of being an inexhaustible field, as in the classical hypothesis, instead of being too large, there is something missing from it: a center which arrests and grounds the play of substitutions," in *Writing and Difference*, trans. Alan Bass (Chicago: University of Chicago Press, 1978), 289, trans. altered; Derrida, "La structure, le signe, et le jeu dans le discours des sciences humaines," in *L'écriture et la difference* (Paris: Seuil, 1967), 423. Derrida's *"jeu"* or *"play"* here does not mean frivolous leisure time, though Derrida comments on Lévi-Strauss's references to games like roulette. Nor does *jeu* mean anything like Friedrich Schiller's *Spieltrieb* (play-drive) in his *On the Aesthetic Education of Man* (1794). As Derrida says, *"jeu"* is a quasi-technical term defining language, and by implication all sign systems, as "a field of infinite substitutions." The "play" of metaphorical displacements in *Middlemarch* is an example of that. On Derrida's use of *"jeu"* in *Of Grammatology*, see my *"jeu,"* in *Reading Derrida's* Of Grammatology, ed. Sean Gaston and Ian Maclachlan (London: Continuum, 2011), 43–7.

14. Princeton: Princeton University Press, 1970, and Baltimore: Johns Hopkins University Press, 1973.

15. See Phillip Bekyros and Helen Tsaggouri, "The Origin of the Tsakonikos Dance," http://users.otenet.gr/~apelon/origin.htm, accessed June 27, 2011.

16. Dorothea also makes the mistake of believing in the explanatory power of origins: "Perhaps even Hebrew might be necessary—at least the alphabet and a few roots—in order to arrive at the core of things . . ." (7: 70). For the search for origins in Casaubon and Lydgate see W. J. Harvey, "The Intellectual Background of the Novel," in *Middlemarch: Critical Approaches to the Novel*, ed. Barbara Hardy (London: University of London, Athlone Press, 1967), 25–37.

17. *The American Heritage Dictionary of the English Language*, 1332a.

18. Nicholas Royle, "On Second Sight: George Eliot," in *Telepathy and Literature: Essays on the Reading Mind* (London: Blackwell, 1991), 89.

19. Though I differ from Wolfgang Iser in placing more emphasis than he does on the generative power of language, my use of the two words "fictive" and "imaginary" is meant as an oblique reference to Iser's distinction

between them in his triad: the real; the fictive; the imaginary. See his *Das Fiktive und das Imaginäre: Perspektiven literarischer Anthropologie* (Frankfurt: Suhrkamp, 1991), translated as *The Fictive and the Imaginary: Charting Literary Anthropology*, trans. David Henry Wilson and Wolfgang Iser (Baltimore: Johns Hopkins University Press, 1993) (cited below as FI), especially the Preface and the first chapter, "Akte des Fingierens" ("Fictionalizing Acts"). As opposed to the long tradition, with its many permutations going back to Aristotelian mimesis, defining the fictive more or less exclusively in terms of its oppositional relation to the real, Iser asserts that a third term, "the imaginary," must be invoked. The imaginary "is basically a featureless and inactive potential" (FI, xvii) in human beings (why not animals too?) for dreaming, fantasizing, projecting, daydreaming, and other kinds of "reveries" (FI, 3), as well as for activating fictions. Fictions are made of transpositions of the real, but the function of the fictional "as if" is to give determinacy, pragmatic form to the formlessness, the featureless and inactive potential, of the imaginary.

20. See Nicholas Royle, "The 'Telepathy Effect': Notes Toward a Reconsideration of Narrative Fiction" in *The Uncanny* (Manchester: Manchester University Press, 2003), 256–76.

21. For a discussion of telepathy from the nineteenth century up to Freud and on beyond to the present day see my *The Medium is the Maker: Browning, Freud, Derrida and the New Telepathic Ecotechnologies* (Brighton: Sussex Academic Press, 2009).

22. His? Her? Its? The fiction of the male narrator is still maintained in *Middlemarch*, even though by this time everyone knew that George Eliot was Marian Evans Lewes, as she then called herself, though she was not legally married to her partner George Henry Lewes. English laws of the time forbade him to divorce his wife because he had condoned her adultery. Royle speaks eloquently, in a passage already cited, apropos of the narrator of *Middlemarch*, of "this narrator-madness," of "this male-female-author-metafictional character-narrator phantasmagoric collage of narratorial positions" ("On Second Sight," 89). I have already written about this issue in the *Adam Bede* section of this book, but, as I said there, the issue of the narrator's gender (and the characters' genders too) keeps coming up as a nagging uncertainty in my readings.

23. See Royle, "On Second Sight," 84–110; Thomas Albrecht, "Sympathy and Telepathy: The Problem of Ethics in George Eliot's *The Lifted Veil*," in *The Medusa Effect: Representation and Epistemology in Victorian Aesthetics* (Albany: State University of New York Press, 2009), 97–116.

24. George Eliot, *The Lifted Veil* (New York: Penguin and Virago, 1985), 19–20.

25. *Die Frohliche Wissenschaft*, paragraph 228, in Nietzsche, *Sämtliche Werke*, 3: 511, my trans.

26. Although several hypothetical originals, including G. H. Lewes, have been suggested for the "eminent philosopher," N. N. Feltes argues persuasively that the philosopher was Herbert Spencer and that the image may be traced back from Spencer to a passage in Ruskin. See "George Eliot's 'Pier-Glass': The Development of a Metaphor," *Modern Philology*, LXVII, 1 (August 1969), 69–71.

27. The metaphor of the key, which I have borrowed from the language of the novel to use as language about the novel, contains the ambiguity I am here exploring. A "key," as in the "Key to all Mythologies," is both an intrinsic pattern organizing from within a large body of apparently heterogeneous material, as when a musical composition is in the key of D major, and at the same time something introduced from the outside that "unlocks" an otherwise hidden pattern. A key is a formula that cracks a code, as when George Eliot, in *Daniel Deronda*, says, "all meanings, we know, depend on the key of interpretation" (*Daniel Deronda*, ed. Barbara Hardy [London: Penguin, 1986], 6: 88). The meaning of a text is both intrinsic to that text and yet present in it only when that meaning is projected by a certain set of extrinsic assumptions about the code or "key." This shifting from intrinsic to extrinsic definitions of "key" is present in the various meanings of the word. These include mechanical, architectural, musical, and botanical senses. See *The American Heritage Dictionary*, 718b.

28. See Feltes, "George Eliot's 'Pier-Glass,'" 69, for a discussion of the passage from Ruskin's letter of February, 1844, to the *Artist and Amateur's Magazine*, reprinted in John Ruskin, *Works*, ed. E. T. Cook and Alexander Wedderburn (London: George Allen, 1903), 3: 656–7.

3: Chapter Seventeen of *Adam Bede*: Truth-Telling Narration

1. "Fra Lippo Lippi," ll. 295–306, in Robert Browning, *The Major Works*, ed. Adam Roberts, Oxford World Classics (Oxford: Oxford University Press, 2005), 181.

2. Gerard Manley Hopkins, "Pied Beauty," ll. 10–11, *Poems*, 4th edn, ed. W. H. Gardner and N. H. MacKenzie (Oxford: Oxford University Press, 1970), 70.

3. See Immanuel Kant, *Critique of Judgment*, trans. J. H. Bernard (New York: Hafner, 1951), especially paragraphs 46–50, pp. 150–64; Kant, *Kritik der Urteilskraft, Werkausgabe*, ed. Wilhelm Weischedel (Frankfurt: Suhrkamp, 1979), 10: 241–57; and for a discussion of these patterns of thought in Kant see Jacques Derrida, "Economimesis," in *Mimesis: Désarticulations* (Paris: Aubier-Flammarion, 1975), 57–93.

4. For discussions of speech act theory in Austin, de Man, and Derrida, see J. Hillis Miller, *Speech Acts in Literature* (Stanford: Stanford University Press, 2001).

4: Returning to *Middlemarch*: Interpretation as Naming and (Mis) Reading

1. Friedrich Nietzsche, *The Will to Power*, trans. Walter Kaufmann and R. J. Hollingdale (New York: Vintage, 1968), 267; Nietzsche, *Nachgelassene Fragmente (1885–1887)*, in *Sämtliche Werke*, ed. Giorgio Colli and Mazzino Montinari, Kritische Studienausgabe, 15 vols. (Berlin: Walter de Gruyter, 1988),12: 315.

2. See Avrom Fleishman, *George Eliot's Intellectual Life*, (Cambridge: Cambridge University Press, 2010), 24–43. See also Fleishman's "George Eliot's Reading: A Chronological List" (available either, in a corrected

version of December 2008, as a separately printed "Supplement to *George Eliot—George Henry Lewes Studies* [No. 54–5 (September 2008)], 76 pp., or, in the first version, as part of that issue of *George Henry Lewes Studies*, pp. 1–106).

3. Wallace Stevens, "Adagia," *Opus Posthumous* (New York: Alfred A. Knopf, 1957), 179.
4. See 2: 21:

> "But now, how do you arrange your documents?" [Mr Brooke asked.]
> "In pigeon-holes partly," said Mr Casaubon, with rather a startled air of effort.
> "Ah, pigeon-holes will not do. I have tried pigeon-holes, but everything gets mixed in pigeon-holes: I never know whether a paper is in A or Z."
> "I wish you would let me sort your papers for you, uncle," said Dorothea.

Google and the Internet have (more or less) solved all such problems these days, though one has some nostalgia for the good old days of pigeon-holes.

5. See Claude Lévi-Strauss, *The Elementary Structures of Kinship*, trans. James Bell, John von Sturmer, and Rodney Needham (Boston: Beacon Press, 1969).
6. See Karl Marx, *The Eighteenth Brumaire of Louis Bonaparte* (New York: International Publishers, 1972), 15: "Hegel remarks somewhere that all facts and personages of great importance in world history occur, as it were, twice. He forgot to add: the first time as tragedy, the second as farce. Caussidière for Danton, Louis Blanc for Robespierre, the *Montagne* of 1848 to 1851 for the *Montagne* of 1793 to 1795, the Nephew for the Uncle." Louis Bonaparte was Napoleon Bonaparte's nephew. Susan Regina Cohen, in her admirable study of family relationships in George Eliot's work, "'The Family Procession': Generational Structures in the Novels of George Eliot," Yale University PhD thesis, 1978, available from Ann Arbor: University Microfilms International, suggests (148) that the source must be Friedrich Schiller's comedy, *Der Neffe als Onkel* (1803). Avrom Fleishman, in "George Eliot's Reading: A Chronological List" (corrected version, 61), includes Schiller's play as alluded to in *Middlemarch*. It is of course more or less certain that Marx was also referring to Schiller's play. It is possible, but unlikely, that George Eliot had both Schiller and Marx in mind. Avrom Fleishman does not list Karl Marx in his authoritative and exhaustive "George Eliot's Reading: A Chronological List."
7. See *Webster's Third New International Dictionary*, under "penny."
8. Walter Benjamin, *Ursprung des deutschen Trauerspiels* (Frankfurt: Suhrkamp, 1978), 152, my trans.
9. For de Man's celebrated and provocative definition of allegory, see his "The Rhetoric of Temporality," in *Blindness and Insight: Essays in the Rhetoric of Contemporary Criticism*, 2nd edn, revised (Minneapolis: University of Minnesota Press, 1983), 207: "We have . . . a relationship between signs in which the reference to their respective meanings has become of secondary importance. But this relationship between signs necessarily contains a constitutive temporal element; it remains necessary, if there is to be allegory,

that the allegorical sign refer to another sign that precedes it. The meaning constituted in the allegorical sign can then consist only in the *repetition* (in the Kierkegaardian sense of the term) of a previous sign with which it can never coincide, since it is of the essence of this previous sign to be pure anteriority." Just how de Man read Kierkegaard or just what he means by "in the Kierkegaardian sense" remains something of a mystery, since he never, so far as I know, spelled out how he read Kierkegaard's *Repetition*.

10. For a discussion of the history and function of zero in mathematics, monetary systems, logic, critical theory, and literature, see my *Zero Plus One* (Universitat de València: Biblioteca Javier Coy d'estudis nord-americans, 2003).

11. For the Nazarenes and some speculations about the originals of Naumann, see Gordon S. Haight, *George Eliot: A Biography* (New York and Oxford: Oxford University Press, 1968), 151–2, and Hugh Witemeyer, *George Eliot and the Visual Arts* (New Haven and London: Yale University Press, 1979), 78–87.

12. New Haven: Yale University Press, 2011.

13. George Eliot, *The Mill on the Floss*, ed. A. S. Byatt (London: Penguin, 1980), bk 2, ch. 1: 206–9. I give book and chapter numbers for the convenience of those using other editions.

14. The *OED* gives several examples under "desert" and "ship," the earliest dated 1615.

15. Aristotle, *Poetics*, trans. S. H. Butcher (New York: Dover, 1951), 1459a, p. 87.

16. Cited by Richard A. Lanham in *A Handlist of Rhetorical Terms* (Berkeley: University of California Press, 1969), 100.

17. William Wordsworth, "Essay upon Epitaphs," in *The Prose Works*, ed. W. J. B. Owen and Jane Worthington Smyser (Oxford: Clarendon Press, 1974), 1: 81.

18. This phrase is part of Socrates's discussion of similitudes in *Phaedrus*, 261d–262b, trans. R. Hackforth, in *Plato: The Collected Dialogues*, ed. Edith Hamilton and Huntington Cairns, Bollingen Series 71 (Princeton: Princeton University Press, 1963), 507–8.

19. George Meredith, *One of Our Conquerors*, in *Works*, Memorial Edition, 27 vols. (London: Constable, 1909–11), 17: 189.

20. Alfred North Whitehead, *Science and the Modern World* (Cambridge: Cambridge University Press, 1926), also available as a recent paperback from New York: Free Press (Simon and Schuster), 1997. References to the fallacy of misplaced concreteness are on pp. 51, 52, and 58 of the latter edition.

21. See, for a major example of Derrida's tropological wisdom, "White Mythology: Metaphor in the Text of Philosophy," in *Margins of Philosophy*, trans. Alan Bass (Chicago: University of Chicago Press, 1986), 207–71; Derrida, "La mythologie blanche: la métaphore dans le texte philosophique," in *Marges: de la philosophie* (Paris: Minuit, 1972), 247–324. For de Man, see, for example, his "Conclusions: Walter Benjamin's 'The Task of the Translator,'" in *The Resistance to Theory* (Minneapolis: University of Minnesota Press, 1986), 73–105. See also my reading of de Man's reading of Benjamin's essay in "Paul de Man at Work: In These Bad Days,

What Good is an Archive," in Tom Cohen, Claire Colebrook, and J. Hillis Miller, *Theory and the Disappearing Future: On de Man, On Benjamin* (London: Routledge, 2011).

22. Robert Moynihan, "Interview with Paul de Man," *Yale Review*, 73, 4 (July 1984), 580.

23. Paul de Man, *Allegories of Reading* (New Haven: Yale University Press, 1979), 10. This essay was originally given as de Man's inaugural lecture upon taking up his professorship at Yale. The passage in question gave offense to some in his audience, not only because they found de Man's references to a popular television character unseemly in such a context, but, in my opinion, for the deeper reason of an instinctive aversion to de Man's irony and word play, as when he makes in the next sentence the vile pun (but are not all puns vile?) of calling Jacques Derrida an "archie Debunker."

24. Some pages from my discussion of the passage in *The Mill on the Floss* are drawn in much revised and extended form from my "The Two Rhetorics: George Eliot's Bestiary," in *Writing and Reading Differently: Deconstruction and the Teaching of Composition and Literature*, ed. G. Douglas Atkins and Michael L. Johnson (Lawrence: University Press of Kansas, 1985), 101–14. A briefer discussion of the passage from *The Mill on the Floss* appears in my "Composition and Decomposition: Deconstruction and the Teaching of Writing," in *Composition & Literature: Bridging the Gap*, ed. Winifred Bryan Horner (Chicago: University of Chicago Press, 1983), 38–56. Avrom Fleishman's authoritative list of George Eliot's astonishing range of reading demonstrates her familiarity with the Western rhetorical tradition down to her own day. (See Fleishman, "George Eliot's Reading: A Chronological List.")

25. *Webster's New Collegiate Dictionary* defines chaos as "the confused state of primordial matter before the creation of orderly forms."

26. See ch. 2, n. 19.

27. For an essay on this passage, in the context of a general discussion of *Middlemarch* apropos of Victorian notions of intersubjectivity, see J. Hillis Miller, "The Roar on the Other Side of Silence: Otherness in *Middlemarch*," in *Rereading Texts/Rethinking Critical Presuppositions*, ed. Shlomith Rimmon-Kenan, Leona Toker, and Shuli Barzilai (Frankfurt: Peter Lang, 1997), 137–48.

28. T. S. Eliot, "Burnt Norton," in *The Complete Poems and Plays: 1909–1950* (New York: Harcourt, Brace, 1952), 118.

29. Trans. Daniel Breazeale, *Philosophy and Truth: Selections from Nietzsche's Notebooks of the Early 1870's* (Atlantic Highlands: Humanities Press, 1979), 83. For the German, see Nietzsche, *Sämtliche Werke*, 1: 880: "ein für uns unzugängliches und undefinirbares X."

30. See especially chapter 4 of *Beyond the Pleasure Principle*, trans. James Strachey, *Works*, Standard Edition (London: Hogarth Press, 1955), 18: 24–33; see also *The Interpretation of Dreams*, ibid., 5: 564–8, 588–609, and "A Note upon the 'Mystic Writing Pad,'" trans. James Strachey, *Collected Papers* (New York: Basic Books, 1959), 5: 175–80.

31. *Youth: A Narrative and Two Other Stories* (London: J. M. Dent, 1923), 93.

32. In *Twilight of the Idols*, section 5. Here is the whole sentence, first in German, then in English: "*G. Eliot.*—Sie sind den christlichen Gott los und glauben nun um so mehr die christliche Moral festhalten zu müssen: das ist eine *englische* Folgerichtigkeit, wir wollen sie den Moral-Weiblein à la Eliot nicht verübeln" (*Sämtliche Werke*, 6: 113); "*G. Eliot*. They are rid of the Christian God and now believe all the more firmly that they must cling to Christian morality. That is an English consistency; we do not wish to hold it against little moralistic females à la Eliot," trans. Walter Kaufmann, in *The Portable Nietzsche* (New York: Viking, 1954), 515. Nietzsche's harsh words for Eliot are drawn from a notebook of spring, 1887 (*Sämtliche Werke*, 12: 550–1). No doubt there is something to what Nietzsche says. The power of sympathy, which many critics sees as the endpoint of Eliot's "message," can indeed be defined as Christian morality without belief in God. My book is arguing throughout, however, that a strong counter-current in Eliot's novels is the constant affirmation of what might be called a Nietzschean rhetorical insight into the power of figurative language to generate illusions and inhibit sympathetic understanding. Eliot's novels, I am arguing, contradict themselves. No evidence exists that I know of that Eliot had read Nietzsche. Of all Eliot's novels, Nietzsche only mentions *Adam Bede* by name in one of his notebooks (summer, 1880, *Sämtliche Werke*, 9: 107). So far as I can ascertain, he never mentions *Middlemarch*.

33. Friedrich Nietzsche, *The Gay Science*, paragraph 322, trans. Walter Kaufmann (New York: Vintage Books, 1974), 254, trans. modified. For the German see *Die fröhliche Wissenschaft*, *Sämtliche Werke*, 3: 322.

34. Benjamin, *Ursprung des deutsches Trauerspiel*, 145. This passage from Benjamin's book, like the one cited earlier, is also cited in Leonardo Francisco Lisi's admirably learned and original *Aesthetics of Dependency: Early Modernism and the Struggle against Idealism in Kierkegaard, Ibsen, and Henry James* (New York: Fordham University Press, 2011). I have learned much from this book through reading it in manuscript. It has helped me in the revision of this present book.

35. Trans. James Strachey, *Works*, 21: 69–71. Here is a bit of this great appropriation of the ruins of Rome as a way to describe the human psyche, to remind the reader of its somber eloquence: "Now let us, by a flight of imagination, suppose that Rome is not a human habitation but a psychical entity with a similarly long and copious past—an entity, that is to say, in which nothing that has once come into existence will have passed away and all the earlier phases of development continue to exist alongside the latest one. This would mean that in Rome the palaces of the Caesars and the Septizonium of Septimus Severus would still be rising to their old height on the Palatine and the castle of S. Angelo would still be carrying on its battlements the beautiful statues which graced it until the siege by the Goths, and so on" (70).

36. George Eliot, *Essays*, ed. Thomas Pinney (New York: Columbia University Press, 1963), 432–6. See Fleischman, *George Eliot's Intellectual Life*, 161–4, for a commentary on this essay that differs somewhat from my own in more emphasizing Eliot's claim that good art is organically unified.

37. Eliot, *Essays*, 432–3.

38. See this ch., n. 34.

39. See R. H. Tawney, *Religion and the Rise of Capitalism* (New York: Harcourt Brace, 1926); available now from: New Brunswick, NJ: Transaction Publishers, 2000.

40. Even Martin Jay, in his authoritative history of the Frankfurt School, makes this error of interpretation, as did, apparently, Benjamin's friends in the Frankfurt Institute. See Jay's *The Dialectical Imagination* (Boston and Toronto: Little, Brown, 1973), 200–1.

41. Benjamin, *Illuminations*, trans. H. Zohn (New York: Schocken, 1969), 262–3; in German: *Illuminationen* (Frankfurt: Suhrkamp, 1961), 278.

42. Benjamin, *Illuminations*, 261.

43. Ibid.; in German: *Illuminationen*, 276.

44. Franz Kafka, *Parables and Paradoxes: In German and English* (New York: Schocken, 1969), 80–1, trans. altered.

45. Benjamin, *Illuminations*, 261; in German: *Illuminationen*, 276.

46. W. B. Yeats, "The Second Coming," ll. 7–8, in *The Variorum Edition of the Poems*, ed. Peter Allt and Russell K. Alspach (New York: Macmillan, 1977), 402.

47. Friedrich Nietzsche, "Vom Nutzen und Nachtheil der Historie für das Leben," *Sämtliche Werke*, 1: 258; Nietzsche, "On the Utility and Liability of History for Life," in *Unpublished Writings from the Period of Unfashionable Observations*, trans. Richard T. Gray, in *Complete Works*, ed. Ernst Behler, 20 vols. (Stanford: Stanford University Press, 1995), 2: 96.

48. George Eliot, "The Antigone and Its Moral," in *Essays*, 261–5. Eliot concludes that, "Whenever the strength of a man's [sic!] intellect, or moral sense, or affection brings him into opposition with the rules which society has sanctioned, *there* is renewed the conflict between Antigone and Creon" (265). Eliot's reading of Philip August Böckh's scholarly edition of Sophocles's *Antigone*, with a translation into German, and a commentary on the play, is mentioned in Fleishman's discussion of Eliot's *Antigone* essay in *George Eliot's Intellectual Life*, 82.

49. Francis Fukuyama, *The End of History and the Last Man* (New York: Free Press, 1992).

50. Henry James, *The Portrait of a Lady*, in *The Novels and Tales*, reprint of the New York Edition (Fairfield: Augustus M. Kelley, 1977), 4: 51. Further references are to volume and page number in this edition.

51. I have explored and exploited in various ways the myth of Ariadne in my *Ariadne's Thread: Story Lines* (New Haven: Yale University Press, 1992). For some obscure reason, obscure to me at least, the story of Ariadne has always struck me as among the most moving of ancient myths.

52. See Felicia Bonaparte, *The Tryptych and the Cross: The Central Myths of George Eliot's Poetic Imagination* (New York: New York University Press, 1979). Especially relevant to my discussion here is the chapter that focuses on the function of the myth of Ariadne in *Romola*: "Bacchus and Ariadne Betrothed," 86-109.

53. In the wake of work on Nietzsche's *The Birth of Tragedy* by Paul de Man, Carol Jacobs, Andrzej Warminski, and Thomas Albrecht, I have, in recent essay, "Globalization and World Literature," discussed the way Apollo and Dionysus, for Nietzsche, turn into one another. My essay has appeared in a special issue of *Neohelicon* (Vol. 58, no. 2[2011], 251–65),

edited by Wang Ning and drawn from lectures given in the summer of 2010 at a conference on world literature at Shanghai Jiaotong University. "Thus," says Nietzsche, "the intricate relation of the Apollonian and the Dionysian may really be symbolized by a fraternal union of the two deities: Dionysus speaks the language of Apollo; and Apollo, finally the language of Dionysus" (*"So ware wirklich das schwierige Verhältniss des Apollinischen und des Dionysischen in der Tragödie durch einen Brunderbund beider Gottgeiten zu symbolisiren: Dionysus redet die Sprache des Apollo, Apollo aber schliesslich die Sprache des Dionysus"*) (Friedrich Nietzsche, *The Birth of Tragedy* and *The Case of Wagner*, trans. Walter Kaufmann [New York: Vintage, 1967], 130; Nietzsche, *Die Geburt der Tragödie*, in *Sämtliche Werke*, 1: 140).

54. See Bonaparte, *The Tryptych and the Cross*, 86-93, for a discussion of some of these sources in relation to the use of the myth of Bacchus and Ariadne in *Romola*. See also Haight, *George Eliot: A Biography*, 152, for George Eliot's response to Johann Heinrich von Dannecker's *Ariadne on the Panther* (*Ariadne auf dem Panther*) (1810–24), which she saw in 1854 in a private house in Germany: "I never saw any sculpture equal to this—the feeling it excites is the essence of true worship—a bowing of the soul before power creating beauty." Eliot seems to have shared my enthusiasm for Ariadne.

55. Jacques Derrida and Bernard Stiegler, *Échographies* (Paris: Galillée, 1996), 19, my trans.

56. Friedrich Nietzsche, *Also Sprach Zarathustra*, in *Sämtliche Werke*, 4: 208; *Thus Spoke Zarathustra*, trans. Kaufmann, in *The Portable Nietzsche*, 277. Kaufmann translates the phrase as "the uncanny, unbounded Yes." Nietzsche's Zarathustra asserts that he shares this yes-saying power with the empty sky before sunrise.

57. See Haight, *George Eliot: A Biography*, for an authoritative account of these relationships, and see also his useful sketches of each of these persons and of their roles in Marian Evans's life in *The George Eliot Letters*, ed. Gordon S. Haight, 7 vols. (New Haven: Yale University Press, 1954), 1: lv–lxi; lxii–lxvii; lxviii–lxx.

58. My ironic allusion is to a famous ironic last sentence of Paul de Man's "Allegory of Reading (*Profession de foi*)," in *Allegories of Reading*, 245: "One sees from this that the impossibility of reading should not be taken too lightly."

Coda

1. See Timothy Clark, "Scale," in *Telemorphosis: Theory in the Era of Climate Change, Vol. 1*, ed. Tom Cohen (Ann Arbor: University of Michigan Press and the Open Humanities Press, 2011). Many of the essays in this remarkable volume are, as the subtitle indicates, relevant to the question of theory's function (and that of literary criticism) in the era of climate change, that is, our era, right now.

2. See this ch., n. 1, and Tom Cohen, "Toxic Assets: De Man's Remains and the Ecocatastrophic Imaginary (An American Fable)," in Tom Cohen, Claire Colebrook, and J. Hillis Miller, *Theory and the Disappearing Future: On de Man, On Benjamin* (London: Routledge, 2011).

3. Jacques Derrida, *Learning to Live Finally: An Interview with Jean Birnbaum*, trans. Pascale-Anne Brault and Michael Naas (Hoboken: Melville House, 2007), 34; *Apprendre à vivre enfin* (Paris: Galilée, 2005), 35.

4. Ed. Pascale-Anne Brault and Michael Naas (Paris: Galilée, 2003). The English version, with slightly different contents, is *The Work of Mourning*, ed. Pascale-Anne Brault and Michael Naas (Chicago: University of Chicago Press, 2001).

5. See my discussion of this in "Derrida Enisled" and "Derrida's Politics of Autoimmunity," in my *For Derrida* (New York: Fordham University Press, 2009), 101–32, 222–44, especially 123–9, 238–41. See also ch. 1, n. 27, for another reference to this material.

Index